AF896825

Studies in Economic History

Series editor

Tetsuji Okazaki, The University of Tokyo, Tokyo, Japan

Editorial Board Member

Loren Brandt, University of Toronto, Canada
Myung Soo Cha, Yeungnam University, Korea
Nicholas Crafts, University of Warwick, UK
Claude Diebolt, University of Strasbourg, France
Barry Eichengreen, University of California at Berkeley, USA
Stanley Engerman, University of Rochester, USA
Price V. Fishback, University of Arizona, USA
Avner Greif, Stanford University, USA
Tirthanker Roy, London School of Economics and Political Science, UK
Osamu Saito, Hitotsubashi University, Japan
Jochen Streb, University of Mannheim, Germany
Nikolaus Wolf, Humboldt University, Germany

Aims and Scope

This series from Springer provides a platform for works in economic history that truly integrate economics and history. Books on a wide range of related topics are welcomed and encouraged, including those in macro-economic history, financial history, labor history, industrial history, agricultural history, the history of institutions and organizations, spatial economic history, law and economic history, political economic history, historical demography, and environmental history.

Economic history studies have greatly developed over the past several decades through application of economics and econometrics. Particularly in recent years, a variety of new economic theories and sophisticated econometric techniques—including game theory, spatial economics, and generalized method of moment (GMM)—have been introduced for the great benefit of economic historians and the research community.

At the same time, a good economic history study should contribute more than just an application of economics and econometrics to past data. It raises novel research questions, proposes a new view of history, and/or provides rich documentation. This series is intended to integrate data analysis, close examination of archival works, and application of theoretical frameworks to offer new insights and even provide opportunities to rethink theories.

The purview of this new Springer series is truly global, encompassing all nations and areas of the world as well as all eras from ancient times to the present. The editorial board, who are internationally renowned leaders among economic historians, carefully evaluate and judge each manuscript, referring to reports from expert reviewers. The series publishes contributions by university professors and others well established in the academic community, as well as work deemed to be of equivalent merit.

More information about this series at http://www.springer.com/series/13279

Hugh Rockoff · Isao Suto
Editors

Coping with Financial Crises

Some Lessons from Economic History

Springer

Editors
Hugh Rockoff
Department of Economics
Rutgers University
New Jersey, NJ
USA

Isao Suto
School of Political Science and Economics
Meiji University
Tokyo
Japan

ISSN 2364-1797 ISSN 2364-1800 (electronic)
Studies in Economic History
ISBN 978-981-10-6195-0 ISBN 978-981-10-6196-7 (eBook)
https://doi.org/10.1007/978-981-10-6196-7

Library of Congress Control Number: 2017951989

© Springer Nature Singapore Pte Ltd. 2018
This work is subject to copyright. All rights are reserved by the Publisher, whether the whole or part of the material is concerned, specifically the rights of translation, reprinting, reuse of illustrations, recitation, broadcasting, reproduction on microfilms or in any other physical way, and transmission or information storage and retrieval, electronic adaptation, computer software, or by similar or dissimilar methodology now known or hereafter developed.
The use of general descriptive names, registered names, trademarks, service marks, etc. in this publication does not imply, even in the absence of a specific statement, that such names are exempt from the relevant protective laws and regulations and therefore free for general use.
The publisher, the authors and the editors are safe to assume that the advice and information in this book are believed to be true and accurate at the date of publication. Neither the publisher nor the authors or the editors give a warranty, express or implied, with respect to the material contained herein or for any errors or omissions that may have been made. The publisher remains neutral with regard to jurisdictional claims in published maps and institutional affiliations.

Printed on acid-free paper

This Springer imprint is published by Springer Nature
The registered company is Springer Nature Singapore Pte Ltd.
The registered company address is: 152 Beach Road, #21-01/04 Gateway East, Singapore 189721, Singapore

This book is dedicated to the memory of Prof. John Allan James of the University of Virginia, who passed away unexpectedly on November 28, 2014. John loved Japan, and had planned on presenting a paper in the session of the World Economic History Congress in Kyoto, where most of the papers in this volume were originally presented. John was an extraordinary scholar, and a kind and generous friend. He was universally admired by his fellow economic historians for his skill, his willingness to wrestle with the most difficult questions, and his commitment to the highest scholarly standards. He is greatly missed by his many friends and colleagues.

Contents

Masato Shizume Faculty of Political Science and Economics, Waseda University, Tokyo, Japan

Isao Suto School of Political Science and Economics, Meiji University, Tokyo, Japan

Anders Ögren Department of Economic History, Lund University, Lund, Sweden

Chapter 1
Reflections on the Evolution of Financial Crises: Theory, History and Empirics

Michael D. Bordo

Abstract The world has seen five global financial crises since 1880. They usually involved shocks transmitted from the core countries to the periphery but sometimes the reverse happened, the shocks were transferred from the periphery to the core countries. Theories of financial crises as well as empirical evidence has evolved greatly in the past century. Here I survey the history, theory and empirical evidence on financial crises. A key development in recent years has been the growing connection between financial crises and fiscal crises. This reflects the increasing importance of government guarantees of the banking system and other parts of the financial sector. I focus on this connection and provide evidence on crisis incidence, the costs of financial crises, the determinants of crisis and the feedback loops between fiscal and financial crises.

Keywords Banking crises · Panics · Debt crises · Fiscal crises
Exchange rate · Gold standard

1.1 Five Global Crises

In "The Global Financial Crisis: Is it Unprecedented" Bordo and Landon-Lane (2012) identified five global banking crises between 1880–2008. The crisis years as shown in Table 1.1 were: 1890–1891, 1907–1908, 1913–1914, 1931–1932, and 2007–2008. We defined global crises in the following way. We first looked at the literature to determine which countries economists have identified as suffering from banking crises. We then counted the number of crises in each year weighting each

---

A preliminary version of this essay was presented at the Conference on Cliometrics and Complexity, Lyon, June 9–10 2016.

M.D. Bordo (✉)
Department of Economics, Rutgers University, New Brunswick, NJ, USA
e-mail: Bordo@econ.rutgers.edu

© Springer Nature Singapore Pte Ltd. 2018

H. Rockoff and I. Suto (eds.), *Coping with Financial Crises*,
Studies in Economic History, https://doi.org/10.1007/978-981-10-6196-7_1

Table 1.1 The countries involved in five global banking crises

Period	Countries
1890–1891	Argentina, Brazil, Chile, Germany, Italy, New Zealand, Paraguay, Portugal, South Africa, UK, USA
1907–1908	Chile, Denmark, Egypt, France, Italy, Japan, Mexico, Sweden, USA
1913–1914	Argentina, Belgium, Brazil, France, Italy, India, Japan, Mexico, Netherlands, Norway, UK, Uruguay, USA
1931–1932	Argentina, Austria, Belgium, Brazil, China, Denmark, Finland, France, Germany, Greece, Italy, Norway, Portugal, Spain, Sweden, Switzerland, Turkey, USA
2007–2008	Austria, Belgium, Denmark, France, Germany, Greece, Ireland, Netherlands, Portugal, Russia, Spain, Sweden, Switzerland, UK, USA

country by GDP. Finally, we defined a period to be a global crisis if it satisfies the following criteria.

1. A period is a local peak of the 2 year moving sum.
2. The local peak is an extreme value

   a. If the weighted sum of the total number of countries in crisis is more than three standard deviations from the mean.
   b. The crisis is considered large and rare if it is in the upper tail of the distribution and has a combined weight that is greater than the combined output of the U.S.

3. The countries involved come from more than one geographical area.

Figure 1.1 shows the annual frequency of financial crises based on the weighted 2-period moving sum of banking crisis frequencies: 1880–2009. Banking crises, evidently, occur frequently. But the crises designated here as global banking crises clearly stand out from the others.

In Bordo and Landon Lane (2013) we also measured the output losses of these global financial crises. The Great Depression was the worst followed by the 1890s, 1907 and the least severe was the recent crisis.

The history of financial crises, however, can be traced back 100s of years (Kindleberger 1978). From Kindleberger's work and that of other scholars who have looked at the long history of financial crises we can derive a number of generalizations. (1) The nature and origins of fiscal crises and their relationship to banking crises has changed over the long-run. (2) Financial crises before deposit insurance were banking panics. (3) Panics would propagate through asset markets via fire sales. (4) Banking crises can occur as a consequence of bank credit driven asset price booms. (5) Banking panics could be caused by shocks to shadow banks. (6) Banking crises have often spread to many countries. (7) Interest rate shocks in the financial center was often the trigger. (8) Advanced countries had many panics in the nineteenth century before central banks learned to be lenders of last resort. (9) With the advent of deposit insurance and other forms of guarantees, banking

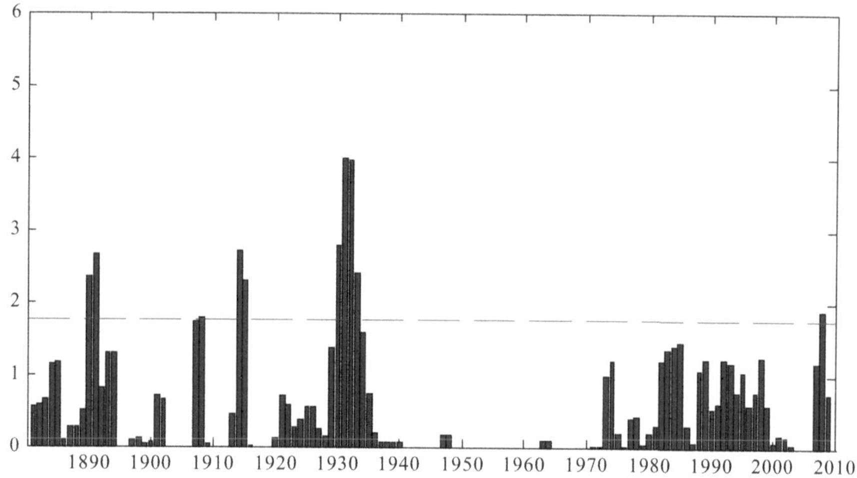

Fig. 1.1 The number of countries suffering from banking crises, weighted 2-period moving sum

panics became banking crises which were resolved by a fiscal rescue. This created a direct link between the banking system and the government's balance sheet. (10) Costly bailouts could lead to fiscal imbalances and, possibly, defaults. (11) Guarantees could create moral hazard which could lead to higher bailout costs and risk of fiscal crisis.

Before the 1930s sovereign defaults had been frequent, especially in emerging countries. They reflected capital flow bonanzas (Reinhart and Rogoff 2009) and sudden stops. Many emerging countries were serial defaulters (Reinhart and Rogoff 2009; Reinhart et al. 2003).

1.2 Theories of Financial Crises (Banking Crises)

The traditional view of a banking crisis was that of a banking panic or liquidity crisis. It occurred in a fractional reserve banking system when the public fearful that their banks would not be able to convert their deposits into currency attempts tried *en masse* to do so. Unless the panic is allayed by a lender of last resort the real economy will be impacted by a decline in money supply, impairment of the payment system, and interruption of bank lending.

Diamond and Dybvig (1983) were the first to formally model banking crisis of this sort. Their model is based on several key ideas. (1) Banks intermediate between demand deposits and long-term investments. (2) This creates the possibility of maturity mismatch between liabilities and assets. (3) A run on a bank or banking system can be triggered by a sunspot because rational depositors, not wishing to be last in line, rush to convert deposits into currency. (4) A panic can be prevented by

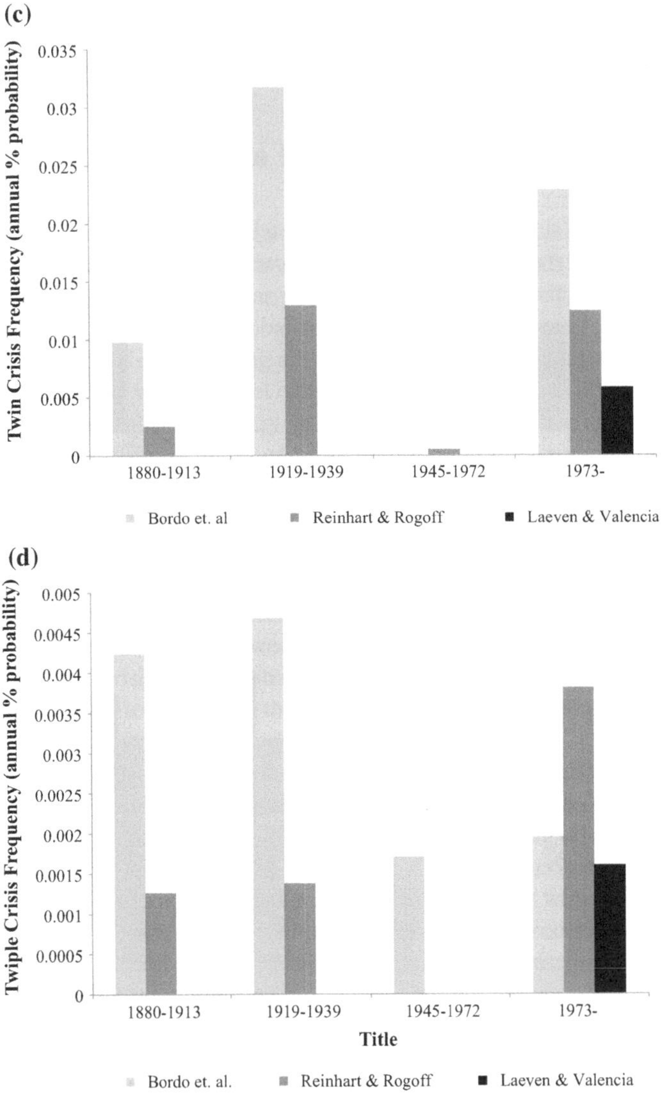

Fig. 1.2 (continued)

financial sector smaller. The losses today are lower than in the interwar when policy was counterproductive.

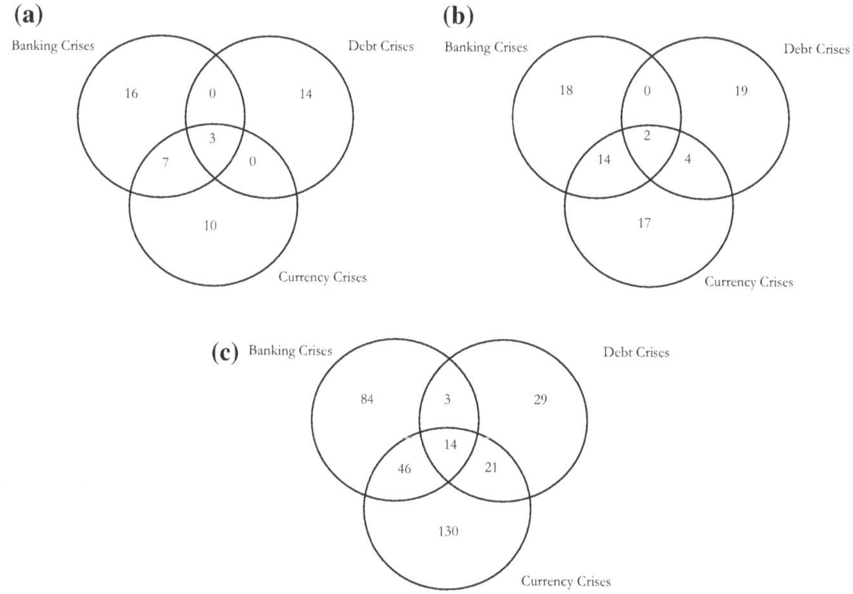

Fig. 1.3 **a** Coincidence of banking, currency and debt crises, 1880–1913 (Bordo et al.). **b** Coincidence of banking, currency and debt crises, 1919–1939 (Bordo et al.). **c** Coincidence of banking, currency and debt crises, 1970–2012 (Laeven and Valencia)

1.5 Fiscal Crises, Banking Crises, and the Fiscal Crisis Trilemma

Recent research (Laeven and Valencia 2013) has focused on the impact of banking crisis on the probability of a debt crisis, especially in advanced countries. Their findings are striking

Average rise in the debt to GDP for all systemic crises was 12%, but for just the advanced economies it was 21.3%. The average rise in debt due to bailouts, rescues and guarantees was 6%

Tagkalakis (2013) empirically examines the feedback loop from fiscal policy to financial markets and back in a sample of 20 OECD countries 1990–2010. Fiscal instability, Tagkalakis found, leads to financial instability and financial instability leads to fiscal instability via bailouts. The rise in debt relative to deficits depends positively on the financial sector. Tagkalakis's results suggest the possibility of a tradeoff for countries along the lines of a trilemma. Assume that most financially developed countries will inevitably face a crisis at some point. Two out of three choices may be possible, but not all three.

(1) A large financial sector.
(2) Debt-financed rescues of the financial sector during a financial crisis.

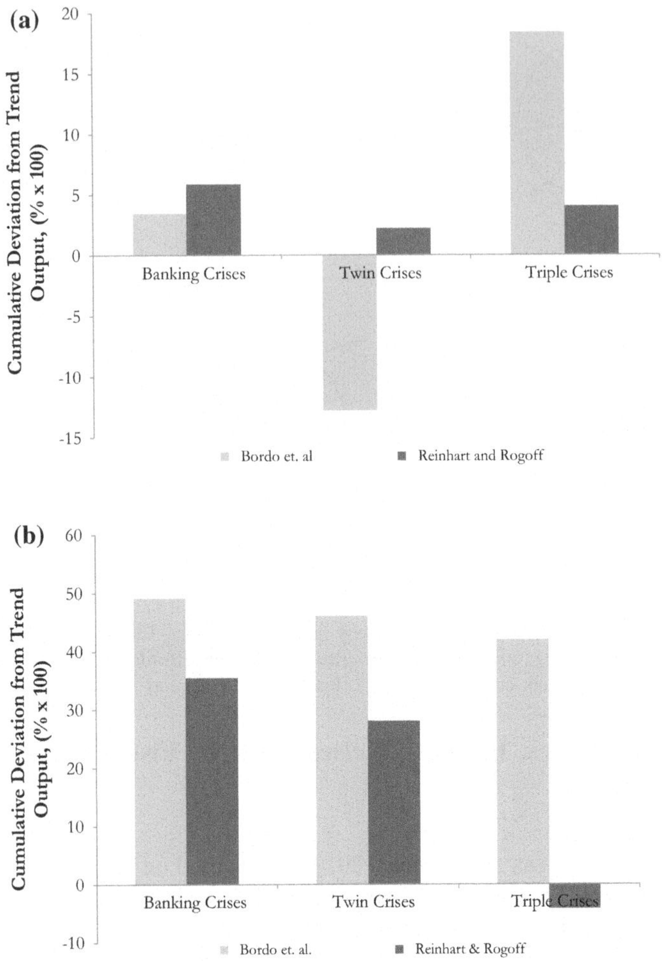

Fig. 1.4 **a** Output loss for three varieties of crises 1880–1913. **b** Output losses, three varieties of crises, 1919–1939. **c** Output losses, three varieties of crises, 1873–1997, 1973–2012, and 1973–2012. **d** Output losses from banking crises 1973–1997

(3) Counter-cyclical/discretionary fiscal policy during financial recessions.

Here is the logic behind this trilemma. A country with a large financial sector will be more likely to have a financial crisis. If so the government can either provide a large bailout package and use up fiscal space. Or else it can reduce the size of the bailout and devote its fiscal space to discretionary fiscal policy. The smaller the financial sector the less binding will be the fiscal constraints since the size of the bailout would be smaller.

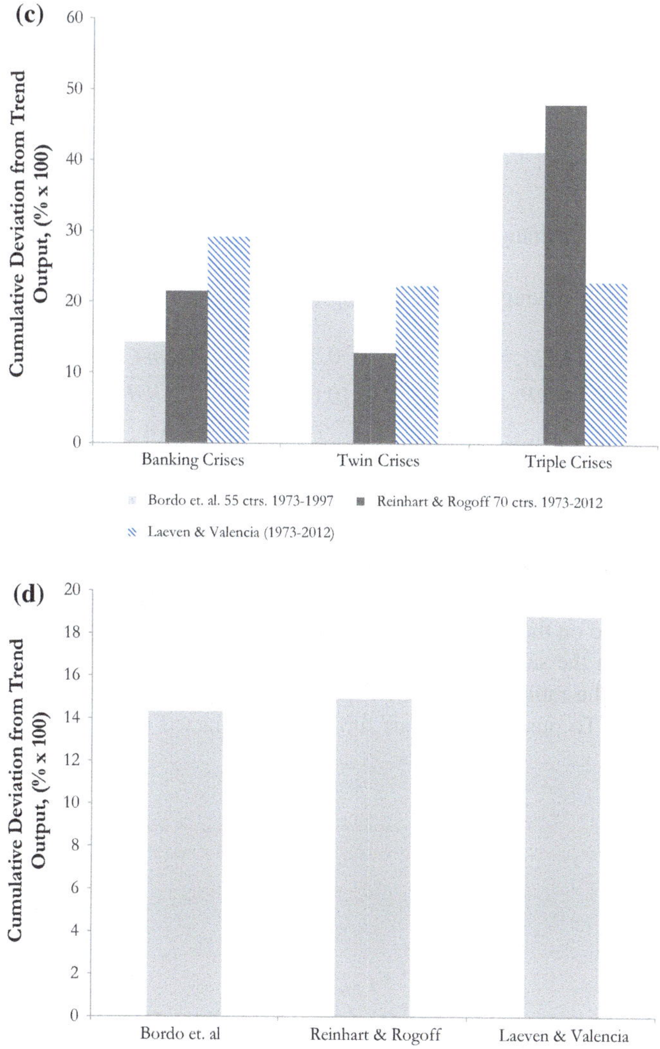

Fig. 1.4 (continued)

For example, the United States post-2007 had a large financial sector but its bailout was relatively small at 4.5% of GDP. The debt GDP ratio rose by 19%. On the other hand, Greece which had an increase in the debt ratio of a similar 17% had a much larger recession and the fiscal bailout costs were 27% (which does not include the external rescues). The ability of countries to finance either a bailout or use discretionary fiscal policy depends on the willingness of capital markets to fund deficits. Thus the trilemma is more applicable foe countries which have better debt sustainability at the beginning of their crisis.

To test the financial trilemma we can use data from Laeven and Valencia (2013) for 19 banking crises in 18 advanced countries since 1970. We estimated the following regression:

$$\ln\left(\Delta\frac{Debt_{it}}{GDP_{it}}\right) = k + \theta_1\left[\ln\left(\Delta\frac{Fiscal\,Costs_{it}}{GDP_{it}}\right)\right] + \theta_2\left[\ln\left(\Delta\frac{Discretion_{it}}{GDP_{it}}\right)\right] + \varepsilon_{it}$$

Discretion is the change in the Debt-to-GDP ratio minus the ratio of fiscal costs to GDP.

Our regression produced the following numerical results.

$$\ln\left(\Delta\frac{Debt_{it}}{GDP_{it}}\right) = \underset{(0.13)}{0.69} + \underset{(0.03)}{0.25}\left[\ln\left(\Delta\frac{Fiscal\,Costs_{it}}{GDP_{it}}\right)\right] + \underset{(0.04)}{0.74}\left[\ln\left(\Delta\frac{Discretion_{it}}{GDP_{it}}\right)\right]$$

The results suggest that the coefficients on the two regressors add up to one and imply a tradeoff between bailout and discretion.

Figure 1.5 plots the predicted iso-line at given levels of the change in the ratio of Debt/GDP based on the estimated regression as well as the data for the 18 countries and 19 crises in the sample.

The rise in the ratios of Debt/GDP predicted by the regression match the data relatively well. To push the analysis further we interacted the fiscal costs variable

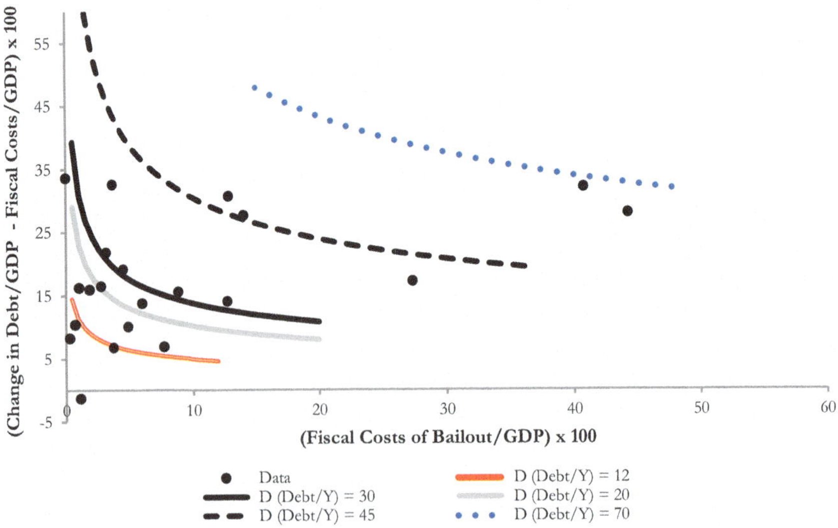

Fig. 1.5 Observed data points and Iso-lines derived from the regression

with the size of the financial sector (domestic private credit over GDP) with the following results.

$$\ln\left(\Delta\frac{Debt_{it}}{GDP_{it}}\right) = \underset{(0.49)}{1.72} + \underset{(0.24)}{-0.27}\left[\ln\left(\Delta\frac{Fiscal\,Costs_{it}}{GDP_{it}}\right)\right]$$
$$+ \underset{0.05}{0.11}\left[\ln\left(\Delta\frac{Fiscal\,Costs_{it}}{GDP_{it}}\right) \times \ln\left(\frac{Domestic\,Credit_{it}}{GDP_{it}}\right)\right]$$
$$+ \underset{(0.04)}{0.72}\left[\ln\left(\Delta\frac{Discretion_{it}}{GDP_{it}}\right)\right] - \underset{(0.10)}{0.22}\left[\ln\left(\frac{Domestic\,Credit_{it}}{GDP_{it}}\right)\right]$$

The positive interaction term implies that countries with large financial sectors devote more of their fiscal space to bailouts. Figure 1.6 shows the relationship between the natural logarithm of the ratio of domestic credit to GDP and the increase in the in the natural logarithm of the debt to GDP ratio in crises. More specifically, Fig. 1.6 presents the predicted regression line/partial regression plot from a univariate regression of the share in the rise in debt as a percentage of GDP against the logarithm of the level of private domestic credit to GDP. We perform a logit transform on the dependent variable prior to estimation. Debt data are from Laeven and Valencia (2013) and credit data are from IMF IFS.

Therefore, as the size of fiscal bailouts increase, the discretionary component of the fiscal response is smaller. Large financial sectors necessitate large bailouts. Hence, the constraints on discretionary fiscal actions are less binding for countries with relatively small financial sectors.

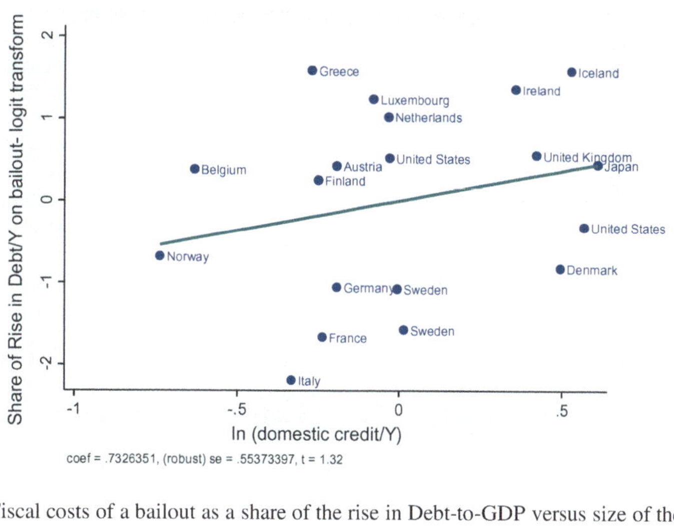

Fig. 1.6 Fiscal costs of a bailout as a share of the rise in Debt-to-GDP versus size of the financial sector

1.6 Conclusions

To sum up:

(1) The history of financial crises shows that there is a crisis somewhere in the world about every decade.
(2) Fiscal and financial crises have been increasingly linked together by the increased use of government guarantees of financial intermediaries.
(3) Government rescues to avoid the costs of old-fashioned banking panics have led to more virulent modern banking crises.
(4) This reflects the general phenomenon that when the government intervenes to prevent costly events from occurring economic agents adjust their behavior accordingly and use more of the protected resource than is optimal in the long-run.
(5) There is a trade-off between the costs of financial crises that accompany financial development and growth and the moral hazard costs of insurance.
(6) Eliminating crises entirely is not desirable, but letting them burn out without intervention is also not ideal.

References

Acharya, Viral V., Itamar Drechsler, and Philipp Schnabl. 2013. A Pyrrhic Victory? Bank Bailouts and Sovereign Credit Risk. Working Paper, Stern School of Business.

Allen, Franklin, and Douglas Gale. 1998. Optimal Financial Crises. *Journal of Finance* 53: 1245–1284.

Barro, R.J. and J.F. Ursua. 2008. Macroeconomic Crises since 1879. Brookings Papers on Economic Activity, 255–335. Spring.

Bhattacharya, S. and D. Gale. 1987. Preference Shocks, Liquidity and Central bank Policy. In *New Approaches to Monetary Economics*, ed. W. Barnett, and K. singleton, 69–88. New York: Cambridge University Press.

Bolton, Patrick, and Olivier Jeanne. 2011. Sovereign Default Risk and Bank Fragility in Financially Integrated Economies. NBER Working Paper 16899 March.

Bordo, Michael D. and John Landon-Lane. 2012. The Global Financial Crisis: Is it Unprecedented. In *Global Economic Crisis: Impacts, Transmission and Recovery*, ed. M. Obstfeld, D. Cho, and A. Mason, 19–57. Cheltenham, UK: Edward Elgar.

Bordo, Michael D. and John Landon-Lane. 2013. Does Expansionary Monetary Policy Cause Asset Price Booms: Some Historical and Empirical Evidence. NBER Working paper 195895 October.

Bordo, Michael D. and Christopher M. Meissner. 2016. Fiscal and Financial Crises. NBER Working Paper No. 22059. Issued in March.

Diaz-Alejandro, Carlos. 1985. Good-Bye Financial Repression, Hello Financial Crash. *Journal of Development Economics*, 19 (1–2), 1–24.

Diamond, Douglas, and Philip Dybvig. 1983. Bank Runs, Deposit Insurance, and Liquidity. *Journal of Political Economy* 91: 401–419.

Diamond, Douglas, and Raghuram Rajan. 2001. Liquidity Risk, Liquidity Creation and financial Fragility: A Theory of Banking. *Journal of Political Economy* 109: 2431–2465.

Diamond, Douglas, and Raghuram Rajan. 2005. Liquidity Shortages and Banking Crisis. *Journal of Finance* 60 (2): 615–647.

Gennaioli, Nicola, Alberto Martin, and Steffano Rossi. 2014. Sovereign Default, Domestic Banks, and Financial Institutions. *Journal of Finance* LXIX (2): 819–886.

Holmstrom, Bengt, and J. Tirole. 1991. Private and Public Supply of Liquidity. *Journal of Political Economy* 106: 1–40.

Kindleberger, Charles. 1978. *Manias, Panics and Crashes: A History of Financial Crises*. New York: Basic Books.

Laeven, Luc, and Fabian Valencia. 2013. Systemic Banking Crises Database: An Update. IMF Working Paper No. 12/163.

McKinnon, Ronald, and Huw Pill. 1986. Credible Liberalizations and International Capital Flows; The "Over Borrowing Syndrome". In *Financial Deregulation and Integration in East Asia*, ed. T. Ito, and A. Kreuger. Chicago: University of Chicago Press.

Mody, Ashoka, and Damiano Sandri. 2012. The Eurozone Crisis: How Banks and Sovereigns came to be Joined at the Hip. *Economic Policy*, April, 199–230.

Reinhart, Carmen, and Kenneth Rogoff. 2009. *This Time is Different: Eight Centuries of Financial Folly*. Princeton: Princeton University Press.

Reinhart, Carmen, Kenneth S. Rogoff, and Miguel A. Savastano. 2003. NBER Working Paper 9908.

Reinhart, Carmen, Kenneth S. Rogoff, and Miguel A. Savastano. 2009. *This Time is Different: Eight Centuries of Financial Folly*. Princeton: Princeton University Press.

Tagkalakis, Athanasios. 2013. The Effects of Financial Crisis on Fiscal Positions. *European Journal of Political Economy* 29: 197–213.

Author Biography

Michael D. Bordo is a Board of Governors Professor of Economics and director of the Center for Monetary and Financial History at Rutgers University, New Brunswick, New Jersey. He has held visiting positions at the University of California at Los Angeles, Carnegie Mellon University, Princeton University, Harvard University, and Cambridge University, where he was the Pitt Professor of American History and Institutions. He is currently a distinguished visiting fellow at the Hoover Institution, Stanford University. He has been a visiting scholar at the International Monetary Fund; the Federal Reserve Banks of St. Louis, Cleveland, and Dallas; the Federal Reserve Board of Governors; the Bank of Canada; the Bank of England; and the Bank for International Settlement. He is a research associate of the National Bureau of Economic Research and a member of the Shadow Open Market Committee. He was also a member of the Federal Reserve Centennial Advisory Committee. He has a BA degree from McGill University, an MSc in economics from the London School of Economics, and PhD from the University of Chicago in 1972. He has published many articles in leading journals including the *Journal of Political Economy*, the *American Economic Review*, the *Journal of Monetary Economics*, and the *Journal of Economic History*. He has authored and coedited fourteen books on monetary economics and monetary history. These include (with O. Humpage and A.J. Schwartz), *Strained Relations: US Foreign Exchange Operations and Monetary Policy in the Twentieth Century* (University of Chicago Press, 2014); (with A. Orphanides), *The Great Inflation* (University of Chicago Press for the NBER, 2013); (with W. Roberds), *A Return to Jekyll Island* (Cambridge University Press, 2013); (with R. MacDonald) *Credibility and the International Monetary Regime* (Cambridge University Press, 2012); (with A. Taylor and J. Williamson), *Globalization in Historical Perspective* (University of Chicago Press for the NBER, 2003). He is also editor of a series of books for Cambridge University Press: *Studies in Macroeconomic History*.

Chapter 2
The International Contagion of Short-Run Interest Rates During the Great Depression

Samuel Maveyraud and Antoine Parent

Abstract The aim of this chapter is to clearly identify the mechanisms of the money market spillovers between the United States, the United Kingdom and France during the interwar period. To describe these mechanisms in detail, a BEKK model, in which we introduce a structural break, is adopted. Our analysis sheds new light on key historical issues: Was the crisis imported into the US? Did France set off interest rate volatility in the rest of the world during the thirties? Does the propagation process of interest rate volatility corroborate the "Golden Fetters" hypothesis?

Keywords Contagion · Financial crisis · Gold exchange standard
Interest rates · Interwar period · GARCH models

Code JEL N12 · N14 · N22 · N24 · E4

2.1 Introduction

In this chapter we focus on the contagion of interest rates before and during the Great Depression and address a key historical issue: Does the "Golden Fetters" hypothesis (Eichengreen 1992) hold regarding the mechanisms of crisis contagion? To that end, we wonder whether the tensions in American money markets spread to

---

Named after the authors of the paper that introduced the technique, (Baba et al. 1991).

S. Maveyraud
University of Bordeaux, GREThA College, bureau E333, Avenue Léon Duguit,
33608 Bordeaux, France
e-mail: samuel.maveyraud-tricoire@u-bordeaux.fr

A. Parent (✉)
Institut d'Etudes Politiques de Lyon, Sciences Po Lyon, 14 Av. Berthelot,
69007 Lyon, France
e-mail: antoine.parent@sciencespo-lyon.fr

© Springer Nature Singapore Pte Ltd. 2018

H. Rockoff and I. Suto (eds.), *Coping with Financial Crises*,
Studies in Economic History, https://doi.org/10.1007/978-981-10-6196-7_2

English and French markets (or conversely), and whether Black Thursday modified the spillover mechanisms more dramatically than the breakdown of the Gold Exchange Standard itself.

To cast new light on these questions, a trivariate BEKK model (Baba et al. 1991) has been adopted. This model reveals, in particular, the spreading mechanisms governing the evolution of variances and covariances in discrepancies between the 3-month Treasury Bond yields of France, Great Britain and the USA. The originality of our modeling is based on the introduction of a structural break in the equation of central tendency and equations of conditional variances and covariances (as proposed by Beirne et al. 2013). Taking this break into account helps to explicitly test the potential modifications of the spillover phenomenon between money markets.

We undertake this analysis in two steps. First, we consider the whole period, from 1921 to 1936, and then as two periods by introducing a structural break. The ensuing model, with its structural break, enables the nature of contagion throughout the whole period to be revealed, once the most relevant shock has been internalized. We have tested five equally important candidates in history in order to determine a break during this period: the triggering of the financial crisis in the US, the devaluation of the pound in September 1931, the declaration of the dollar inconvertibility in March 1933, the London Conference in June 1933, and the official devaluation of the dollar in January 1934.

Once having identified, with the maximum of likelihood, the most relevant break among the five candidates, we distinguish two sub-periods: before and after this break. The first goes from 1921m01 to 1929m06, the second one from 1930m06 to 1936m12. As is usual in this literature, we deliberately do not take into account the period around the structural break, in order to avoid turbulence and noise. Thus, we manage to assess appropriately the two sub-periods as two distinct periods, and then compare the dynamics of the relationship between interest rates[1] during those two periods.

This chapter is organized as follows: the first section recapitulates comparative studies of contagion using historical data; the second section surveys existing literature on contagion; the third one draws connections between the contagion mechanisms during the Great Depression and the "Golden Fetters" hypothesis; in the fourth section, we present data, methodology, and the econometric model (BEKK with a structural break); our findings are explored in Sect. 2.5; discussion is given in Sect. 2.6; the last section concludes.

[1]The word interest rate must be understood as actuarial interest rate (a synonym for yield).

2.2 Comparative Studies of Contagion Based on Historical Data

Very few articles use elaborated tools to study contagion in historical perspective. The seminal paper in economic history which addresses the question of contagion in financial crises is that of Bordo and Murshid (2001). Two levels of analysis can be distinguished in their study: a comparison of contagion phenomena over time; a specific analysis of contagion over the Gold Exchange Standard (GES) period. Bordo and Murshid's initial research goals are quite straightforward. They aim at comparing empirical data on contagion and crises from the past with modern episodes of contagion, in order to elaborate a more thorough explanation of present-day crises, but also in order to destroy common misconceptions about the intensity and supposedly "exceptional" severity of modern crises. They want to obtain better insights into the most suitable economic and monetary regimes that would help to avoid favouring contagion across financial markets. They conduct this research not only to infer which economic policies and regulations could best suit a given country with its own particular monetary regime and economic situation, but also to find inspiration for policy suggestions to solve current crises.

To carry out their comparative analysis of contagion, Bordo and Murshid (2001) use the weekly data of NYSE-traded bonds emitted by the following countries: Argentina, Belgium, Brazil, Canada, Chile, Denmark, Finland, France, Germany, Italy, the Netherlands, Sweden, Switzerland, the UK and the US. Their purpose is to ascertain whether there are stronger market co-movements after turbulent periods (i.e. the financial crises at the end of the 19th century, the Great Depression of 1929, and the Asian crises of the 1990s). They examine, in six-month time frames, the evidence of increased cross-market correlations after a major shock. During the interwar, there seems to be stronger cross-market linkages, notably via a higher co-movement of bond prices after a shock. On the contrary, during the Mexican crisis at the beginning of the 1980s, and after the speculative attack against Thailand in 1997, Bordo and Murshid (2001) find no evidence of stronger cross-market co-movements, thus making it impossible to assert that contagion now is stronger than it was in the past.

When assessing for regional patterns of contagion, Bordo and Murshid (2001) note that, in the past, contagion patterns usually found their source in the UK, and were then propagated toward other European countries. Another common historical pattern of crisis transmission in the last century has been from the core European countries to the peripheral ones. This pattern of shock transmission seems to have remained unchanged in recent times.

Finally, Bordo and Murshid (2001) find that tangible cross-market co-movements have occurred in *both* tranquil and tumultuous periods, but they are not able to establish a strong case for contagion today.

Concerning the Great Depression itself, Bordo and Murshid (2001) provide a review of the basic facts which, they consider, characterized the 1929 contagion. The spread of contagion was manifested in two effects: first, price and output decreased all over the world, a series of decreases that led the US to stop foreign lending. Second, the depression was accompanied by the banking panics sparked off, not only in the US, but throughout the world.

They sum up the main features of the 1929 contagion, and adopt as their own the explanations provided by Eichengreen (1992), acknowledging that the "US-induced crisis notoriously experienced international propagation. [...] The depression spread through the channels of international gold flows, money supplies, and the capital flight" (Bordo and Murshid 2001). Do they actually provide evidence that the "Golden Fetters" hypothesis which they endorse is the key to understanding contagion during the interwar period, and do their outcomes corroborate this view? One point remains unclear in their analysis: they provide evidence of intense co-movements in the aftermath of the 1929 crisis, notably after sterling and the dollar were devalued, respectively in 1931 and 1933. Why then should contagion be stronger only once the gold exchange system exploded and not before? Does this finding correctly reproduce the "Golden Fetters" hypothesis? This point needs further clarification (see Discussion, Sect. 2.3).

The second paper that deals with contagion over the interwar period is that of Accominotti (2011). Contagion is assessed via Principal Component Analysis performed on an exchange market pressure index (EMP), sovereign bond spreads and stock market returns (1928–1936). The EMP index, first introduced by Girton and Roper (1977), is built as a weighted average of the monthly changes in a country's international reserves and exchange rate volatilities. This index has been generalized by Eichengreen et al. (1995, 1996, July 1996) and built by Accominotti (2011) for the interwar period. Spreads on sovereign bonds traded in New York (monthly prices for 29 countries from January 1928 to February 1934) relative to the yield on long-term United States bonds, measure the default risk. Monthly series for stock market returns covering 14 national stock exchanges, from February 1928 to December 1936, are also included in the database. Accominotti's subsequent analysis of contagion consists of a principal component analysis that explores the co-movements between the series of EMP index, spreads on sovereign bonds and stock market returns.

> The author finds that global stress in the early 1930s was related to …
>
> a liquidity shortage on international capital markets, which culminated in the huge capital flow reversal of the year 1931. The geography of financial troubles at the beginning of the 1930s closely matched the distribution of countries between creditors and debtors. The crisis first propagated to the large importers of capital. With the huge liquidation of international investments, countries that were previously relying on foreign borrowing to finance their current account deficits fell victim of speculative attacks.[2]

By contrast, the largest creditors of the 1920s repatriated those capital flows in the early 1930s, a situation which, according to Accominotti (2011), is the main characteristic of this period. Unfortunately, in Bordo and Murshid (2001), the

[2]The same idea is repeated in a more recent Working Paper by Accominotti and Eichengreen (2013): The sharp increase in stock market volatility in the major financial centers that exported capital at the end of the 1920s is described as being at the origin of the decline in foreign lending to borrowing countries.

definition of contagion is only based on the correlation of prices. Additionally, the three indicators estimated by Accominotti (2011) cannot be considered as relevant indicators of contagion: in particular, an increase in the spread of government bonds does not necessarily reveal an increase in contagion, but almost always signifies a higher risk premium.

In order to propose a rigorous econometric approach taking into account, most notably, problems due to auto-regressive conditional heteroskedasticity on time series, and the direction of contagion, we base our analysis of contagion on the most recent research on the subject in order to re-examine the "Golden Fetters" hypothesis.

2.3 Contagion: A Survey

The existing literature includes many studies involving contagion, but scholars do not seem to agree on one generally accepted definition of this phenomenon. A recent paper on contagion gives up to eleven definitions of this concept (Forbes 2012). As Sebastian Edwards (2000) points out, the use of the term "contagion" in economics is relatively new, only dating back from the early 1990s. However, the word itself is not new: it stems from the Latin verb "contingere", which means "to come in contact with" or "to pollute" and, initially, the term was coined in the 14th century to describe a pathological phenomenon, i.e. the "transmission of a disease by direct or indirect contact". More exactly, in epidemiology, contagion designates the very vast—greater than originally expected—spread of a disease (Edwards 2000).

The only clear-cut certitude found in the literature is that contagion cannot be assimilated to causality (Forbes 2012). Whereas causality is a strong, direct link between two distinct phenomena, cause and effect, contagion is not as clear-cut and direct. Hence, these two phenomena should be differentiated. Two main conceptions of contagion can be distinguished in the literature: a global and systemic definition, mainly based on macroeconomic aggregates, and another one founded on price movements.

2.3.1 The Global and Systemic Approach

Eichengreen et al. (July 1996) define contagion as "a situation where the knowledge that there is a crisis elsewhere increases the probability of a domestic crisis." Following this broad definition, several papers focus more on the extent of contagion than on its origin and direction, defending the idea that contagion can concern not only specific, correlated markets or countries, but that it can become global. According to a popular definition by Masson (1998, 1999), there exist three types of contagion mechanisms: "monsoonal effects", "spillover effects"—a term integrated in one of Forbes' latest papers (Forbes 2012) and in several other pieces of literature—and residual contagion mechanisms. Whereas monsoonal effects focus on contagion in a group of countries stemming from a common cause, such as policies in common adopted wholesale by industrialized countries, spillover effects are crises that originate in one specific market or country and that then "may affect the macroeconomic fundamentals" [i.e. GNP, prices, the balance of payments situation, the level of unemployment] in another market or country (Masson 1998). This type of contagion is also acknowledged by Kaminsky and Reinhart, who call it "fundamentals-based contagion" (Kaminsky and Reinhart 2000). Finally, residual contagion phenomena are "those that cannot be identified with observable changes in macroeconomic fundamentals", i.e. the crises that originate in one country and spread to another because those countries, or the markets involved, are subject to "multiple equilibria", i.e. "self-fulfilling expectations" held by investors in the country or market involved (Masson 1999). A similar, popular definition of contagion as a residual, negative effect has been adopted by Edwards (2000), who indicates three scales of shock propagation: global, that coming from one correlated country, and residual. He classifies residual contagion as being "all that exceeds market participants' expectations" (Edwards 2000). As mentioned by this author, it appears more useful to apply the notion of contagion to more restricted—and perhaps more quantifiable—phenomena.

2.3.2 The Price Movements Approach: From Interdependence to Shift Contagion

Kodres and Pritsker (2002) observe that contagion has been defined by some authors as any price movement, i.e. as "a price movement on one market resulting from a shock in another market", and hence can be assimilated to a spillover effect. Moreover, this approach considers contagion as being a correlation between several markets, countries or groups of countries. In her survey of literature of the existing definitions of contagion, Kristin Forbes (2012) shows that contagion is used to refer to:

- a co-movement across several markets or countries. Morgenstern (1959) asserts that financial crises are likely to spread either simultaneously to several countries or in multiple phases, from those countries where the crisis started to the other, "peripheral" ones. It is implicit that contagion usually traces its roots in one market or country and then, at a later stage, spreads to another (or several other) markets or countries (Kindleberger and Aliber 2011).
- a phenomenon that needs multiple occurrences in order to exist. For example, in Boyer et al. (2006), contagion is described as the excess correlation between stock markets. Dungey et al. (2010) provide us with a more explicit definition, saying that contagion is the bunch of "effects of contemporaneous movements in asset returns across countries".

We see, then, that this literature is starting to admit the existence of contagion and its specificity, as compared to mere market interdependence or minor spillover phenomena. For instance, Forbes and Rigobon (2002) and Bordo and Murshid (2001) measure interdependence as cross-market correlations, and treat contagion as a stronger degree of cross-market correlation.

The first-ever work to mention "excess" is a 2003 article (Bae et al. 2003), cited by Forbes (2012), which defines contagion as the "exceedance events in a region that are not explained by covariates"—i.e. interest rates, volatility, exchange rates—but rather by severe shocks in excess or in defect of the "5th and 95th quantile of marginal return distribution" in equity indexes. This definition paves the way to quantifying excessive or abnormal contagious phenomena—and, hence, to defining contagion more accurately. Boyer et al. (2006) define contagion as the "excess correlation"—i.e. a tangible increase in correlation of accessible and investable securities across financial markets—"between stock markets during periods of high volatility". A slightly more inclusive definition of contagion is that elaborated by Bekaert et al. (2014), according to which contagion is "the co-movement in excess of that implied by the factor model, i.e. above and beyond what can be explained by fundamentals taking into account their natural evolution over time".

Contagion, however, is not only "excess correlation": it also implies an alteration of the nature of the cross-market relationship, i.e. whether there is a change in market interdependence before and after the shock. Hence, some scholars advocate the use of the expression "shift contagion", which refers to a tangible shift in cross-market correlation after a shock in one single country, as opposed to interdependence, which is a mere "continuation of the same cross-market linkages that exist during more tranquil periods" (Forbes and Rigobon 2001).

As Forbes and Rigobon (2001) point out, this notion of change is what distinguishes contagion from simple correlation: as such, the existence of a shift in market correlation before and after the contagious event is worth analyzing. Forbes and Rigobon (2001) aim at proving that the term contagion—or, in their words, "shift-contagion"—"implies that cross-market linkages are fundamentally different after a shock to one market". In order to do so, they analyze the correlation between the concerned markets before and after the shock: if their correlation has increased "significantly", then that episode can be classified as shift-contagion. Moreover, what characterizes shift-contagion is the fact that pre-crisis transmission mechanisms are different than transmission mechanisms that occur during or after the crisis. This implies that, during the crisis, contagion channels appear that would not exist in "normal" or more tranquil periods: hence, Forbes and Rigobon (2001) assert that shift contagion occurs when a crisis considerably transforms a market and its mechanisms by inducing a "structural shift". However, Forbes and Rigobon (2001) fail to provide generally accepted indications as to the minimal increase or value range that need to be covered by contagion in order for it to be significant.

2.3.3 BEKK Model with a Structural Break

Implementing a BEKK model with a structural break provides an accurate tool to measure contagion which, moreover, allows the limitations mentioned above to be overcome. First, it measures spillover effects via the transmission of volatility from one variable to another. Second, it identifies both the origin and direction of contagion. Third, the excess volatilities are taken into account in the variances-covariances equation, since the BEKK model is based on a GARCH approach. Fourth, the introduction of a structural break in the BEKK model enables shift contagion phenomena to be studied. This regime-switching analysis is particularly appropriate for studying contagion over the interwar period, and also for testing its dominant explanation, the "Golden Fetters" hypothesis.

2.4 Contagion During the Great Depression and the "Golden Fetters" Hypothesis

In this section, we recall the key features of the "Golden Fetters" hypothesis. According to Eichengreen (1992), two factors produced the stability of the pre-war Gold Standard (GS): credibility (commitment to par was not violated prior to 1914), and cooperation between central banks, which rendered the commitment an international one. This cooperative management by central bankers was quite different from the leader/follower approach of the "Theory of hegemonic stability" developed by Kindleberger (1973). Over the pre-war GS period, Eichengreen (1992) argues, the Bank of England acted in fact as an "international borrower of last resort" (not a lender, as defended by Kindleberger 1973), and, was "hostage to international cooperation, reduced to dependence on the assistance of European central banks" (Eichengreen 1992, p. 8). During the interwar period, international cooperation collapsed, provoking the disappearance of one of the pillars of the pre-war GS. Eichengreen (1992) assesses this imperfect GS (Subsequently, the Gold Exchange Standard, GES), as being at the origin of the propagation of the Great Depression worldwide. Capital flows were the *vector* of this crisis: "The asymmetry in the GS system under which countries in surplus can shift the burden of adjustment to countries in deficit, forcing them to deflate, was the last thing needed [...] Monetary authorities outside the US were forced to respond vigorously to the decline in capital inflows if they wished to stay on the GS (p. 15)". Due to the commitment to gold, monetary and fiscal policies in the world remained restrictive, aggravating the contractionary effects on economic activity. Eichengreen highlights the fact that "governments hazarding expansionary initiatives were forced to draw back (p. 16)" (Britain in 1930; the US in 1931–1933; Belgium in 1934). The trade-off was whether to defend the GES, or to renew it with international cooperation to implement expansionary policies in the world. Under the GES, the lack of international cooperation precluded these initiatives. What "amplified this destabilizing impulse

[…] and gave rise to the great economic contraction? The answer lies in *the spread of financial instability* […] the bank failures and financial chaos that led to the liquidation of bank deposits (p. 18)". "Why didn't policy makers intervene to head off the collapse of their financial systems? They failed to do so because the GES posed an insurmountable obstacle to unilateral action. Containing bank runs required policy makers to inject liquidity into the banking system, but this could be inconsistent with the GS rules (p. 18)". After that, "realizing that convertibility might be compromised and that devaluation might cause capital losses on domestic assets, investors rushed to get their money out of the country […] the destabilizing linkages between domestic and international financial systems operated most powerfully where foreign deposits were more prevalent: Europe's banking systems were interconnected by a network of foreign deposits (p. 18)". *This is the vehicle through which contagion comes into play in Eichengreen's analysis*. European countries illustrate these mechanisms: disturbing revelations about the cover ratio (of gold reserves to notes and coins) in countries like Germany and Austria, accelerated capital flight and favored foreign deposit withdrawals. "Far from being a bulwark of financial stability, the GS was the main impediment to its maintenance (p. 19)". Domestic authorities could not fund the banking system without jeopardizing the GS rules. Saving banks required international cooperation, which never materialized. This is why the author first designates the GES as the main cause of the Great Depression and then goes on, in a striking formula, to *assimilate the end of the Depression with the end of the GES* (Eichengreen 1992, p. 21). Ultimately, unlike Kindleberger (1973) and Nurkse (1944), he asserted that countries that left Gold experienced economic recovery, whereas those remaining on Gold exacerbated their economic situation. Accordingly, "breaking the Golden Fetters" constituted the solution.

Our purpose here is to focus on the implications of contagion raised by the "Golden Fetters" hypothesis. Following Eichengreen (1992), Bordo and Murshid (2001) identify and retain one major contagion channel under the imperfect Gold Exchange Standard (GES), explicitly gold flows between countries and capital flights. They contend that their findings on contagion corroborate Eichengreen's "Golden Fetters" hypothesis. Their explanation relies on the absence of coordination between central banks during the GES, in which case the defense of parity should have implied a copycat of central banks in the use of interest rate. In order to respect par and without cooperation between Central Banks, each central bank had to monitor its domestic metallic holdings. In that respect, the best tool was the use of the discount rate. To control for this consequence, each central bank had no choice but to base its own discount rate on that of the others. In the absence of cooperation over the GES, the will to preserve metallic holdings in order to respect the gold par should have meant that each central bank had to adopt a follow-the-herd attitude. However, in case of currency attacks, if there had been efficient coordination, this would have led the central bank with a weak currency to raise its interest rate, while the central bank with a strong currency would have lowered its interest rate.

It is this specific link between the international contagion of interest rates and the "Golden Fetters" hypothesis that we want to test in the present chapter. If the "Golden Fetters" hypothesis holds, then interest rate contagion should have been more pronounced under the GES than when it collapsed. This is because as soon as the GES was abandoned, each country was free to pursue its own domestic goals, resulting in far more disconnected interest rates. Was this the case? This is the key historical issue we address in our analysis of the international contagion of short-term interest rates during the interwar period.

To this end, we have chosen to consider the three implications of Eichengreen's "Golden Fetters" thesis as sub-hypotheses, in order to assess their validity:

(1) H1: "The financial crisis has been imported into the US" (Eichengreen 1992). The BEKK model with a structural break will enable this issue to be decided.
(2) H2: "France caused the disruption of the International Monetary System in the thirties" (Eichengreen 1992). Comparison of the two sub-periods (twenties versus thirties) will help to reveal whether or not contagion moved from France to other countries.
(3) H3: "The GES was responsible for contagion" (which is *stricto sensu* the "Golden Fetters" hypothesis): The origin of the 1929 crisis is considered as indissociable from the unsustainable international monetary system (Gold Exchange Standard), with its presumed complete absence of central bank cooperation. Theoretically, such a lack of cooperation should have led to a stronger copycat policy of instrument rates while the GES was in operation, rather than after its breakdown. This was because, throughout the whole GES period, lack of cooperation resulted in competition for gold species between issuing institutions; this, in turn, led each central bank to copy its rate on that of its "partners/competitors". After the breakdown of the GES, each central bank was assumed to act independently, so interest rate contagion should have been less apparent.

   We propose to test the validity of H3 through two indicators derived from our BEKK model:

   (a) We test contagion with five distinct structural breaks[3]: the triggering of the financial crisis (end of 1929), September 1931 (devaluation of the Pound), March 1933 (suspension of the Dollar convertibility), June 1933 (London conference), January 1934 (official devaluation of the Dollar). Our purpose is to identify which structural break constitutes the defining moment of the period. Finding that one of the dates corresponding to the breakdown of the GES is more statistically significant than the financial crisis of 1929 would, undoubtedly, support the "Golden Fetters" hypothesis (H3). We contend, however, that an additional condition is required.
   (b) By counting the number of scenarios of absence of contagion during the two sub-periods, we are able to characterize the plausibility of

[3]These breaks are the most significant ones over the considered period. For reasons of space, tests that enable the presence of structural breaks in 1931, 1933, 1934 to be rejected, are not presented here, but are available upon request. It should be noted that for these dates, the BEKK model never converges, which means that these dates cannot be considered as indicating relevant structural breaks.

Eichengreen's statement: if there were more scenarios of non-contagion in the thirties than in the twenties, H3 would be corroborated; conversely, more scenarios of non-contagion in the twenties than in the thirties would weaken H3.

2.5 Data and Methodology

The data used here refer to the 3-month Treasury Bond interest rates in the USA, Great Britain and France, based on a monthly frequency. The considered period goes from 1921M01 to 1936M12 (Fig. 2.1). The database has been elaborated by Pierre Villa.

The choice of this data is driven by the two following considerations. First, the three-month government bond yields incorporate the effects of monetary policy: by means of open market policies, central banks could purchase or sell Treasury bonds in function of their particular objectives. Second, our choice of the three countries is based on the outcomes of Accominotti (2011), who indicates that the crisis that came from debtor countries was provoked by creditor countries repatriating their capital. In the present chapter, we further assess the role played in the contagion phenomena by the three main creditor countries' use of strictly similar short-run interest rates.

When considering the possible specifications required to model the co-movements of spreads, we finally decided to adopt a BEKK model. We immediately discarded the VECH model of Bollerslev et al. (1988) as it was extremely unwieldy (more than 70 coefficients to evaluate in a trivariate

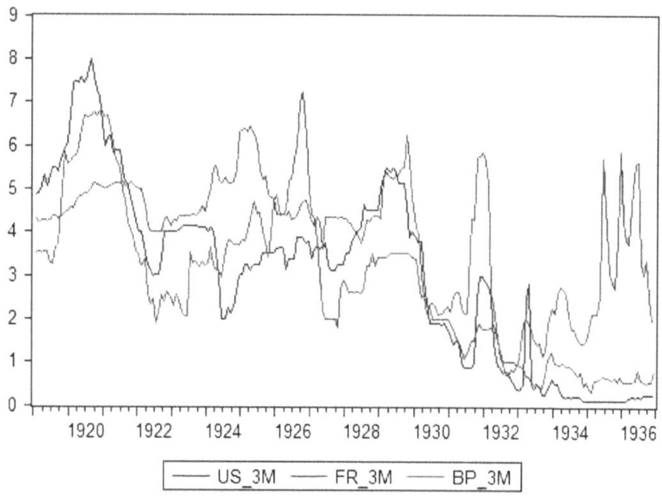

Fig. 2.1 The 3-month interest rates of France, Great Britain and the USA (1920m01–1936m12)

framework); moreover, that model could generate time series on conditional variances featuring negative values. We also rejected the DVECH model (Diagonal VECH) which imposes prior restrictions on the structure of coefficient matrices: the conditional variance of the interest rate of a given country is dependent on its own past values and the innovation square related to them. The number of coefficients to be evaluated is certainly considerably reduced, thereby making estimation easier, but it then becomes impossible to test the reality of many schemes of influence between the volatilities of various variables, precisely because that model imposes its own pre-defined scheme. As for the dynamic correlations DCC scheme (Engle 2002; Tse and Tsui 2002), this is not suitable for tests on hypotheses relating to propagation phenomena because, like the VECH model, it does not guarantee the positivity of the values calculated from conditional variances.

Finally, the BEKK model was chosen, because (i) it is the only model that can test the hypothesis of the appropriate propagation scheme of volatilities, (ii) without having to estimate too many coefficients, and (iii) while guaranteeing the positivity of the values calculated from conditional variances. However, as we want to test H3 by identifying the defining moment of the period, we introduce a structural break into the model.

2.5.1 Writing Conventions for Propagation Schemes of Volatilities and Modeling

A variety of propagation schemes based on the monthly levels of the 3-month interest rates (Y1, Y2, Y3) and, above all, on their volatilities, can be found in the 3 zones (USA, Great Britain and France). A scatter plot analysis confirms that a positive correlation prevails between the 3-month interest rates (Fig. 2.2).

As the unit root tests implemented on the monthly series systematically confirm level stationarity (Table 2.1), we have retained monthly levels of interest rates.

Consequently, the implemented BEKK model will focus on the dynamics of the monthly levels of interest rates and their associated second-order moments.

The BEKK model enables the simultaneous modeling of conditional expectations, variances and covariances of the short-run interest rates. It allows for a fairly easy testing of different propagation schemes of volatility between the three zones and, unlike the standard VECH model, the estimated coefficients provide, in all circumstances, positive conditional variances.

The unrestricted reference model M1 explicitly allows for volatility propagation schemes in all directions between the three zones. The model consists of two systems of equations, S1 and S2. Conditional expectations, variances and covariances are specified as:

$$\mathrm{S1}\; Yt = \Delta t\, \alpha + [I - \Delta t]\, \beta + \varphi\, Yt - 1 + \varepsilon t$$

$$\mathrm{S2}\; Ht = C'\Delta t\, C + D'[I - \Delta t]D + A'\, \varepsilon t\, \Delta t\, \varepsilon t' A + B'\, \varepsilon t\, [I - \Delta t]\varepsilon t' B + G' Ht - 1 \Delta t\, G + F' Ht - 1[I - \Delta t]F$$

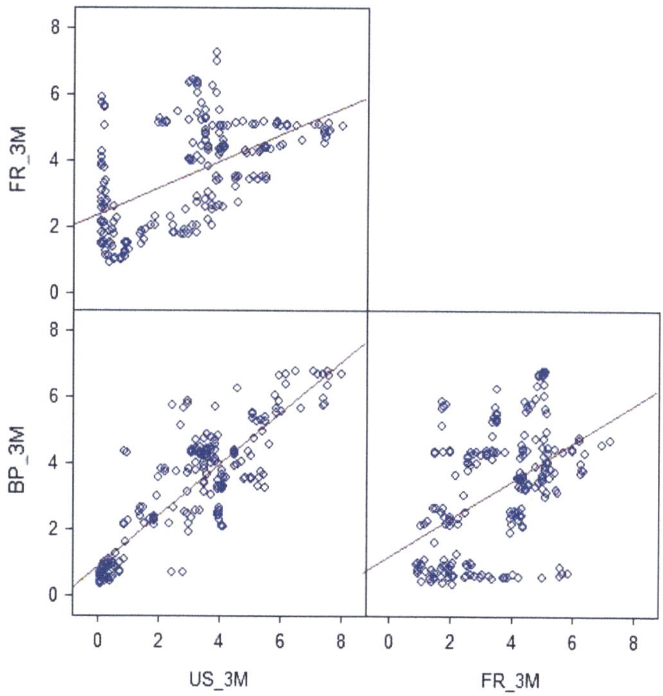

Fig. 2.2 The correlation between the 3-month interest rates of France, Great Britain and the USA (1921m01–1926m12)

Table 2.1 Unit-root tests

	3-month interest rates			
Period: 1921M01–1936M12	1921m01–1929m06		1930m06–1936m12	
	t-Statistic	Prob.	t-Statistic	Prob.
Im, Pesaran and Shin W-stat	−1.78	0.04	−2.09	0.01

The number of lags is automatically determined on the basis of the Min(SIC) criterion. The Prob. column indicates the risk threshold from which it becomes possible to reject H0

where Δt is an identity matrix from the date of the structural break and a null matrix before this date, and I is the identity matrix of dimension 3. The matrices α, C, A and G (respectively β, D, B and F) are the matrices of prevailing coefficients after (respectively before) the date of the structural break. The restrictions made on the matrix components β, D, B and F, when we move from the propagation scheme «RRR» to another scheme, can easily be deduced from the restrictions mentioned in a non-exhaustive way in Appendix 1. The first system, S1, depicts the conditional expectations of the short-run interest rates Y_{jt} (j ∈ {1, 2, 3). For the sake of simplicity, each equation has been indicated in an AR(1) form. As for the S2 system, it models the 3 conditional variances and the 3 conditional covariances $h_{ij,\,t}$ where (i, j) ∈ {1, 2, 3}).

It should be noted that the H_t matrix of conditional variances and covariances is symmetric, which is not the case, however, of matrices **C**, **A** and **G** (respectively D, B and F). The g_{ij} and f_{ij} coefficients (resp. a_{ij} and b_{ij}) determine the degree of dependence of the conditional variance $h_{jj,\ t}$ of Y_j on date t toward the lagged conditional variance $Y_{ii,\ t-1}$ of Y_i (resp. toward the lagged squared innovation $\varepsilon_{i,\ t-1}{}^2$). Consequently, a restriction of nullity on these coefficients ($a_{ij} = b_{ij} = g_{ij} = f_{ij} = 0$) suggests the absence of propagation of the volatility from i toward j. Many diffusion schemes can be considered between conditional volatilities, with each being bound up with particular restrictions on some coefficients of matrices **A**, **G**, **B** and **F**. Some prior conventions are useful to describe these diffusion schemes. To begin with, on the basis of the three monetary zones (1 = USA, 2 = Great Britain, 3 = France) three pairwise relationship can be observed (1, 2), (1, 3) and (2, 3). These pairwise relationships can take four alternate forms:

(a) Total absence of propagation between the two zones, a scheme indicated by the letter N (No contagion). N(1, 2) depicts the absence of any volatility propagation between zone 1 and 2.
(b) Reciprocal propagation, identified by the letter R.[4]
(c) Univocal propagation of the first component of the couple toward the second is indicated by the letter U.[5]
(d) Inverted univocal propagation of the second component of the couple toward the first one; the letter I identifies this scheme.[6]

The description of the global diffusion scheme between the three pairs (1, 2), (1, 3) and (2, 3) will take the form of a triplet, whose components are chosen from the set {N, R, U, I}. For instance, the total absence of diffusion mechanisms between any of the three monetary pairs is described by the triplet N(1, 2), N(1, 3), N(2, 3) or, in short, «NNN» if we admit that the first component of the triplet always refers to the couple (1, 2), the second to the couple (1, 3), and the third one to the couple (2, 3).[7] Therefore, the model of reference M1 is also, according to these conventions, the model «RRR». Each possible restriction of the model RRR relates to a specific propagation scheme, and has been tested using a Wald test.

---

[4]R(1, 2) suggests a recursive scheme of propagation 1 ↔ 2.

[5]U(1, 2) means that there is one scheme of propagation between zones 1 and 2 working in the sense 1 ⟶ 2.

[6]I(1, 2) enables a 1 ⟵ 2-type of diffusion scheme to be to identified.

[7]For example, UIR suggests the existence of a scheme such as:

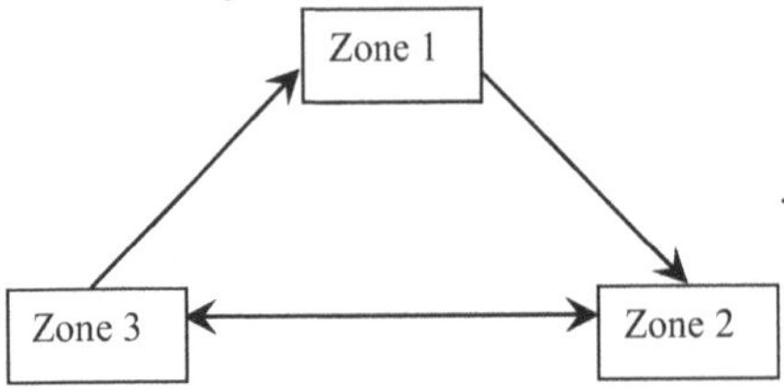

The set of possible schemes is stated in the Appendix (1); it sums up, for each scheme, the corresponding restrictions on the components of the initial matrices **A**, **B**, **G** and **F**.

2.5.2 *Calibration and Coefficient Estimations*

The «RRR» model is estimated using the method of maximum likelihood. Assuming normality of the joint distribution ε_{1t}, ε_{2t} and ε_{3t}, the likelihood of the *t*th observation for a set of coefficients $\Theta = \{\alpha, \Phi, C, D, A, B, G \text{ and } F\}$ is:

$$L_t = \frac{1}{2\pi}|H_t|^{-1/2}\exp^{-\hat{\varepsilon}_t' H_t^{-1}\hat{\varepsilon}_t}$$

where $|H_t|$ is the determinant of $\mathbf{H}_t$ and $\hat{\varepsilon}_t = \begin{bmatrix} \hat{\varepsilon}_{1,t} \\ \hat{\varepsilon}_{2,t} \\ \hat{\varepsilon}_{2,t} \end{bmatrix}$ is the residuals matrix stemming from ε. The log-likelihood of the whole sample is then:

$$\mathrm{LogL} = \sum_{t=1}^{T}\left(-\frac{1}{2}\mathrm{Log}(|H_t|) - \mathrm{Log}(2\pi) - \hat{\varepsilon}_t' H_t^{-1}\hat{\varepsilon}_t\right)$$

The numerical resolution of the optimization problem needs an appropriate choice of the first guess of the coefficients. To that end, we start by evaluating a univariate GARCH model for each of the three variations Y_{jt} ($j \in \{1, 2, 3\}$) of interest rates. On the basis of the resulting estimated coefficients and residuals, the *first guests* for matrices α, Φ, C, D, A, B, F and G are calibrated.[8]

In the same way, the conditional covariance time series are initially set as:

$$h_{ij,t} = \mathrm{Cov}(\hat{\varepsilon}_{i,t}, \hat{\varepsilon}_{j,t}) \forall i, j, t$$

while the initial conditional variances time series of the BEKK model correspond to their estimated counterpart in the univariate models.

[8]Calibration of the initial coefficient values is here only described for the case of the system with no structural break. Calibration of the model with a structural break does not present, conceptually, any additional difficulties except for the fact that it requires, even for the same spread, the estimation of two univariate Garch models for each of the two sub-periods separated by the date-event of 1929m11.

2.6 Findings

The unrestricted model RRR is evaluated for the whole period. The structural break introduced in the BEKK model has been selected by using the maximum of likelihood methods among five candidates. Contrary to the hypothesis of Accominotti (2011) and Eichengreen (1992), the triggering of the financial crisis of 1929 surpasses by far the other four dates, which correspond to the breakdown of the GES. None of these other four dates, which characterize the 1931–1934 "Golden Fetters" hypothesis, gives significant results regarding contagion schemes.

Estimation of the possible schemes of contagion is presented in Table 2.2.

In Table 2.3 we have ranked restrictions of M1 model via decremented values of type I errors: the most acceptable restrictions appear at the top of the list. We found 10 scenarios of possible contagion schemes, with a probability of occurrence superior to 80%. We have also decided to reject 18 scenarios with a probability of occurrence inferior to 15%.

Table 2.2 Propagation schemes of volatilities for 3-month interest rates (1921m01–1936m12) Break on 1929M11: Wald restriction tests

1–2 USA↔ FRA	1–3 USA↔GB	2–3 FRA↔GB	Wald Stat	% P-val
R	*R*	*I*	*0.493137*	*97.42*
I	*R*	*U*	*2.434867*	*96.47*
I	*I*	*I*	*4.871141*	*96.21*
R	*R*	*U*	*0.631324*	*95.95*
I	*I*	*U*	*5.023761*	*95.72*
I	*R*	*I*	*3.165346*	*92.36*
I	*I*	*R*	*3.682484*	*88.46*
R	*I*	*I*	*3.856801*	*86.98*
I	*R*	*R*	*1.296504*	*86.2*
R	*I*	*U*	*4.498451*	*80.96*
I	U	R	5.639672	68.75
R	R	N	5.783262	67.15
I	U	U	9.838523	63.01
R	I	R	3.016483	55.51
R	U	U	7.175579	51.78
R	U	I	7.669387	46.64
N	I	R	11.79841	46.2
I	N	R	12.2358	42.69
U	U	I	12.37814	41.58
N	I	I	16.64276	40.91
R	U	R	4.085821	39.45
I	U	I	12.67004	39.35
U	R	R	4.173033	38.31

(continued)

Table 2.2 (continued)

1–2 USA↔ FRA	1–3 USA↔GB	2–3 FRA↔GB	Wald Stat	% P-val
U	R	I	8.74197	36.45
R	N	R	8.877864	35.27
N	R	R	9.061661	33.71
I	N	I	17.87961	33.1
U	U	N	18.38672	30.17
U	I	R	9.532098	29.94
U	R	U	9.537282	29.9
U	R	N	14.07094	29.62
R	N	I	14.15778	29.07
I	N	U	18.72683	28.31
R	N	U	14.28863	28.27
R	U	N	14.30124	28.19
U	I	I	14.30569	28.16
N	R	I	14.37414	27.75
N	N	I	23.24544	27.69
N	U	I	19.44487	24.63
U	U	R	10.40044	23.8
N	N	R	19.8765	22.58
U	U	U	15.30949	22.49
U	N	I	20.39068	20.31
N	U	R	16.1511	18.44
U	N	R	16.92651	15.24
N	*I*	*U*	*22.33523*	*13.27*
N	*R*	*U*	*17.49013*	*13.21*
N	*U*	*U*	*24.99994*	*6.98*
U	*I*	*U*	*20.54314*	*5.75*
I	*I*	*N*	*27.06526*	*4.08*
N	*N*	*U*	*32.75582*	*3.59*
I	*R*	*N*	*22.34018*	*3.39*
I	*U*	*N*	*29.80802*	*1.9*
U	*N*	*U*	*29.89013*	*1.86*
R	*I*	*N*	*24.74377*	*1.61*
N	*U*	*N*	*36.46109*	*1.36*
N	*R*	*N*	*31.84416*	*1.05*
N	*I*	*N*	*39.32954*	*0.61*
U	*I*	*N*	*37.46111*	*0.18*
I	*N*	*N*	*44.15522*	*0.14*
N	*N*	*N*	*50.93498*	*0.11*
R	*N*	*N*	*40.9662*	*0.06*
U	*N*	*N*	*49.05617*	*0.03*

Table 2.3 Selection of propagation schemes based on Wald restriction tests (1921m01–1936m12)—break on 1929M11

Rejected schemes at a 15% level				
	1–2 USA↔ FRA	1–3 USA↔GB	2–3 FRA↔GB	Total
R	2	3	0	5
U	4	3	5	12
I	4	5	0	9
N	7	6	12	25
Most probable schemes (P-value >80%)				
	1–2 USA↔ FRA	1–3 USA↔GB	2–3 FRA↔GB	Total
R	3	5	2	10
U	0	0	3	3
I	6	4	4	14
N	0	0	0	0

In order to select the most probable scheme of contagion, Table 2.3 recapitulates the number of scenarios whose probability of occurrence is higher than 80% or inferior to 15%. For each pair of countries, we retain (respectively, we reject) the scheme observed the largest number of times, with a probability superior to 80% (respectively, inferior to 15%).

We obtain the following results:

- an inverted propagation process between the 3-month interest rates of the USA and France
- an inverted or reciprocal propagation process between the USA and Great Britain
- an inverted propagation process between France and Great Britain

Moreover, according to Table 2.3 we can reject the total absence of propagation between the zones throughout the whole period.

Having determined that the structural break occurred in November 1929, we distinguish two sub-periods, in order to compare the dynamics of the relationship between interest rates before and after this structural break. The first sub-period corresponds, then, to the 1920s, and the second to the 1930s. This allows us to analyze the extent to which Black Thursday has modified the propagation schemes of interest rates.

The ranked restrictions of M1 model (Table 2.4) offer quite different results than those obtained for the reference period.

At the 80% level, 42 contagion schemes could be good candidates and, unlike the whole period, we cannot reject any propagation scheme at a 15% level.

Table 2.5 indicates that the most probable scheme of propagation is the following: a reciprocal propagation process from the 3-month interest rate of the USA to the 3-month interest rate of Great Britain, and reciprocal propagation between the interest rates of the USA and France and also between France and Great Britain.

Table 2.4 Propagation schemes of volatilities for 3-month interest rates (1921m01–1929m06): Wald restriction tests

1–2 USA↔ GB	1–3 USA↔FRA	2–3 GB↔FRA	Wald Stat	% P-val
I	*N*	*R*	*0.10*	*100.00*
N	*I*	*R*	*0.18*	*99.99*
I	*I*	*U*	*0.17*	*99.99*
N	*I*	*I*	*0.57*	*99.98*
I	*U*	*R*	*0.06*	*99.96*
I	*I*	*R*	*0.06*	*99.96*
R	*N*	*R*	*0.09*	*99.91*
N	*R*	*I*	*0.46*	*99.83*
U	*I*	*I*	*0.47*	*99.82*
I	*I*	*I*	*0.47*	*99.82*
I	*R*	*U*	*0.13*	*99.80*
N	*R*	*R*	*0.14*	*99.75*
U	*U*	*R*	*0.15*	*99.75*
U	*I*	*R*	*0.16*	*99.71*
R	*I*	*U*	*0.16*	*99.70*
U	*U*	*I*	*0.57*	*99.68*
U	*R*	*U*	*0.21*	*99.51*
U	*R*	*N*	*0.70*	*99.46*
R	*U*	*R*	*0.01*	*99.31*
I	*R*	*R*	*0.02*	*99.17*
I	*N*	*U*	*1.57*	*99.14*
R	*I*	*R*	*0.04*	*98.22*
I	*R*	*I*	*0.41*	*98.20*
R	*R*	*U*	*0.04*	*98.02*
R	*I*	*I*	*0.43*	*98.01*
U	*R*	*I*	*0.45*	*97.78*
R	*U*	*I*	*0.51*	*97.25*
I	*U*	*U*	*1.42*	*96.49*
R	*N*	*U*	*1.43*	*96.37*
R	*R*	*N*	*0.62*	*96.04*
U	*U*	*U*	*1.55*	*95.59*
U	*R*	*R*	*0.11*	*94.85*
U	*N*	*R*	*1.80*	*93.73*
U	*N*	*U*	*3.02*	*93.28*
U	*N*	*I*	*3.62*	*88.99*
U	*I*	*U*	*2.49*	*86.98*
R	*U*	*U*	*1.33*	*85.55*
N	*N*	*U*	*5.58*	*84.94*
N	*N*	*R*	*4.27*	*83.17*

(continued)

Table 2.4 (continued)

1–2 USA↔ GB	1–3 USA↔FRA	2–3 GB↔FRA	Wald Stat	% P-val
I	*U*	*I*	*2.91*	*82.02*
R	*R*	*I*	*0.40*	*81.95*
I	N	I	4.43	81.64
N	N	I	6.45	77.64
R	N	I	3.33	76.70
U	U	N	5.04	75.36
N	U	U	5.29	72.65
N	I	U	5.36	71.80
N	U	I	5.38	71.68
R	U	N	3.73	71.32
N	U	R	4.07	66.79
U	I	N	5.98	64.95
N	R	U	5.01	54.22
I	R	N	5.26	51.12
U	N	N	9.33	50.09
R	I	N	5.76	45.06
I	I	N	7.83	44.99
N	N	N	12.04	44.29
N	U	N	10.15	42.77
N	I	N	10.18	42.45
N	R	N	8.60	37.74
I	U	N	8.64	37.38
I	N	N	10.83	37.10
R	N	N	9.08	33.52

Table 2.5 Selection of propagation schemes based on Wald restriction tests (1921m01–1929m06)

Rejected schemes at a 15% level				
	1–2USA↔ GB	1–3 USA↔FRA	2–3 GB↔FRA	Total
R	0	0	0	0
U	0	0	0	0
I	0	0	0	0
N	0	0	0	0
Most probable schemes (P-value >80%)				
	1–2USA↔ GB	1–3 USA↔FRA	2–3 GB↔FRA	Total
R	11	12	14	37
U	13	9	13	35
I	12	11	13	46
N	6	10	2	18

The ranked restrictions of M1 model for the 1930m06–1936m1 period (Table 2.6) indicate that 6 scenarios of possible contagion schemes with a probability of superior to 80% occur, and that 27 schemes with a probability of occurrence inferior to 15% should be rejected.

Table 2.6 Propagation schemes of volatilities for 3-month interest rates (1930m06–1936m12): Wald restriction tests

1–2 GB↔ FRA	1–3 GB↔US	2–3 FRA↔US	Wald Stat	% P-val
R	*R*	*N*	*0.087257*	*99.91*
R	*R*	*I*	*0.05316*	*97.38*
R	*R*	*U*	*0.053929*	*97.34*
I	*R*	*N*	*1.779036*	*93.89*
I	*R*	*I*	*1.297166*	*86.19*
I	*R*	*U*	*1.541508*	*81.93*
N	R	U	3.417805	75.49
R	U	I	1.972047	74.09
N	R	N	5.526478	70.01
I	I	U	4.098324	66.34
R	I	U	2.496221	64.53
R	U	N	4.255086	64.22
U	R	N	4.453052	61.56
I	R	R	1.099971	57.7
U	R	U	2.995865	55.85
R	U	U	3.225842	52.08
N	R	R	3.39723	49.37
N	R	I	5.43646	48.92
I	I	R	3.575559	46.65
I	U	N	8.054405	42.82
R	U	R	1.859954	39.46
R	N	R	4.252468	37.29
U	R	I	4.424572	35.16
U	U	I	6.836071	33.63
R	I	R	2.227796	32.83
U	U	N	9.742889	28.35
I	U	I	7.677891	26.27
I	U	U	7.731055	25.85
N	U	N	12.52656	25.14
N	U	I	10.35847	24.08
N	I	U	10.40154	23.8
U	R	R	2.994214	22.38
U	U	R	5.861161	20.98
R	N	U	8.484417	20.47

(continued)

Table 2.6 (continued)

1–2 GB↔ FRA	1–3 GB↔US	2–3 FRA↔US	Wald Stat	% P-val
N	U	U	11.56852	17.15
U	U	U	9.163999	16.46
N	*U*	*R*	*9.81462*	*13.27*
I	*N*	*U*	*12.54106*	*12.86*
U	*I*	*U*	*10.08558*	*12.11*
I	*U*	*R*	*7.45553*	*11.37*
N	*I*	*R*	*10.38553*	*10.93*
N	*N*	*U*	*17.67896*	*6.06*
I	*N*	*R*	*12.06443*	*6.05*
U	*N*	*R*	*12.22209*	*5.72*
N	*N*	*R*	*15.91356*	*4.36*
U	*N*	*U*	*16.10408*	*4.09*
U	*I*	*R*	*10.0646*	*3.94*
R	*N*	*I*	*14.16441*	*2.79*
R	*I*	*N*	*14.47251*	*2.48*
I	*I*	*N*	*19.09318*	*1.44*
R	*I*	*I*	*13.02208*	*1.12*
N	*I*	*N*	*23.70769*	*0.84*
I	*I*	*I*	*17.52413*	*0.75*
R	*N*	*N*	*21.34454*	*0.63*
U	*I*	*N*	*22.60246*	*0.39*
U	*N*	*I*	*22.80762*	*0.36*
N	*I*	*I*	*23.4974*	*0.28*
N	*N*	*N*	*31.86781*	*0.15*
U	*I*	*I*	*21.82563*	*0.13*
U	*N*	*N*	*29.01136*	*0.12*
I	*N*	*N*	*29.06539*	*0.12*
N	*N*	*I*	*31.31883*	*0.05*
I	*N*	*I*	*28.92165*	*0.03*

Table 2.7 indicates that the following scheme may well prevail during the second sub-period:

- there is a propagation scheme from France to Great Britain
- there is reciprocal propagation between the 3-month interest rates of Great Britain and the USA
- There is a univocal propagation scheme between the 3-month interest rates of France and the USA.

Table 2.7 Selection of propagation schemes based on Wald restriction tests (1930m06–1936m12)

Rejected schemes at a 15% level				
	1–2 GB↔ FRA	1–3 GB↔US	2–3 FRA↔US	Total
R	4	0	7	11
U	8	2	4	14
I	7	11	8	26
N	8	14	8	30
Most probable schemes (P-value > 80%)				
	1–2 GB↔ FRA	1–3 GB↔US	2–3 FRA↔US	Total
R	3	6	0	9
U	0	0	2	2
I	3	0	2	5
N	0	0	2	2

To summarize our results, we can reasonably assume that the following contagion scheme prevailed throughout the interwar period and its associated sub-periods (Fig. 2.3).

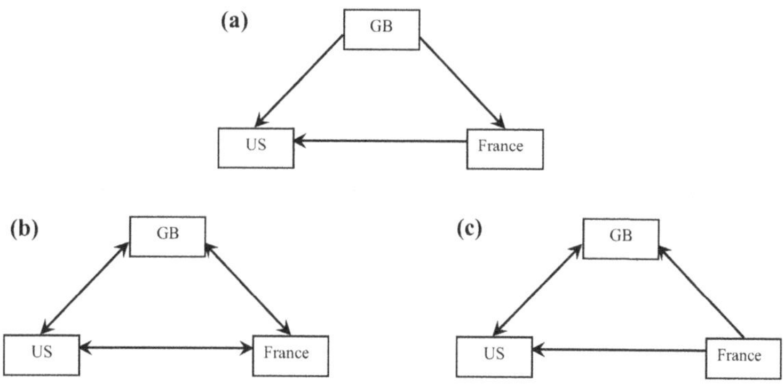

Fig. 2.3 The most probable schemes of propagation. **a** The most probable scheme of contagion throughout the interwar period. **b** The most probable scheme of contagion throughout the 1920s. **c** The most probable scheme of contagion throughout the 1930s

2.7 Discussion

Our results shed new light on the "Golden Fetters" thesis. We recall here that the aim of this chapter was to test the implications of the "Golden Fetters" hypothesis as three sub-hypotheses, in order to assess their validity:

(1) Regarding H1 (proposal: "the financial crisis has been imported into the US", Eichengreen 1992), the BEKK model with structural break (see Fig. 2.3) corroborates Eichengreen's view: the US suffered from the contagion that originated in Europe. We find that Great Britain and France were at the origin of changes in the volatility of US interest rates. We cannot, therefore, reject the idea that the financial crisis was imported into the US.

(2) H2: (proposal: "France caused the disruption of the International Monetary System in the thirties", Eichengreen, 1992). Comparison of the two sub-periods (twenties versus thirties) indicates contrasted dynamics of contagion. By retaining the real propagation mechanisms at the 1% error level, the twenties seem marked by perfect interaction between the three countries: over this period, recursion (mutual contagion) stands out as dominant. Conversely, in the thirties, the contagion moves from France both to the UK and to the US. The volatility of French interest rates controls both the UK and the US rates: At issue, according to Eichengreen (1992), the "policy of species" of the Bank of France, which drained the gold species in order to maintain the gold parity of its currency. Our econometric results tend to support hypothesis (H2): we cannot reject the possibility that, in the thirties, the sources of interference between interest rates might have come from the "mercantilist" policy of the Bank of France. Nonetheless, this finding should not be over-interpreted. It is, admittedly, one of the most probable schemes of contagion, but not the only one. We have also detected the presence of reciprocal propagation between GB and the USA.

(3) H3: Was the GES ultimately responsible for contagion? This strong claim, advanced by Eichengreen (1992), implies that the origin of the 1929 crisis lies in an unsustainable international monetary system (Gold Exchange Standard), characterized by the presumed complete absence of central bank cooperation: this lack of cooperation should, logically, lead to a stronger copycat policy of instrument rates under the GES than after its break.

    (a) By mobilizing the BEKK model with a structural break, we first determined which date revealed the most significant structural break. We tested contagion mechanisms with five plausibly distinct structural breaks: the triggering of the financial crisis of 1929, September 1931 (devaluation of the pound), March 1933 (suspension of the dollar convertibility), June 1933 (London conference), January 1934 (official devaluation of the dollar). Using the method of maximum likelihood to order our results, we have found that only 1929 marked a significant break in the transmission mechanism of interest rate volatility. The change in the transmission of shocks of interest rate volatility appears at the end of the year 1929, clearly as a result of the financial crisis, not of the progressive collapse of the GES. This result undermines the thesis of the "Golden Fetters", because none of the key dates of the breakdown of the GES appears to be significant here.

(b) We then counted the number of scenarios of absence of contagion in the two sub-periods: under the hypothesis of non-cooperation between central banks over the GES period, as explained above, the transmission of interest rate volatility should be strong (with each central bank mapping its interest rates on its "partners/competitors"). Yet, we have found that the scenario of no link between interest rates (complete absence of contagion) was rejected 30 times during the period 1930–1936, while we cannot reject it for the period 1921–1929. This means that the absence of contagion is more characteristic of the twenties than the thirties, which is in contradiction with H3. We have also found that the scenario of absence of contagion could be accepted (with a probability of 80%) for 18 episodes over the twenties, against only two episodes over the thirties. Both the rejection and acceptance of scenarios of absence of contagion indicate that H3 should be reconsidered.

2.8 Conclusion: Does the "Golden Fetters" Hypothesis Hold?

Our study reveals somewhat contrasting effects regarding the incidence of contagion during the GES period. Our findings suggest that the disappearance of the GES did not have the effects implicitly assumed by Eichengreen (1992), and that the absence of contagion was more probable in the twenties than in the thirties. If one follows the conclusions of Eichengreen (1992), then contagion due to the GES should have been stronger in the twenties than in the thirties. We provide empirical evidence here that goes against this scenario. We show that, in the mechanism of short-run interest rate contagion, the key date was the triggering of the financial crisis, not the steps leading to the collapse of the GES. However, the other two propositions drawn from the work of Eichengreen (1992) resist our analysis: the assumption of the financial crisis being imported in the US cannot be ruled out; a possible French source in the transmission of short run interest rate shocks cannot be ignored, but it is not the only source. Ultimately, it emerges from our results that two of the scenarios proposed by Eichengreen (1992) are possible (H1 and H2, although not entirely in the case of H2), with the third one (H3) remaining far less plausible.

Appendix 1

Propagation schemes of interest rate volatilities, and corresponding restrictions on A, B, G and F components (BEKK model with structural break)

Scheme	Corresponding restrictions
RRR	No restriction
III	A1(2) = A1(3) = A2(3) = G1(2) = G1(3) = G2(3) = B1(2) = B1(3) = B2(3) = F1(2) = F1(3) = F2(3) = 0
IIN	A1(2) = A1(3) = A2(3) = A3(2) = G1(2) = G1(3) = G2(3) = G3(2) = B1(2) = B1(3) = B2(3) = B3(2) = F1(2) = F1(3) = F2(3) = F3(2) = 0
IIR	A1(2) = A1(3) = G1(2) = G1(3) = B1(2) = B1(3) = F1(2) = F1(3) = 0
IIU	A1(2) = A1(3) = A3(2) = G1(2) = G1(3) = G3(2) = B1(2) = B1(3) = B3(2) = F1(2) = F1(3) = F3(2) = 0
INI	A1(2) = A1(3) = A3(1) = A2(3) = G1(2) = G1(3) = G3(1) = G2(3) = B1(2) = B1(3) = B3(1) = B2(3) = F1(2) = F1(3) = F3(1) = F2(3) = 0
INN	A1(2) = A1(3) = A3(1) = A2(3) = A3(2) = G1(2) = G1(3) = G3(1) = G2(3) = G3(2) = B1(2) = B1(3) = B3(1) = B2(3) = B3(2) = F1(2) = F1(3) = F3(1) = F2(3) = F3(2) = 0
INR	A1(2) = A1(3) = A3(1) = G1(2) = G1(3) = G3(1) = B1(2) = B1(3) = B3(1) = F1(2) = F1(3) = F3(1) = 0
INU	A1(2) = A1(3) = A3(1) = A3(2) = G1(2) = G1(3) = G3(1) = G3(2) = B1(2) = B1(3) = B3(1) = B3(2) = F1(2) = F1(3) = F3(1) = F3(2) = 0
IRI	A1(2) = A2(3) = G1(2) = G2(3) = B1(2) = B2(3) = F1(2) = F2(3) = 0
IRN	A1(2) = A2(3) = A3(2) = G1(2) = G2(3) = G3(2) = B1(2) = B2(3) = B3(2) = F1(2) = F2(3) = F3(2) = 0
IRR	A1(2) = G1(2) = B1(2) = F1(2) = 0
IRU	A1(2) = A3(2) = G1(2) = G3(2) = B1(2) = B3(2) = F1(2) = F3(2) = 0
IUI	A1(2) = A3(1) = A2(3) = G1(2) = G3(1) = G2(3) = B1(2) = B3(1) = B2(3) = F1(2) = F3(1) = F2(3) = 0
IUN	A1(2) = A3(1) = A2(3) = A3(2) = G1(2) = G3(1) = G2(3) = G3(2) = B1(2) = B3(1) = B2(3) = B3(2) = F1(2) = F3(1) = F2(3) = F3(2) = 0
IUR	A1(2) = A3(1) = G1(2) = G3(1) = B1(2) = B3(1) = F1(2) = F3(1) = 0
IUU	A1(2) = A3(1) = A3(2) = G1(2) = G3(1) = G3(2) = B1(2) = B3(1) = B3(2) = F1(2) = F3(1) = F3(2) = 0
NII	A1(2) = A2(1) = A1(3) = A2(3) = G1(2) = G2(1) = G1(3) = G2(3) = B1(2) = B2(1) = B1(3) = B2(3) = F1(2) = F2(1) = F1(3) = F2(3) = 0
NIN	A1(2) = A2(1) = A1(3) = A2(3) = A3(2) = G1(2) = G2(1) = G1(3) = G2(3) = G3(2) = B1(2) = B2(1) = B1(3) = B2(3) = B3(2) = F1(2) = F2(1) = F1(3) = F2(3) = F3(2) = 0
NIR	A1(2) = A2(1) = A1(3) = G1(2) = G2(1) = G1(3) = B1(2) = B2(1) = B1(3) = F1(2) = F2(1) = F1(3) = 0
NIU	A1(2) = A2(1) = A1(3) = A3(2) = G1(2) = G2(1) = G1(3) = G3(2) = B1(2) = B2(1) = B1(3) = B3(2) = F1(2) = F2(1) = F1(3) = F3(2) = 0
NNI	

(continued)

(continued)

Scheme	Corresponding restrictions
	A1(2) = A2(1) = A1(3) = A3(1) = A2(3) = G1(2) = G2(1) = G1(3) = G3(1) = G2(3) = B1(2) = B2(1) = B1(3) = B3(1) = B2(3) = F1(2) = F2(1) = F1(3) = F3(1) = F2(3) = 0
NNN	A1(2) = A2(1) = A1(3) = A3(1) = A2(3) = A3(2) = G1(2) = G2(1) = G1(3) = G3(1) = G2(3) = G3(2) = B1(2) = B2(1) = B1(3) = B3(1) = B2(3) = B3(2) = F1(2) = F2(1) = F1(3) = F3(1) = F2(3) = F3(2) = 0
NNR	A1(2) = A2(1) = A1(3) = A3(1) = G1(2) = G2(1) = G1(3) = G3(1) = B1(2) = B2(1) = B1(3) = B3(1) = F1(2) = F2(1) = F1(3) = F3(1) = 0
NNU	A1(2) = A2(1) = A1(3) = A3(1) = A3(2) = G1(2) = G2(1) = G1(3) = G3(1) = G3(2) = B1(2) = B2(1) = B1(3) = B3(1) = B3(2) = F1(2) = F2(1) = F1(3) = F3(1) = F3(2) = 0
NRI	A1(2) = A2(1) = A2(3) = G1(2) = G2(1) = G2(3) = B1(2) = B2(1) = B2(3) = F1(2) = F2(1) = F2(3) = 0
NRN	A1(2) = A2(1) = A2(3) = A3(2) = G1(2) = G2(1) = G2(3) = G3(2) = B1(2) = B2(1) = B2(3) = B3(2) = F1(2) = F2(1) = F2(3) = F3(2) = 0
NRR	A1(2) = A2(1) = G1(2) = G2(1) = B1(2) = B2(1) = F1(2) = F2(1) = 0
NRU	A1(2) = A2(1) = A3(2) = G1(2) = G2(1) = G3(2) = B1(2) = B2(1) = B3(2) = F1(2) = F2(1) = F3(2) = 0
NUI	A1(2) = A2(1) = A3(1) = A2(3) = G1(2) = G2(1) = G3(1) = G2(3) = B1(2) = B2(1) = B3(1) = B2(3) = F1(2) = F2(1) = F3(1) = F2(3) = 0
NUN	A1(2) = A2(1) = A3(1) = A2(3) = A3(2) = G1(2) = G2(1) = G3(1) = G2(3) = G3(2) = B1(2) = B2(1) = B3(1) = B2(3) = B3(2) = F1(2) = F2(1) = F3(1) = F2(3) = F3(2) = 0
NUR	A1(2) = A2(1) = A3(1) = G1(2) = G2(1) = G3(1) = B1(2) = B2(1) = B3(1) = F1(2) = F2(1) = F3(1) = 0
NUU	A1(2) = A2(1) = A3(1) = A3(2) = G1(2) = G2(1) = G3(1) = G3(2) = B1(2) = B2(1) = B3(1) = B3(2) = F1(2) = F2(1) = F3(1) = F3(2) = 0
RII	A1(3) = A2(3) = G1(3) = G2(3) = B1(3) = B2(3) = F1(3) = F2(3) = 0
RIN	A1(3) = A2(3) = A3(2) = G1(3) = G2(3) = G3(2) = B1(3) = B2(3) = B3(2) = F1(3) = F2(3) = F3(2) = 0
RIR	A1(3) = G1(3) = B1(3) = F1(3) = 0
RIU	A1(3) = A3(2) = G1(3) = G3(2) = B1(3) = B3(2) = F1(3) = F3(2) = 0
RNI	A1(3) = A3(1) = A2(3) = G1(3) = G3(1) = G2(3) = B1(3) = B3(1) = B2(3) = F1(3) = F3(1) = F2(3) = 0
RNN	A1(3) = A3(1) = A2(3) = A3(2) = G1(3) = G3(1) = G2(3) = G3(2) = B1(3) = B3(1) = B2(3) = B3(2) = F1(3) = F3(1) = F2(3) = F3(2) = 0
RNR	A1(3) = A3(1) = G1(3) = G3(1) = B1(3) = B3(1) = F1(3) = F3(1) = 0
RNU	A1(3) = A3(1) = A3(2) = G1(3) = G3(1) = G3(2) = B1(3) = B3(1) = B3(2) = F1(3) = F3(1) = F3(2) = 0
RRI	A2(3) = G2(3) = B2(3) = F2(3) = 0
RRN	A2(3) = A3(2) = G2(3) = G3(2) = B2(3) = B3(2) = F2(3) = F3(2) = 0
RRU	A3(2) = G3(2) = B3(2) = F3(2) = 0
RUI	A3(1) = A2(3) = G3(1) = G2(3) = B3(1) = B2(3) = F3(1) = F2(3) = 0

(continued)

(continued)

Scheme	Corresponding restrictions
RUN	A3(1) = A2(3) = A3(2) = G3(1) = G2(3) = G3(2) = B3(1) = B2(3) = B3(2) = F3 (1) = F2(3) = F3(2) = 0
RUR	A3(1) = G3(1) = B3(1) = F3(1) = 0
RUU	A3(1) = A3(2) = G3(1) = G3(2) = B3(1) = B3(2) = F3(1) = F3(2) = 0
UII	A2(1) = A1(3) = A2(3) = G2(1) = G1(3) = G2(3) = B2(1) = B1(3) = B2(3) = F2 (1) = F1(3) = F2(3) = 0
UIN	A2(1) = A1(3) = A2(3) = A3(2) = G2(1) = G1(3) = G2(3) = G3(2) = B2 (1) = B1(3) = B2(3) = B3(2) = F2(1) = F1(3) = F2(3) = F3(2) = 0
UIR	A2(1) = A1(3) = G2(1) = G1(3) = B2(1) = B1(3) = F2(1) = F1(3) = 0
UIU	A2(1) = A1(3) = A3(2) = G2(1) = G1(3) = G3(2) = B2(1) = B1(3) = B3(2) = F2 (1) = F1(3) = F3(2) = 0
UNI	A2(1) = A1(3) = A3(1) = A2(3) = G2(1) = G1(3) = G3(1) = G2(3) = B2 (1) = B1(3) = B3(1) = B2(3) = F2(1) = F1(3) = F3(1) = F2(3) = 0
UNN	A2(1) = A1(3) = A3(1) = A2(3) = A3(2) = G2(1) = G1(3) = G3(1) = G2 (3) = G3(2) = B2(1) = B1(3) = B3(1) = B2(3) = B3(2) = F2(1) = F1(3) = F3 (1) = F2(3) = F3(2) = 0
UNR	A2(1) = A1(3) = A3(1) = G2(1) = G1(3) = G3(1) = B2(1) = B1(3) = B3(1) = F2 (1) = F1(3) = F3(1) = 0
UNU	A2(1) = A1(3) = A3(1) = A3(2) = G2(1) = G1(3) = G3(1) = G3(2) = B2 (1) = B1(3) = B3(1) = B3(2) = F2(1) = F1(3) = F3(1) = F3(2) = 0
URI	A2(1) = A2(3) = G2(1) = G2(3) = B2(1) = B2(3) = F2(1) = F2(3) = 0
URN	A2(1) = A2(3) = A3(2) = G2(1) = G2(3) = G3(2) = B2(1) = B2(3) = B3(2) = F2 (1) = F2(3) = F3(2) = 0
URR	A2(1) = G2(1) = B2(1) = F2(1) = 0
URU	A2(1) = A3(2) = G2(1) = G3(2) = B2(1) = B3(2) = F2(1) = F3(2) = 0
UUI	A2(1) = A3(1) = A2(3) = G2(1) = G3(1) = G2(3) = B2(1) = B3(1) = B2(3) = F2 (1) = F3(1) = F2(3) = 0
UUN	A2(1) = A3(1) = A2(3) = A3(2) = G2(1) = G3(1) = G2(3) = G3(2) = B2 (1) = B3(1) = B2(3) = B3(2) = F2(1) = F3(1) = F2(3) = F3(2) = 0
UUR	A2(1) = A3(1) = G2(1) = G3(1) = B2(1) = B3(1) = F2(1) = F3(1) = 0
UUU	A2(1) = A3(1) = A3(2) = G2(1) = G3(1) = G3(2) = B2(1) = B3(1) = B3(2) = F2 (1) = F3(1) = F3(2) = 0

References

Accominotti, Olivier. 2011. *Asymmetric Propagation of Financial Crises During the Great Depression*. London School of Economics: Mimeo.

Accominotti, Olivier, and Barry Eichengreen. 2013. *The Mother of All Sudden Stops: Capital Flows and Reversals in Europe, 1919–1932*. London: Mimeo, London School of Economics.

Baba, Yoshi, Engle, Robert F., Kraft, Dennis F., and Ken F. Kroner. 1991. Multivariate Simultaneous Generalized ARCH. Manuscript, Department of Economics, University of California, San Diego.

Bae, H., G.A. Karolyi, and R.M. Stulz. 2003. A New Approach to Measuring Financial Contagion. *Review of Financial Studies* 16 (3): 717–763.

Beirne, John, Guglielmo Maria Caporale, Marianne Schulze-Ghattas, and Nicola Spagnolo. 2013. Volatility Spillovers and Contagion from Mature to Emerging Stock Markets. *Review of International Economics* 21 (5): 1060–1075.

Bekaert, Geert, Michael Ehrmann, Marcel Fratzscher, and Arnaud J. Mehl. 2014. The Global Crisis and Equity Market Contagion. *Journal of Finance* 69 (6): 2597–2649.

Bollerslev, Tim, Engle, Robert F., and Jeffrey M. Wooldridge. 1988. A Capital Asset Pricing Model with Time-Varying Covariances. *Journal of Political Economy* 96(1): 116–131.

Bordo, Michael D., and Antu P. Murshid. 2001. Are Financial Crises Becoming Increasingly More Contagious? What Is the Historical Evidence on Contagion? In *International Financial Contagion*, ed. by S. Claessens and K. J. Forbes, Chap. 14, 367–403. Boston: Kluwer Academic.

Boyer, Brian H., Tomomi Kumagai, and Kathy Yuan. 2006. How Do Crises Spread? Evidence From Accessible and Inaccessible Stock Indexes. *The Journal of Finance* 61 (2): 957–1003.

Dungey, Mardi, Fry, Renee A., Gonzalez-Hermosillo, Brenda, and Vance L. Martin. 2010. *Transmission of Financial Crises and Contagion: A Latent Factor Approach*. New York: Oxford University Press.

Edwards, Sebastian. 2000. Contagion. *World Economy* 23 (7): 873–900.

Eichengreen, Barry. 1992. *Golden Fetters: The Gold Standard and The Great Depression, 1929–1933*. New York: Oxford University Press.

Eichengreen, Barry, Andrew K. Rose, and Charles Wyplosz. 1995. Exchange Market Mayhem: The Antecedents and Aftermath of Speculative Attacks. *Economic Policy* 21: 249–312.

Eichengreen, Barry, Andrew K. Rose and Charles Wyplosz. 1996. Speculative Attacks on Pegged Exchange Rates: An Empirical Exploration with Special Reference to the European Monetary System. In *The New Transatlantic Economy*, ed. by Matthew Canzoneri, Wilfred Ethier, and Vittorio Grilli. Cambridge: Cambridge University Press.

Eichengreen, Barry, Andrew K. Rose and Charles Wyplosz. 1996. Contagious Currency Crises. NBER Working Paper No. 5681, Cambridge, MA, July 1996.

Engle, Robert F. 2002. Dynamic Conditional Correlation: A Simple Class of Multivariate Generalized Autoregressive Conditional Heteroskedasticity Models. *Journal of Business and Economic Statistics* 20 (3): 339–350.

Forbes, Kristin J. 2012. The Big C: Identifying and Mitigating Contagion. NBER Working Paper No. 18465, Cambridge, MA, October 2012.

Forbes, Kristin J., and Roberto Rigobon. 2002. No Contagion, Only Interdependence: Measuring Stock Market Comovements. *Journal of Finance* 57 (5): 2223–2261.

Forbes, Kristin J., and Roberto Rigobon. 2001. Measuring Contagion: Conceptual and Empirical Issues. In *International Financial Contagion*, ed. by Stijn Claessens and Kristin J. Forbes, 43–66. New York: Springer US.

Girton, Lance, and Don Roper. 1977. A Monetary Model of Exchange Market Pressure Applied to the Postwar Canadian Experience. *American Economic Review* 67 (4): 537–548.

Kaminsky, Graciela L., and Carmen M. Reinhart. 2000. On Crises, Contagion, and Confusion. *Journal of International Economics* 51 (1): 145–168.

Kindleberger, Charles P. 1973. *The World in Depression, 1929–1939*. Berkeley and Los Angeles: University of California Press.

Kindleberger, Charles P., and Robert Z. Aliber. 2011. *Manias, Panics and Crashes: A History of Financial Crises*. New York: Palgrave Macmillan.

Kodres, Laura E., and Matthew Pritsker. 2002. A Rational Expectations Model of Financial Contagion. *Journal of Finance* 57 (2): 769–799.

Masson, Paul R. 1998. Contagion: Monsoonal Effects, Spillovers, and Jumps Between Multiple Equilibria. IMF Working Paper No. 98/142, Washington, DC, September 1998.

Masson, Paul R. 1999. Multiple Equilibria, Contagion, and the Emerging Market Crises. IMF Working Papers 99/164, Washington, DC, December 1999.

Morgenstern, Oskar. 1959. *International Financial Transactions and Business Cycles*. Princeton: Princeton University Press.

Nurkse, Ragnar. 1944. *International Currency Experience: Lessons of the Interwar Experience*. Geneva: League of Nations.

Tse, Y. K., and Albert K. C. Tsui. 2002. A Multivariate Generalized Autoregressive Conditional Heteroscedasticity Model with Time-Varying Correlations. *Journal of Business and Economic Statistics* 20 (3): 351–362.

Author Biographies

Samuel Maveyraud is a Professor of Economics at the University of Bordeaux, GREThA, College of Law, Political Science, and Economics. He has done extensive research and published many papers on financial history, central banking, financial markets, and macroeconomics. His most recent paper is "La structure du réseau de commerce international en 1850" in Economies et Sociétés. A fuller list of his published articles and working papers can be found at ideas.repec.org.

Antoine Parent is a Professor of economics at the Institut d'Etudes Politiques de Lyon, (Sciences Po Lyon). He has written extensively on monetary and financial history and the history of economic thought. His most recent paper written with Olivier Damette is "Did the Fed follow an implicit McCallum rule during the Great Depression?" in *Economic Modelling*. A fuller list of his published articles and working papers can be found at ideas.repec.org.

Chapter 3
Banking Crises and Lender of Last Resort in Theory and Practice in Swedish History, 1850–2010

Anders Ögren

Abstract This paper is a first attempt to make a comparative analysis of Swedish banking crises over time—focusing on how the crises were handled. The empirical material is also compared to economic theories on crises management, i.e. lender of last resort and bank bailouts. The main questions are: How do the crises management relate to economic theories, i.e. to what extent did the crises management follow any economic rationale? To what extent were the crises management seen as necessary by authorities and market agents, and to what extent were the designs of the crises management made by market agents and/or by authorities? Were there any common features of the crises management over time that can explain why crises were handled in a certain fashion? I also make an estimation of the relative costs for the state to manage each crisis.

Keywords Bank bailouts · Currency crises · Financial crises · Foreign debt
Lender of last resort · Monetary policy · Monetary regimes

3.1 Introduction

Banking crises are costly. In Reinhart and Rogoff's seminal study on sovereign debt crises and banking crises a banking crises costs in the three years after it occurrence on average 86% of a country's GDP.[1] In his paper "The Lender of Last Resort: Some Historical Insights", Bordo concludes that successful lender of last resort policies, on several historical occasions, have prevented costly banking panics.[2] Managing financial market instabilities in general and banking crises in particular is by many economists seen as one of the main reasons for the existence of central

[1]Reinhart and Rogoff (2009).
[2]Bordo (1989, p. 220).

A. Ögren (✉)
Department of Economic History, Lund University, Lund, Sweden
e-mail: anders.ogren@ekh.lu.se

© Springer Nature Singapore Pte Ltd. 2018

H. Rockoff and I. Suto (eds.), *Coping with Financial Crises*,
Studies in Economic History, https://doi.org/10.1007/978-981-10-6196-7_3

banks in modern economies.[3] While much theoretical focus on banking support is placed on the central bank, historical experiences on crisis management shows a more complex organization involving also treasuries and other state agencies. In this paper I compare the experiences of banking crises with the special focus of banking support from the state to what economic theories on banking support claim.

The chapter first goes through theories on banking support, second cases of banking crises and banking support are described in chronological order, and third there is a short discussion of the interpretations of the cases in question.

3.2 Banking Support in Theory[4]

To paraphrase Wicksell on monetary economics, there is more written on banking support than any man can ever read during his entire life. But even though there are many ways that banking support has been handled through history the theoretical basics behind banking support are quite limited. Banking support is about making sure that market instabilities are minimized in a manner which does not lead to moral hazard or distorts competition.

The most well-known kind of banking support is that of a "Lender of Last Resort" as it was distilled and described by Bagehot in *Lombard Street* 1873. However, we all know that this had been put into practice in different ways long before the writings of Bagehot. The interesting part about this economic rationale and way of providing banking support, which I follow Bordo in labeling the "classical lender of last resort," is that it still is the way which banking support is supposed to be provided—but as the reader will see—practice has come a long way from it.

There are several reasons why practice differs from the way that banking support is supposed to be organized in accordance to this classical view, and this means that the rationale behind Lender of Last Resort and as a consequence the way it is supposed to be provided has changed in an ad hoc kind of way. This was the case for the ideas on banking support in the twentieth century and following Bordo I label this the "evolutionary lender of last resort."

Finally, as a result of this evolution (if this indeed is the right word) of the concept of lender of last resort there has emerged a confusion between lender of last resort and the establishment of targeted operations to save specific banks—what is known as life-boat operations, banking recapitalization, toxic asset funds and so on.

---

[3]Goodhart argued that the possibility of incurring credit losses, together with the right of the public to make quick withdrawals or to redeem notes, obviously makes banks vulnerable to a lack of short term capital. The banking system therefore requires the special services of a central bank or, more specifically, of a lender of last resort that can support them in case of difficulties (Goodhart 1987, pp. 3–4). Kindleberger also argued that central banks arrived to impose control over the instability of credit (Kindleberger and Aliber 2005).

[4]This section draws heavily on Ögren (2007).

It should be made clear that even if this is one way of banking support which is often resorted to it is not the same as Lender of Last Resort, and to understand the logic in how banking support may be provided in different ways it is important not to confuse these two concepts of Lender of Last Resort and, what I chose to label Banking recapitalization. Below I shortly go through the theories behind these ways of providing banking support.

3.2.1 Classical Lender of Last Resort

There are many originators of the concept of Lender of Last Resort, such as Bagehot, Baring, Goschen and Thornton to name those who arguably are the most well-known describers of the concept.[5] A lender of last resort was needed because banks operated with fractional reserves, the less cash reserves in legal tender the more vulnerable the bank for a bank run. Hence the lender of last resort was, and still is, about ensuring that banks have sufficient legal tender reserves to meet demand for withdrawing deposits or redeeming issued bank notes. The more legal tender liquidity pumped into the banking system the less the risk for a bank run. Since the run for what in fact is endogenous bank money (deposits or bank notes) expresses itself as a run for exogenous base money (legal tender) it will be the issuer of such exogenous base money that will be responsible for the provision of liquidity. Thus in the classical lender of last resort the monetary authority, the central bank, shall act as the lender of last resort. And to avoid moral hazard and distortion of competition the central bank should lend freely (that is not take into account who the borrower is) on good collateral, but at their pre-crisis value. This will be done at a high interest rate, meaning higher than normal circumstances, as money is scarcer during times of crises.

This specific idea on how to provide lender of last resort support is usually attributed to Bagehot[6] and has been distilled into four basic rules: (1) The central bank should be the sole lender of last resort. (2) During panics illiquid banks should be granted loans backed by any collateral that would be marketable under normal conditions. (3) The central bank should provide large loans and advances, but at

[5]For an analysis of the historical development of the concept of lender of last resort, see Wood (2000, pp. 204–209).

[6]Bagehot's original aim was to create awareness of how the Bank of England, on the basis of experience from 1848 and 1857, could limit the banking crisis of 1866. He did this first as editor of The *Economist* during the 1860's, and later in his classic book *Lombard Street* (1873). It is therefore somewhat unfair to criticize Bagehot's views from a more general perspective. Regarding Bagehot and central banking see Rockoff (1986).

above market interest rates. (4) The previous three rules should be clearly stated beforehand and strictly followed during crises.[7]

The economic rationale behind this scheme is quite straightforward: The central bank is assumed to be lender of last resort not only because it is the monopoly issuer of bank reserves (base money) but also because it is probable that the central bank due to its close relations to the banking system has an information advantage. It should be the first to know if there are any difficulties in the banking sector that may cause a general alarm and then bank runs.[8] In times of runs banks that were illiquid but solvent could borrow from the central banks, and the guarantee that these banks were merely suffering from illiquidity and not from insolvency was that they could offer good collaterals that were marketable under normal circumstances, that is when the market is not frozen. Moreover, discretionary lending by the central bank was avoided by the demand for such collaterals as basis for the loan. Thus the demand for high quality collateral was the mechanism ensuring not only that only prudent and well managed banks were saved but also used to avoid moral hazard and limit the impact of the lender of last resort activities on competition. Arguably it is this demand for collateral that makes classical lender of last resort as far away as it can be from the modern Troubled Asset Relief Program form of support used in the United States (and in other cases) recently.

Finally, we come to the issue of a high interest rate being charged by central banks during a crisis, which from time to time has been seen as a penalty interest rate. But historically the use of high rates during crises seems to have reflected the fact that during times of crisis money market interest rates are driven up as a result of the sudden increase in demand, and thus to lend at lower rates than current market rates would be to subsidize those in need of liquidity.[9] There is also a link between the central banks way of handling the lender of last resort function and its way of handling monetary policy. An increased interest rate would halt a possible outflow of capital and thus protect the reserves of the central bank as described by Goschen. And as lender of last resort means supplying more base money, preventing an outflow of central bank reserves was of utmost importance for not turning the banking crisis also into a currency crisis.[10] Altering the discount rate was also seen as the least oppressive way of keeping the ratio between issued monetary liabilities and reserves in a fractional banking system.[11]

The idea of making the interest rate fight outflows and discourage unnecessary lending in times of crisis has been referred to as the Bagehot rule, and an additional rule was that the central bank in times of short run liquidity crisis should engage in

[7]Bordo (1989) p. 25 Footnote 6. (From Meltzer (1986) "Financial Failures and Financial Policies" in Kaufman, G.G. and Kormendi, R.C. (Ed) *Deregulating Financial Services: Public Policy in Flux*. Ballinger Publishing Company. Cambridge. p. 83), see also Goodhart (1999, pp. 340–341).

[8]Capie and Wood (1995, pp. 215, 223).

[9]Bignon et al. (2009).

[10]Bagehot (1866, pp. 236–237), Bagehot (1916, pp. 265–267, 270) "The notion that the Bank of England can stop discounting in a panic, and so obtain fresh money, is a delusion.".

[11]Sayers (1976, p. 28).

lender of last resort activities even if it meant temporary abandoning the monetary policy objective. In the rhetoric of the gold standard and according to the rules of the game the central bank should temporarily abandon free convertibility between the gold and the domestic currency, to restore it as soon as possible, after the crisis.[12]

Thus lender of last resort means a conflict between the monetary regime and the provision of liquidity during crisis management. And as is evident today, and has been through all central bank history, it does not matter what monetary regime the central bank lives by, it may be a fixed exchange rate as the gold standard or a currency board or a floating exchange rate targeting domestic price stability, either way an excessive liquidity provision will threaten the monetary regime. This fact means that also classical lender of last resort hinges on the possibility for central banks to break monetary policy rules without losing confidence.[13]

It should be noted that the recipe for how to provide lender of last resort has been frequently revised by economists and economic historians but that it seem that the classical lender of last resort often comes back into fashion.[14] So why is it that lender of last resort in practice does not follow this set of rules?

3.2.2 Evolutionary Lender of Last Resort

From the 1970s the theoretical view on lender of last resort has been expanded based on observations of practical problems in the classical recipe. In this literature information problem is key for how to solve lender of last resort. As is the case with the classical view of a lender of last resort has to provide liquidity to restore confidence in the market and by doing so prevent costly bank runs and ultimately bank failures.

The problem with the classical view is that holders of bank liabilities do not possess full information about the status of their bank. This means that saving only illiquid but insolvent banks will not suffice because any bank failure, even of a

---

[12]McKinnon (1993, p. 4).

[13]Following the implementation of the gold standard in 1871 and the establishment of the Reichsbank as a central bank in 1876, Germany constructed a system of lending of last resort that operated outside the requirements of the specie standards. The Reichsbank operated a type of giro, or checking, system for the transfer of funds. Since these checks were non-note liabilities, the Reichsbank was not required to back them with reserves, the gold cover rules only being applicable to the issuance of bank notes. This giro system guaranteed the liquidity of the credit banks. The Reichsbank provided liquidity by discounting the credit banks' holdings of bills of exchange, thus allowing these to functions as substitutes for Reichsbank notes. The discount rate was volatile, reaching high levels during periods of capital shortage. Nonetheless, this policy allowed the Reichsbank to function as a lender of last resort for the private banking system (McGouldrick 1984, p. 313; Tilly 1986, pp. 195–196).

[14]Wood (2000, pp. 222–223). Or in Wood's words: "Reconsideration of the role of lender of last resort shows revision of it to be unnecessary".

mismanaged and insolvent bank, will trigger runs also on well managed banks suffering only from illiquidity. So the risk of contagion makes it necessary to step in and provide liquidity also to insolvent banks. Moreover, the argument is that basing the decision on which bank to save on solvency requires an accurate estimation of the bank's assets and liabilities and the distinction between illiquid and insolvent is not clear especially not during rapid economic downturns as banking crises when assets tend to rapidly fall in value. This is especially the case for bank customers who seldom are as well informed as a perfect financial market would assume. Because of this problem of information and in the interest of banking and financial stability Goodhart (and others who in this paper are said to represent the evolutionary view) argues that all banks in times of banking panics should be saved.[15]

As all banks should be saved due to the "collateral damage" on the market the moral hazard problem that was solved in the classical lender of last resort by the demand for good collaterals becomes apparent. If banks know they will be saved what grounds are there for prudence? Such incentive structures may well actually lead to a financial crisis a problem which is seriously discussed in the economic literature.[16] But the question is if the existence of moral hazard has been taken too seriously? Goodhart argued for instance that the occurrence of moral hazard is overstated and thus that it does not constitute a valid reason for refraining from last-resort lending.[17]

The evolution of lending of last resort points in a direction of a solution for crisis management that instead of leaning on general liquidity provision opens up for targeted bank bailout operations. Historically a shift has happened, Bordo showed that bailouts of insolvent banks were an exception before the 1970s.[18] A question is why it seems as bank bailouts have increased during the period when market forces are supposed to be operational—that is after the 1980s.

The big issue in bank bailouts, or banking recapitalization, is how to do it in a manner which has the least negative impact on the disciplinary forces of the market —that is to avoid moral hazard. Thus the way successful interventions through bail outs are described in economic literature is that it should not affect competition, it should be neutral and as cost efficient as possible.[19] The question is if this is possible at all—once an agent is targeted, this takes away the competitive aspect, it also provides room for discretionary decisions. But it is possible to punish banks by given severe haircuts to those financial assets in which over investments have occurred, making bank owners pay or lose their ownership and so on. The question here is to what extent this really is done.

---

[15]Goodhart (1999, pp. 343–344), Bordo (1989, pp. 9–10).

[16]Bordo (1998, pp. 16–17), Fisher (1999, pp. 92–94), Freixas et al. (2000, pp. 73–78).

[17]Goodhart (1999, pp. 352–356).

[18]Bordo (1989, pp. 22–23).

[19]Beck et al. (2010).

3.2.3 *Liquidity Provision Under Zero Interest Rates: Quantitative Easing*

Quantitative easing has been widely used during the recent crisis by some central banks, and the reason for this is that central banks in today's crisis are operating in economies with low interests rates close to the liquidity trap. This situation with low interest rates and crisis management is a result of the fact that recession fighting and crisis management are not completely following the same logic. Thus in an economy fighting recession by low interest rates an important part of the classical lender of last resort has been taken away. Originally the idea was that interest rates in times of a rush for liquidity should make this liquidity cost according to the situation (not necessarily as a penalty but as a result of a lack of supply). Another idea in relation to this had to do with international capital flows during a fixed exchange rate (as the gold standard), an increased interest rate should prevent capital from flowing out of the country. In present economic policymaking low interest rates are seen as *the* monetary policy tool to fight recession and crisis and capital outflow is translated into depreciating exchange rate which may boost exports.

With interest rates close to zero it is difficult to stimulate the economy using interest rate cuts, and after the example of Japan quantitative easing has been promoted by economists and policy makers as a "new way" of providing lender of last resort when interest rates no longer can be cut. For those who are not into central bank jargon quantitative easing is simply the central bank providing liquidity by buying financial assets directly from the agents in need of capital. Evidently, as seen above, this adds nothing new to the traditional lender of last resort which actually was constructed on the basis that the central bank would provide liquidity by buying or discounting (good quality) financial assets from market agents in need of capital.

Since it adds nothing new the problems it seeks to avert are still there: First if the agents have to sell their highest quality financial assets (say government bonds) this will weaken the agent's balance sheets and make them more vulnerable for a run. Second, the central bank will pump in fresh capital for these assets, which means that the central bank will increase its monetary liabilities in exchange for financial assets. This may not be a problem if the financial assets are of top quality; they may then be seen as close to legal tender cash in solvency and thus it means no more than an increased balance sheet for the central bank by increasing both assets and liabilities almost at the same. But in times of crisis this is hardly the case, the financial assets issued by market agents are not of the same quality. Moreover, the most high quality asset in the economy is government debt, and the exchange of legal tender cash for government debt is in fact to monetize the state debt, which, if the state's economy is under pressure, will lead to falling currency value, domestic inflation and thus further fuel the economic problems into a banking, debt and currency crisis.

Still during the crisis the Bank of England officially maintained the idea that using the central bank to purchase assets (government bonds and debt issued by private companies) would not mean that it weakened its balance sheet nor that it monetized the debt issued by the state.

> The MPC's decision to inject money directly into the economy does not involve printing more banknotes. Instead, the Bank buys assets from private sector institutions—that could be insurance companies, pension funds, banks or non-financial firms—and credits the seller's bank account. So the seller has more money in their bank account, while their bank holds a corresponding claim against the Bank of England (known as reserves). The end result is more money out in the wider economy.[20]

But, of course the claim on the Bank's reserves are monetary liabilities, that is money (legal tender cash) and of course these transactions are weakening the Bank's balance sheet (as long as the financial assets bought are not regarded as of higher quality than the cash, or the claim's, on the Bank of England—which with all certainty is not the case especially not during a crisis). And of course if the Bank buys government bonds with its money, issued as a claim on the Bank or as printed notes, it monetizes the state debt all the same. Thus whatever rhetoric is used by policy makers and economists there is no way round the fact that saving financial institutions costs money and makes central banks weaken their balance sheets.

3.3 Financial Crises and Lender of Last Resort in Swedish History

There follows below short descriptions of each banking crisis in Sweden focusing on how liquidity provision and bank bailouts were managed, as well as what the stated reasons were for the market intervention by the authorities.

3.3.1 The Crisis of 1857/58

In the crisis of 1857/58 the Bank of Sweden did provide liquidity. The crisis emerged in the early fall 1857 as a result of an international crisis when many Swedish agents had their credits in the Hamburg credit market cancelled. On November 4, 1857 British trading companies important for Sweden suspended their payments. The situation on the market made the Bank of Sweden openly declare its commitment to support the credit market. But, as stressed in the classical lender of last resort doctrines, the Bank of Sweden was constrained in its liquidity provision by its commitment to the silver standard. Thus a lot of the discussion on the Board was devoted to the issue of how to work around the constraints imposed by the specie standard. It included ideas on classifying all of the Bank's assets as reserves, an effective devaluation of the currency by adding two percent over par when

[20]Bank of England (N/A) "Quantitative easing explained" Pamphlet on-line and printed, p. 9.

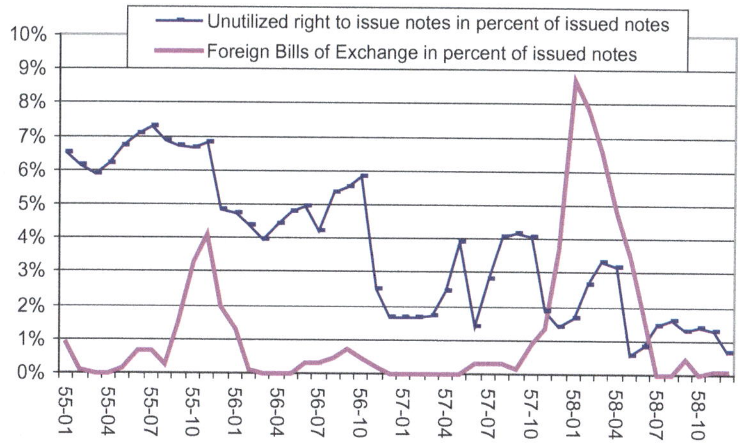

Fig. 3.1 Monthly data on the Riksbank's unutilized rights to issue notes and foreign bills of exchange as a percentage of issued notes, January 1855–December 1858 (Ögren 2007; Finanskommittén 1858, vol. I)

buying domestic silver (which was adopted in December 1857), and there were even ideas on openly grabbing for citizens silver holdings by officially claiming them to be held by the bank as collaterals in a kind of repurchase agreement (this however was not put into practice).[21] The most effective and most criticized solution was to engage in cooperation with the Stockholm Stock Exchange and aiding them in opening an office in Hamburg providing foreign bills of exchange that the Bank of Sweden could buy or discount to keep the supply of domestic liquidity up. New regulations made it possible for the Bank of Sweden to include foreign bills of exchange in its reserves. As seen in Fig. 3.1 below this arrangement helped the Bank keep liquidity up without officially abandoning the silver standard.

Figure 3.1 also shows how the liquidity provision by the Bank of Sweden, that was based on these foreign bills of exchange issued by Swedish merchants in Hamburg, was most important during the most acute stage of the crises, December 1857 until February 1858. Arguably, this general supply of liquidity to avoid banking panics was in line with classical ideas on lender of last resort—with one exception—that the Bank of Sweden had to stick to low interest rates in accordance with the law on usury. Money market rates, if there was a market (both Copenhagen and Hamburg were described as frozen in December 1857) were probably between two and three times as high.

[21]Ögren (2007) RbFP No 151 December 10, 17 1857. The Bank of Sweden included in its reserves silver and gold it held as collateral. This was officially motivated by the borrowers having sold them to the Bank of Sweden, subject to the right of repurchase by repaying their loans. Only one member of the Board opted for the solution of allowing the note issuance to temporary exceed its legal limits.

However, this textbook provision of liquidity was a temporary solution. At the same time as it was put into practice a more rigorous scheme for bank bailouts was put into practice. The most important bank in trouble at the time, *Skåne Enskilda Bank*, was the market agent who approached the authorities asking for, or rather demanding, support. Such support directly violated the Banking act of 1846 which stated in §1 that no private bank should expect aid from the public. This bank had increased its lending right up to the beginning of the financial difficulties in September 1857 and like most banks at the time it funded its lending by note issuance. It was at the time the largest bank and also the largest note issuer among the banks, and many of its notes also circulated in the market of Copenhagen in neighboring Denmark. With the prolonged and deepened crisis a general distrust towards the Skåne Enskilda Bank notes started, and in Copenhagen they were traded for large discounts thus putting pressure on the *Skåne Enskilda Bank's* reserves. On December 5, *Skånes Enskilda Bank* failed to raise the capital needed to consolidate its reserves so two days later it contacted the Minister of Finance threatening to stop redeeming its notes. This initiative resulted in a meeting between representatives from the Minister of Finance, the Parliamentary Standing Committee on Supply, the National Debt Office and the Bank of Sweden on December 10. The outcomes of the meeting was an immediate credit granted by the Bank of Sweden of 200,000 SEK to be raised to 500,000 SEK within a short time. This amount can be compared with the total turnover of the bank of 5.6 MSEK and its note issuance of 2.2 MSEK. The Bank of Sweden openly acknowledged its fear that a failure of the *Skåne Enskilda Bank* would affect the Swedish currency and thus the position of the Bank of Sweden. The loan was collateralized in bonds form the Mortgage Association and a personal IOU from one of the Bank's representatives in Stockholm.[22] In exchange for its bonds the Mortgage Association from *Skånes Enskilda Bank* was given the collaterals from their lending. Needless to say, there was no market for any of this paper at the time.

To solve the situation more permanently it was decided in early January 1858 that the bank of Sweden should tap international capital markets for 12 MSEK, to be directed as emergency credit to the commercial banks. The sum was important, approximately one third of the monetary liabilities of the Bank of Sweden by the end of 1857, and it was instructed that as soon as the loan contract was signed the Bank of Sweden should include this sum as part of its reserves and issue notes of an equivalent amount.[23]

On January 28, 1959 a representative of the Bank of Sweden borrowed the sum in Hamburg. The fund created to save banks was labeled the State Loan Fund

[22]Kock (1931, pp. 162–169). The actual representative of the bank in Stockholm refused to guarantee the credit in person, instead the founder of the Stockholm Enskilda bank, A.O. Wallenberg, stepped in. See also Brisman (1934, pp. 102–103, 105–106), Nilsson (1989, pp. 9–29), Schön (2000, p. 165).

[23]Ögren (2007) RbFP No 152 January 7, 28 1858. Some Bank of Sweden board members questioned the idea of supporting the Enskilda banks whom they blamed for the problems of the credit market.

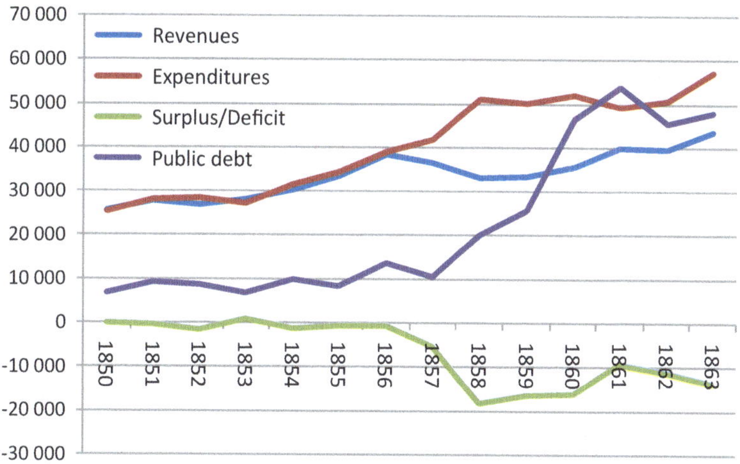

Fig. 3.2 State finances, 1850–1863 (1000's SEK) (Fregert and Gustafsson 2008, pp. 68–76)

(*Statslånefonden*) and it was administered by the Bank of Sweden who also received a special parliamentary authorization to exceed the usury limit of six percent interest.[24] The entire 12 MSEK was lent out within a year despite the resulting interest rate of nine percent. How this was done is not entirely clear as the General Ledger of the Fund does not reveal what happened to the Fund's assets in Sweden.[25] Loans from the fund were short term, up to three years. The day after, January 29, a representative of the National debt Office managed to sign for another loan of 20 MSEK in Frankfurt am Main, this loan was long term and designed to fund the building of Railroads in Sweden but the capital was immediately used to ease the situation on the domestic money market.[26]

Ironically, the efforts of the Bank of Sweden to provide liquidity during the crisis were criticized by those groups in parliament that supported the private commercial banks. It was argued that these actions had severely damaged the Swedish currency's reputation and thus endangered the silver standard—a somewhat odd criticism given that the reason for the intervention of the Bank of Sweden was to secure the currency value and after all the silver standard was successfully kept.[27]

Figure 3.2 above shows the structure of the state's finances during the period 1850–1863. The engagements of the Bank of Sweden, counting only the size of its foreign loan, plus the capital imported by the national Debt Office amounted to 32

[24]Ögren (2007) RbFP No 152 February 2, 4, 11 1858. In England it was said that an interest rate of 7% would draw gold from the moon (Goodhart 1999, p. 342).

[25]Ögren (2007) RbDA No 4352, Pag. 1810 1858, RbFP No 152 February 4, 8, 11, 1858, RbSLF No 4812 Pag.306 1858, Pag. 306 1859, RbSLFH No 4817 1858.

[26]Ögren (2007) RbFP No 152 February 11, 24 1858, RGKLKT No 9061 1858 §1.

[27]Ögren (2012).

MSEK—almost the entire state's revenues in 1856, and the by far largest part of the expenditures. The lag in the state's commitment from the acute banking crisis when the bank of Sweden upheld its liquidity is also visible as the public debt shifted up substantially in 1859 and 1860, showing that when the state engages in bailing out banks it is a commitment over the longer term.

3.3.2 The Railroad Crisis of 1878/79

The 1878/1879 crisis in Sweden was a delayed reaction to the international crisis of 1873. In Sweden 1873 was at the height of the boom and the Bank of Sweden even over issued notes to meet demand from the credit market that showed no response to the increased interest rates. The investment vehicle of the time was the railroad bonds that were issued to fund the building of private railroads in connection to the state's main line. Many banks came to hold large shares of such bonds in their portfolios. A first sign of a weakening business cycle was when the banking firm C. G. Cervin suspended its payments in 1875, and the minutes of the board of the bank of Sweden already in January 1875 shows concern over the situation. Thus it took more than three years before this recession turned into a banking crisis. One of the reasons may be that the Bank of Sweden actively supported the credit market by what in modern rhetoric would be labeled "quantitative easing;" that is it bought or discounted bonds and commercial bills of the market agents to keep up liquidity. It also opened up an exchange office in Copenhagen to keep up the par value of its notes.[28] But as discounting these bills weakened the balance sheet of the Bank of Sweden it started to lower its interest.[29] The commercial banks, however, did the opposite of the bank of Sweden, they reduced their lending to the extent that the bank of Sweden had to sustain the market even more—a development which in late 1877 and early 1878 forced the Bank of Sweden to deny discounting due to risk of having to abandon the gold standard. But the board of the Bank of Sweden also requested the National Debt Office to launch new loans by placing bonds abroad and in that way to sustain the capital market by importing capital.[30] In doing so the Bank of Sweden did not have to violate the rules of the fixed exchange rate system as is seen in Fig. 3.3.

[28]Ögren (2007) RbFP No 169 January 20 1875, RbFSP No 252 January 14, February 18, April 22 1875. According to the Board of the Riksbank, the decision to open an office in Copenhagen was motivated by a desire to protect the Riksbank's credit worthiness (RbFSP No 252 February 18 1875).

[29]Ögren (2012) and Ögren (2007). RbFSP No 252 October 14 1875. The decision stated that "bank and banker bills of exchange on foreign credits were to be sparingly discounted at the lower rate established by the Board." See also Söderlund (1964, p. 99).

[30]Ögen (2007) RbFP No 170–172 July 1, November 25 1876, March 22, July 12, November 29 1877, January 15, 24 1878, RbFSP No 252–253 June 17, July 9, December 16 1875, June 15 1876 July 5, September 24, November 15 1877, RbR No 429 December 11 1876.

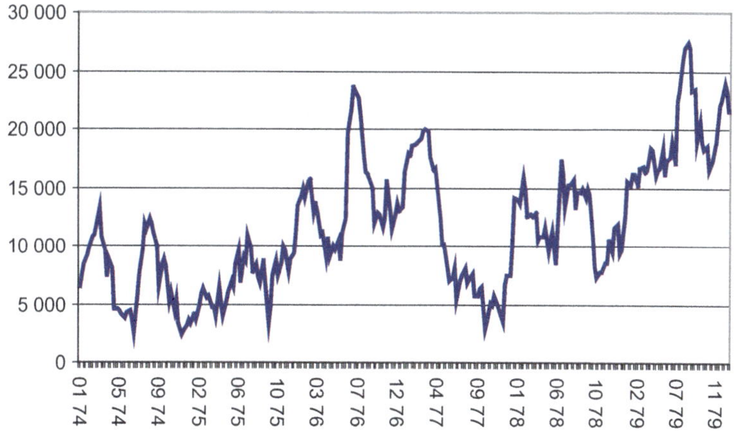

Fig. 3.3 Weekly data on the Riksbank's unutilized rights to issue notes in 1000's of SEK, January 1874–December 1879 (Ögren 2007) BaU No 1 1875–1880, RdRB 1875–1880

The jump in unutilized note issuing in January 1878 shows when the National Debt Office started to import capital and thus helped consolidate the Bank of Sweden reserves. In December 1878 the then largest Swedish commercial bank, *Stockholms Enskilda Bank,* was subjected to a run due to its large exposure to railroad bonds. This was a run on deposits as this bank hardly issued any notes but instead relied on deposits as source of funds and most of those were payable on demand up to six months, which gave the bank some respite. But the problems of the bank continued and in February 1879 the liberal Minister of Finance, Forsell, against the banking laws and against his own ideological support for "laissez faire" had to pronounce public support of the banks in order to "*free the capital that had been made illiquid*" and prevent a credit crunch.[31] The solution was to establish a "toxic asset fund" to recapitalize banks by extending credit using aforementioned railroad bonds as collaterals—the Railroad Mortgage Fund (*Jernvägshypoteksfonden*) that, unlike *Statslånefonden* in 1858, was to be administered by the National Debt Office.[32]

Establishing the fund however took months of bureaucratic work but on May 17, 1879 the fund was enacted. In short all assets that were tied to the funding of the railroads were allowed to be used as collaterals when borrowing from the fund: railroad bonds, promissory notes, IOUs from Swedish railway companies, etc. Total

[31]Ögren (2007) In 1879, the National Debt Office cancelled its credits due to a shortage of funds and expected future receipts. The effect on Stockholm Enskilda bank was especially severe because, in addition to the loans of the Bank, its founder and principal owner, A.O. Wallenberg, had a personal debt of 250,000 SEK, collateralized by railroad bonds, to the Office. Having repaid 50,000 SEK, Wallenberg was allowed to extend the rest of his loan and with only half of the collateral originally pledged. This after Wallenberg makes reference to this Riksbank credit of 200,000 SEK secured by bonds in the same (Gefle-Dala) railroad company (RGKLP No 4462 January 16, 23 1879).

[32]Ögren (2007, Kprop 1879 No 29, pp. 1, 7–10).

capitalization of the fund was 23 MSEK, to be borrowed by the National Debt Office on international markets after each loan had been approved. The Bank of Sweden was working as underwriter and the capital was to be kept in the bank until lent out.[33] Banks had until June 1, 1880 to file for loans from the fund but their collaterals had to be assessed by representatives of the Royal Railway Traffic Board (*Kungliga Styrelsen för Statens Järnvägstrafik*) before any loan was granted.[34] Thus flexibility of the fund was quite limited.

The fund was officially put into practice on June 4, 1879 but given its precarious situation *Stockholms Enskilda Bank* had applied for a loan of 5 MSEK in late May and on its first day 1 MSEK was paid out from the bank of Sweden to *Stockholms Enskilda Bank*. To react this quickly the board of the National Debt Office had to violate the rules of the fund.[35]

The way the fund developed it came to be more or less completely devoted into saving the *Stockholm Enskilda Bank*. As the cost for borrowing from the fund was below market price the CEO and founder of *Stockholm Enskilda Bank*, A.O. Wallenberg, was quick to use the fund to the extent possible and by July 1879 the bank had borrowed 4 MSEK from the fund.[36] The situation in the market improved quite quickly and as a result of the late establishment of the fund it does not seem to have been that vital for the recovery of the financial system, with the exception of *Stockholms Enskilda Bank*—which after all was the largest bank in terms of total

[33]Ögren (2007, RdSkr No 53, pp. 2–3). The state was to be fully repaid for this commitment and any eventual profit was to be used to repay the loans used to build the state railways or other state debts. The Railroad Mortgage Fund eventually generated a surplus of just over 155,000 SEK (RGKJHFH No 7907 1894, pp. 3–4, 7). The Fund's upper limit had been reduced from thirty to twenty three million SEK at the prompting of those groups in the Parliament who blamed the commercial banks for creating the crisis and who wished to devote the saved amounts to alternative, noncredit market approaches to providing lender of last resort services. Thus, through the *Sågverksegarnas Garantiförening* (Saw Mill Owners' Guarantee Association), the saw mill industry was provided with a fund of three million SEK to be lent on the security of stored timber. The remaining four million SEK were allocated to the purchase of the private *Hallsberg-Motala-Mjölby* railway by the state (StU No 53, pp. 3–5). RGKJHFM No 8514, pp. 23–27.

[34]Ögren (2007) RGKLP No 4462 May 26, June 5 1879. All this was done to prevent misuse of the Fund. Nonetheless, the railway bonds were valued at close to their nominal value, that is at approximately twice their current market value. A special collateral valuation board was also used by the toxic asset fund *Securum AB* that was established to assist the banks during the crisis of 1992.

[35]Ögren (2007), RGKLP No 4462 May 30, June 3 1879, RGKJHFH No 7893 1879, pp. 40–41, RGKJHFM No 8514 p. 23. In order to lend such a large amount so quickly, the National Debt Office had to violate the regulations. For a time it even accepted the Bank's own promissory notes as collateral. Two of the Office's board members noted their reservations in the loan protocol.

[36]Ögren (2007), RGKJHFM No 8514, pp. 23–24, RGKLP No 4462 May 30, July 24, 31 1879. Once the Fund came into being, Wallenberg switched the railroad bonds he had provided as collateral for his personal loans from the National Debt Office and the Bank of Sweden over to his own bank, Stockholms Enskilda Bank. The certificate of deposit he received from Stockholms Enskilda Bank was then used to back those loans, while the bonds were offered as collateral when Stockholms Enskilda Bank applied for a loan from the Railroad Mortgage Fund (RGKLP No 4462 June 12 1879).

Table 3.1 Borrowers from the Railroad Mortgage Fund (Ögren 2007) RGKJHFH 1879, 1880, RGKJHFL and RGKLP 1879, 1880

Date granted	Date paid	Bank	Collateral (nominal value) as a percent of loan	Loan amount (SEK)
June 3–July 24 1879	June 4 1879–Jan. 31 1880	Stockholm Enskilda Bank	149	4,000,000
June 12 & Nov. 13 1879	18/6 & 5/12-1879	Stockholm Handelsbank	249	775,000
June 12 & Aug. 7 1879	June 23 & Aug. 16 1879	Göteborg Köpmannabank	200	350,000
June 19 1879	July 5 1879	Göteborg Inteckningsgaranti AB	277	50,000
June 19 1879	July 17 1879	Södermanland Enskilda Bank	200	115,000
July 24 & Nov. 13 1879	Aug. 4 & Dec. 30 1879	Kalmar Enskilda Bank	207	470,000
Aug. 13 1879 & May 27 1880	Sept. 12 1879 & July 1 1880	AB Gefle Bank	131	80,000
Aug. 21 1879	Oct. 1 1879	Sundsvall Enskilda Bank	111	540,000
Oct. 23 1879	Oct. 31 1879	Kristinehamn Enskilda Bank	134	180,000
	March 6 1880	Gotland Enskilda Bank	100	30,000
June 16 1880	July 1 1880	Wermland Enskilda Bank	350	1,000,000
June 16 1880	July 7 1880	Ulricehamn Folkbank	219	50,000
July 8 1880	July 26 1880	Skaraborg Län Enskilda Bank	100	200,000

assets at the time.[37] As seen in Table 3.1 below the total amount lent out was far from the stipulated 23 MSEK; 7.56 MSEK or 33% of the capital was used by thirteen different banks. However, *Stockholms Enskilda Bank* not only borrowed 4 MSEK they also kept the loans, with their favorable interest rates, for the longest

[37]Ögren (2007), RGKLP No 4462 August 24 1879. In late July, the National Debt Office lowered the rate of interest on its loans to the Railroad Mortgage Fund to five percent, since loans at that rate were readily available to the Fund from other sources.

time. In 1890, the account heading loans from the Fund was changed from "various borrowers" to "Stockholm Enskilda Bank"[38]

The funding of the Railroad Mortgage Fund came mainly from the Bank of Sweden; 1.4 MSEK were lent directly to the National Debt Office and instantly passed on and in addition the bank bought bonds issued by the National Debt Office for 3.5 MSEK during 1879.[39]

Still the Bank of Sweden officially refused to act in a manner that endangered its possibility of maintaining the gold standard. This was, as the first objective, always more important than lending support to the banks no matter what collateral the banks could offer. The solution was different than in the 1857/58 crisis insofar as it was the National Debt Office that was to import funds and administer the banking support—an arrangement which has been repeated ever since with the exception of the Kreuger crisis in 1931/32 (see below)[40] The Bank of Sweden's new responsibility for the gold standard that was adopted in 1874 was also an important variable in the Bank's decision not to sustain the credit market further, unlike in the crisis 1857/58 when the Bank did not hesitate to provide liquidity in a manner which clearly violated the rules of the fixed exchange rate. The reason is not tied to the monetary regime as much as to the fact that the Swedish state in 1878/79, unlike in 1857/58, had increased its foreign debt quite substantially, and this foreign debt was all denominated in foreign currencies, meaning thata currency default would be very costly in 1878/79 when compared with 1857/58.[41]

As seen in Fig. 3.4 above the economic consequences of the Railroad crisis for the state was less substantial than what had been the case in 1857/58. It engaged in saving banks to an amount of 7.56 MSEK (of guaranteed 23 MSEK) plus 3 MSEK to purchase the shares of one failing private railroad and another 4 MSEK devoted to provide loans to the sawmill industry. All in all, these 14.56 MSEK were substantial but far from the state's total revenues of 73 MSEK in 1879. The increase in the public debt was linked more to the investments in the infrastructure than to the salvage of the financial system.

---

[38]Ögren (2007), RGKJHFH No 7903–7906, 1890, pp. 18–19, 1891, pp. 18–19, 1892, pp. 18–19, 1893, pp. 20–21.

[39]Ögren (2007), RGKJHFL No 4851, pp. 22–23, 26–27. These payments were one million SEK on June 4 and 400,000 on October 1 on 1879. They were originally registered as a special entry labeled "The Riksbank", but this was later changed. Since the bank of Sweden in fact lent to the National Debt Office which, in turn, lent to the Fund, it is possible that the total credit provided by the Bank of Sweden exceeded these amounts. RGKLHFM No 8514 p. 23. In addition to the Bank of Sweden, two other principal actors were instrumental in providing funds for the Railroad Mortgage Fund, the banking firm of Ehrlanger & Söhne, Frankfurt am Main and C.J. Hambro & Son, London.

[40]Ögren (2007) RbFP No 172 January 15, 24 1878. RbR No 430 February 26 1880. In response to Wallenberg's Parliamentary proposal (No. 37) concerning a guaranteed right to borrow from the Riksbank against certain specified types of bonds. RbFSP No 252 June 15, 29 1876, RbR No 429 April 15 1875, June 26 1876, December 11 1877, Schön (2000, pp. 262–263), Simonsson (1931, pp. 40–41).

[41]See Ögren (2012) for details.

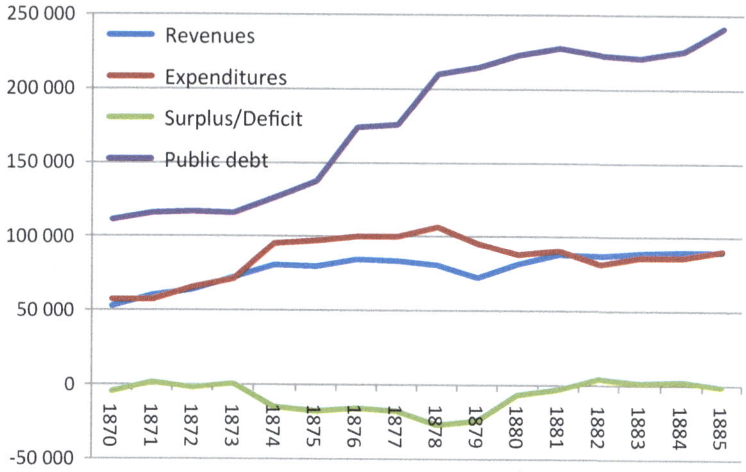

Fig. 3.4 State finances, 1870–1885 (1000's SEK) (Fregert and Gustafsson 2008, pp. 68–76)

3.3.3 Deflation Crisis 1921/23

The acute banking crisis in 1921 until 1923, and the following industrial crisis, is still the most profound Swedish crisis in terms of the decrease in GDP and financial costs. The crisis was preceded by a strong boom which was fed by the economic circumstances during WWI. Capital flowed into neutral Sweden, the currency appreciated, and prices, especially asset prices, skyrocketed. The banking system increased its lending even to the extent that the regulations that demanded a certain reserve coverage were removed during the peak year 1917 by the government for the main banks, after pressure from the very same banks. In addition, legal changes stemming from the new and detailed Banking act of 1911 had allowed banks not only hold shares as collateral but also to own and trade shares. As a result, the banks became important investors in industrial shares on the stock market. As the economy changed after the war with falling demand for Swedish industrial products, many industrial companies found themselves with excessive inventories of industrial products with very limited demand. The result was fire sales, losses, and falling share values—a situation which affected the banks portfolios.[42]

The first signals of the Banking crisis were experienced in 1920, not counting the bank *AB Privatbanken* which was liquidated due to economic fraud in 1919, when both *AB Nya Banken* and *AB Köpmannabanken* were liquidated. Both of these failures were seen as due to exceptional circumstances as the former had invested in Russia before the Bolshevik revolution in 1917 and the latter had invested too heavily into one single agent. History shows that at least the latter reason is more

[42]Lönnborg et al. (2011).

rule than exception when banks find themselves in distress. *AB Nya Banken* was recapitalized as *Bank AB Norden* without state intervention. While these banks experienced grave difficulties many banks that just one year later would find themselves in need of support were still paying high dividends.

Problems in the financial sector mounted under 1921 and by the end of the year the Banking inspection signaled alarm for the future state of the banking system. Given the focus on reestablishing the gold standard the Bank of Sweden was impeded from sustaining the market by providing liquidity. In fact, the deflationary monetary policy that had begun in 1919 made interest rates peak at 7.5%, higher than any agent had experienced before. (The gold standard was adopted, at the pre-WWI par, in 1924). But the governor of the Bank of Sweden, Victor Moll, was not insensitive to the situation, instead the Bank of Sweden guaranteed emergency credits targeting specific banks in trouble to sustain their recapitalizations. The governor of Bank of Sweden was also early in frequent discussions with the banking elite (CEOs of the main banks *Skandinaviska Kreditaktiebolaget* (Rydbeck), *Stockholms Enskilda Bank* (Nachmanson, Wallenberg (deputy CEO)), *Svenska Handelsbanken* (Philipson) and representatives of the banks in trouble to solve the situation. The Banking inspector, von Krusentjerna was also involved and later also the governor of the National Debt Office (Kinander) and the Minister of Finance (Thorsson). Having worked closely with the banks and even presented a proposal for a special Toxic Asset Fund, Victor Molls was surprised to find that the initiative and the design in many vital ways (for instance the funding) of the emergency fund was taken over by the CEOs of *Stockholm Enskilda Bank* and *Skandinaviska Kreditaktiebolaget.* In this proposal the state should guarantee 50 MSEK, the banks 5MSEK, the state should take the losses (and if there would be a profit this too would belong to the state). The Board of the fund, that was named *AB Kreditkassan,* should consist of three state representatives and two from the commercial banks. This was quite far from the original idea that the banks should provide one third of the capital—still this proposal was what laid the foundation for the establishment of *AB Kreditkassan* that after intense parliamentary debates was established in April 1922. Originally the fund was meant to save one bank, *Sydsvenska Kredit AB*, and the capital provided by the banks, 5 MSEK, was meant to cover one third of this action and as quickly as possible the banks withdrew their capital from the fund. But to salvage *Sydsvenska Kredit AB* was just the tip of the iceberg. Within the year *Kreditkassan AB* had to recapitalize four more banks, pumping in not less than 83 MSEK into bank recapitalization, thus extending its obligations with two-thirds just to banks.[43]

As seen below in Table 3.2 the fund also had to take on and recapitalize several companies that were parts of the banks portfolios—to a value of no less than 77 MSEK. This means that the state, through the National Debt Office provided credits to an amount of 160 MSEK, not counting the 20 MSEK guaranteed by the Bank of

[43]BaU (1922: 25), RdAK (1922: 23), RdFK (1922: 20), Hagberg (2007), Kprop (1922: 149), RdS (1922: 78).

Table 3.2 Total recapitalization by Kreditkassan AB 1922–1923 (1925 in parantheses) (Hagberg 2007)

Bank	Support in SEK
AB Sydsvenska Banken	13,200,000
Smålands Enskilda Bank	6,900,000
Wermlands Enskilda Bank	31,900,000
AB Jordbrukarebanken	8,100,000
AB Göteborgs Handelsbank	22,900,000
Total Bank support	83,000,000
Industries	*Support in SEK*
Steel industry	
Wargön AB	20,000,000
Ludvika Bruksägare	4,800,000
Fagersta Bruk AB	7,800,000
Forsbacka Järnverk AB (1925)	10,500,000
Pulp industry	
Sulfit AB Göta	5,800,000
Mackmyra Sulfit AB	3,900,000
Agriculture	
AB Malmö Valvskvarn	2,700,000
Svenska lantmännens kvarnandelsförening	4,650,000
Sveska lantmännens kvarnförening	2,400,000
Shipping	
Rederi AB Transatlantic (1925)	9,000,000
Svenska Lantmännens Rederi AB	3,500,000
Construction	
Vallevikens Cement AB	2,000,000
Total industrial support	77,000,000
Total write off (until 1928)	68,000,000
Total losses (until 1928)	70,910,000

Sweden at the outset of the crisis. The losses were substantial as well, almost 45% of the capital pumped in by the state was lost mostly as write offs in value.

The outcome of the crisis was that the main banks consolidated their positions even further. Small provincial banks were not supported by the state, some of them were taken over by the main banks. In the long term the main banks also came to hold a strong position with close ties to important industrial companies.[44] The fund *Kreditkassan AB,* had initially been seen as a five year project, to be concluded in 1927 but due to the prolonged crisis and the heavy involvement by the state it had early been viewed as the Fund's existence had to be prolonged but the then, at the time for the Funds planned dismantling in 1927, liberal Minister of Finance wanted

[44]See Larsson (1998) There is a concept to define this strong relationship between one bank and one industrial company that arose and was cemented as a result of the crisis —"*Husbankförbindelse*" [~House-bank relationship].

to end its existence and consequently it was only prolonged one year until the end of 1928 but was then replaced by "The Fund for dealing with the losses of Kreditkassan AB" (*Fonden för mötande av förluster å AB Kreditkassan av år 1922*). Criticism in parliament was fierce—focusing on the fact that the representatives of the state: the Bank of Sweden (through the Standing Committee on Banking) and the National Debt Office, had presented the plan as a more or less risk free way to salvage the financial system without incurring any losses on the state.

3.3.4 The Kreuger Crisis in 1931/32

The crisis in Sweden in 1931 was related to the Great Depression and is seen as much less severe than the prior crisis in the 1920s had been. Usually this is explained as a result of more cautious industry and banking sectors in terms of investments as a result of the recent crisis experiences. Moreover, the massive recapitalization that had occurred in the early 1920s made them comparably invulnerable as they did not have to carry the burden of bad assets to the same extent.

As the capital flooding from the US to Europe ended with the great crash in 1929 the crisis did hit the Swedish banking system all the same. Two main banks had initially been involved in the activities of Ivar Kreuger and his famous empire based on safety matches, monopoly positions for sovereign debt and an aggressive financial strategy based on the issuing of corporate debt and financial innovations (such as the infamous "participating debentures" on international capital markets; *Svenska Handelsbanken* and *Skandinaviska Kreditaktiebolaget"*. This involvement had its origin during the WWI boom but it was not until the tide turned on international capital markets, countries defaulted on their debt, and credits were cancelled to Kreuger's corporate group. In 1931 to repay his loans mainly to French banks Kreuger negotiated a huge loan from the Bank of Sweden of approximately fifty percent of its' entire foreign exchange reserves, guaranteed by the bank most involved in his business, *Skandinaviska Kreditaktiebolaget*. As a new due date was to arrive in February 1932 Kreuger again had to involve the Swedish credit market. He even approached the Swedish Prime Minister C: G: Ekman, which can be explained by the fact that at this time a stunning more than 60% of the entire loan portfolio of Swedish commercial banks was related to the Kreuger Group. By far mostly involved was *Skandinaviska Kreditaktiebolaget,* somewhat surprising considering that the CEO of *Skandinaviska Kreditaktiebolaget* still was aforementioned Oscar Rydbeck who had been deeply involved in the 1920s crisis only ten years before (and whom actually had started his career with the reconstruction of *Hernösands Enskilda Bank* in 1907/1908). Kreuger's call for help made the Bank of Sweden meet with representatives for all commercial banks (except for *Stockholm Enskilda Bank*) to guarantee funds. One of the activities called for was to go through the books of the Kreuger Group to find out the situation—the result showed that another 135 MSEK was needed to meet the claims on the Kreuger

Group in 1932 alone. This made the Bank of Sweden call for an immediate meeting with Rydbeck at *Skandinaviska Kreditaktiebolaget* and Ivar Kreuger in person. Unfortunately Kreuger never came to the meeting, he committed suicide in a hotel in Paris March 12, 1932.[45]

On March 31 the government launched a parliamentary proposition to save the financial system—or rather to save *Skandinaviska Kreditaktiebolaget* which was argued as vital for the survival of the financial system. The proposition was prepared by the Minister of Finance, Hamrin. The official reason for the proposition was a letter which he had received March 24 from the *Skandinaviska Kreditaktiebolaget* where the bank argued, something the Minister of Finance, the Bank of Sweden and the Banking Inspection agreed upon, that it in fact was solvent but that the recent events had made it illiquid and thus its public trust was endangered. As a result the bank asked for public support to ease its constrained situation.

What the bank was granted in credit, however, points to more than a problem of illiquidity. The state, through the National Debt Office, guaranteed credits of 215 MSEK, and other commercial banks were supposed to deposit "for some time" (not specified) a sum of 40 MSEK in the bank. First in total this was around fifty percent of the bank's public liabilities at the time it called for help. Second, this was more than the supposed 135 MSEK that was needed to salvage the Kreuger Group—one reason probably being that these assets had fallen in value since. Third, the state decided to make additional sum of 30 MSEK available to the banks due to the general situation on the market—thus almost covering for the 40 MSEK the banks loosely were supposed to deposit in *Skandinaviska Kreditaktiebolaget.* Again, the state was to take the majority share of the cost and risk for salvaging the banks, no other banks opted for the possibility to acquire the supposedly solvent assets.

The liberal government, and the representatives of the Bank of Sweden, the National Debt Office and the Banking Inspection, had no criticism on the bank despite its significant commitment of 245 MSEK (a sum comparable to the more spread crisis in 1921/23) to save one bank who had repeated the problems of the former crisis by investing too heavily into one agent. Loans were guaranteed without any consequences for *Skandinaviska Kreditaktiebolaget* other than a stipulated 5.5% minimum dividend while its emergency debt towards the state lasted. Leading Social democrats in parliament motioned against the bank's right to pay out dividends plus for the possibility of the state (National Debt Office) to have a Board member at *Skandinaviska Kreditaktiebolaget.* The Standing Committee on banking did not support these motions, the former on the ground that denying the bank the right to pay out dividends would "work against the purpose of the banking aid" but it was never explained in what way, and for the latter it was argued that if the state had a representative in the Board this: "… could lead to an unsuitable

[45]Lönnberg et al. (2011, pp. 239–242).

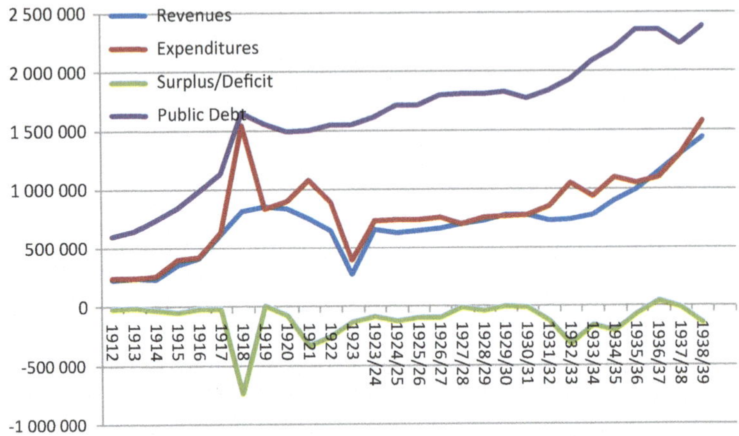

Fig. 3.5 State finances, 1912–1937/38 (1000's SEK) (Fregert and Gustafsson 2008, pp. 68–76)

division of the responsibility of the bank's management and also in addition be fitted to bring about consequences, which now can not be foreseen."[46]

A possible reason for the state's leniency were in the light of the currency crisis the engagements of the Bank of Sweden that had been guaranteed by *Skandinaviska Kreditaktiebolaget*. But instead of the Bank of Sweden taking over assets to a comparative value it concluded in its recommendation on the proposition that it would be good if the capital advanced by the National Debt Office to *Skandinaviska Kreditaktiebolaget* would be used to pay *Skandinaviska Kreditaktiebolaget's* debt to the Bank of Sweden so that the Bank of Sweden would not have to print more money for the National Debt Office to sustain *Skandinaviska Kreditaktiebolaget.*[47]

In the end the management of the Kreuger crisis was made under a floating exchange rate as Sweden decided to abandon the gold standard in 1931. Thus in this sense the possibility to manage the crisis and provide liquidity was the opposite of the situation in the early 1920s when the monetary policy was tied to the objective of restoring the gold standard, even at pre-WWI par, which was done in 1924.

Figure 3.5 below shows the state's finances during the period 1912 until 1937/1938. It should be noted that unfortunately the year 1923 marked the change of the fiscal year from the prior use of calendar year, thus 1923 in the graph is only six months. This makes a clearer difference for the flow variables (Expenditures, Revenues and Deficit/Surplus) and explains the fall in these during 1923. Both the crises in the 1920s and the 1930s were marked by deficits, and in this respect that is in terms of state finances the crisis in 1932 was as severe as the prior crisis in 1921–1923. The shock in 1918 is tied to the end of WWI's effect on Swedish exports and

[46]MoAK (1932: 346, 509) and BaU (1932: 22, pp. 8–9) [Standing Committee on Banking No 22 April 4, pp 8–9].

[47]Kprop (1932: 248 p. 6).

should have been a warning signal—but as stated above asset values and credit expansion continued.

3.3.5 Real Estate Crisis 1991/92

The Swedish crisis in the early 1990s was of significant magnitude to be compared only with the crisis in 1921–1923. The fall in GDP was less than in the crisis in the 1920s but the crisis meant a significant shift not least on the labor market where unemployment became established at four times the level of the pre-crisis period. Thus the 1990s crisis had longer lasting consequences but a less volatile cycle than the crisis in the 1920s. Also in this case the Swedish crisis was part of an international crisis with the ongoing currency turbulence and the breakdown of the European Exchange Rate Mechanism. But, again as was the case in the 1920s, Sweden also had its own problems that helped make the crises as severe. In short currency and fiscal policies were mismatched, financial deregulations and incentives to borrow spawned credit expansion and inflation with exploding assets values, not least in the real estate sector.[48]

The boom was curbed in 1990 and signs of distress were usually attributed to the fall of one real estate company (*Nyckeln)* which meant more pessimistic future valuations of assets and properties. When the crisis hit in 1991 the Bank of Sweden was fiercely defending the fixed exchange rate. Nevertheless, focus had to be turned to the banking sector where the banks that had been most aggressive during the boom found themselves with rapidly deteriorating balance sheets due to credit losses. The two banks most in trouble were somewhat ironically two banks that during the late 1980s had fought to fend off their reputation as somewhat dull, careful and stable banking institutions: *Första Sparbanken* and *Nordbanken. Första Sparbanken* [the First Savings bank] was a result of the regulatory change making savings banks into commercial banks. It became the flagship of the associated savings banks. It was intended to operate as a full-fledged commercial bank, but apparently took on more risk than a normal commercial bank in order to gain market share. Between 1988 and 1990 it doubled its lending, and to new market segments such as financial and real estate corporations. *Nordbanken* was the other bank most in trouble, and even though the government ideologically adhered to a liberal belief in *laissez faire* the fact that *Nordbanken* was a remnant of *AB Kreditkassan* from 1928 (then *Sveriges Kreditbank*) and the postal bank (merged in 1974 into *Post och Kreditbanken* or *PK Banken*) which was owned to 70.6% by the Swedish state, made it difficult for the government to decide not to intervene. It was also the bank that, due to its position as a state owned bank with access to the postal infrastructure, had the most private individuals as clients of all commercial banks. But it was not from the households that the losses mounted but from business

[48]Englund (1999).

activities undertaken by the bank in the late 1980s to gain more corporate market shares with the aspiration to become, as had been the case with *Första Sparbanken,* a modern commercial bank.

Thus, when *Nordbanken* was bleeding and needed fresh capital from its owners it was natural to turn to its main owner, the Swedish state. It was decided that the bank needed an injection of not less than 5160 MSEK. The banking problems had been communicated to the Social democratic government by the banks and the Banking inspection. After their defeat in the election in September 1991 the problems were handed over to the new conservative liberal government and in October 1991 this government decided to take on its share of new shares in the bank and guarantee the remaining, almost 30%. Still, credit losses were higher in 1991, almost 10,000 MSEK. But without this immediate capital injection by the owners, the bank would have had to cut credits to an amount of around 73,000 MSEK. The capital injection was carried out *Nordbanken* and it is an excellent example of how ideological convictions seems to play a small role when banks are on the verge of collapsing. The liberal minister of finance (Anne Wibble) claimed that in principle the state should not own banks and thus these new shares should be sold as soon as possible, the problem of course being who would want to invest in those shares given the future prospect of the bank, thus it should be "when it was suitable for the state" and "when it did not affect the credit grading of the bank".[49] As credit losses of the bank continued to pile up events moved in the opposite direction. Facing credit losses of more than 60,000 MSEK the same government, that through its guarantee to support the share issuance in 1991 had increased its ownership share of *Nordbanken* to 77.6%, in May 1992 decided to take over the bank in full by buying up remaining shares at 17% over market value (in total 2050 MSEK). This was part of the plan to reconstruct the bank by initiating a special "toxic asset fund," *Securum AB,* that could take on these estimated 60,000 MSEK of *Nordbanken's* bad assets. It was decided that above the cost for buying up the shares another 20,000 MSEK would be made available as capital for *Nordbanken* and *Securum AB.* The task of administering this fund was again given to the National Debt Office.[50]

The same remark concerning the unsuitability of the state intervening in the market was made in the case of *Första Sparbanken* who two weeks after the first guarantee for *Nordbanken* (October 24, 1991) was granted an interest free loan of 3800 MSEK as part of its reconstruction due to credit losses of 4500 MSEK. The stated reason was to protect the depositors. In this case, as the state was not the owner, but it was decided that as long as the state guaranteed this credit to the bank the state had the right to decide on the bank's board members. Moreover, no dividends were allowed during this time.[51] Also in this case mounting credit losses made the state increase its support in May 1992 by another 3500 MSEK. The

[49]Prop (1991/92: 21).

[50]Prop (1991/92: 153).

[51]Prop (1991/92: 63).

motivation behind the decision is illustrative of the dilemma inherent in providing banking support as a common good:

> Normally in the banking sector it is the owners' responsibility to solve their economic problems without the support of the state. The circumstance that Sparbankstiftelsen Första lacks sufficient financial resources, as well as the circumstance that the situation in the capital market presently is such that it is not possible to bring in the necessary capital addition, make state support in this case necessary. The proposed steps mean that the state contributes to bridge the acute problems to achieve a tenable solution in the long term where the bank continues to be managed within a more stable financial structure and with partly new owners.[52]

In the early fall of 1992 the situation even made this government instigate a specific authority on the side of Bank of Sweden, the National Debt Office and the Banking inspection (now *Finansinspektionen*) that was responsible for supporting bank and credit institutions with "some connection to the state" (as the bill read). The motivation behind the liberal government's desire to increase its involvement in the financial sector was threefold: (1) to secure the continuation of the banking recapitalization—the initial 20,000 MSEK were not sufficient given that the credit losses of *Nordbanken* alone was more than 60,000 MSEK—and more banks started to ask for support. Apart from the support to *Nordbanken* and *Första Sparbanken* support was also given to those who had liabilities in *Gota Banken AB*—but the bank in question had to file for bankruptcy. (2) To secure the stability of the Swedish payment system, and (3) as part of the overall structural changes of the economy that the government had agreed upon with the Social Democratic Party.[53]

All of this was done while defending the fixed exchange rate. Even when Italy and the UK decided to abandon European Exchange Rate Mechanism on September 16–17, 1992, the Swedish government decided to fight—setting a record interest rate of 500%. But on November 19 Sweden also caved in and allowed the SEK to float—a decision which has been seen as fundamental for the Swedish economic recovery. It may also explain why the Bank of Sweden was not present as a liquidity provider during the initial crisis.

But it is also in the light of the increasing credit losses and need for recapitalization in 1992 that the choice of the state to allow the currency to depreciate should be seen. The decisions to save the banks were made in late October just before the currency was set afloat. All in all, the state's commitment to save the banks amounted to almost 73,000 MSEK (or more than five percent of GDP). In 1991 and 1992 the interest free loans to *Första Sparbanken* of 7300 MSEK, equity to *Nordbanken* of 16,300 MSEK, and to *Securum* of 24,000 MSEK and in 1993 the

---

[52]Prop (1991/92: 168, p. 4).

[53]Prop (1992/93: 135), Prop (1992/93: 50). This program marked the dismantling of the welfare system including the retirement system in a manner which makes it remarkable how such a program could gain support among such broad political lines, unions and other interest groups.

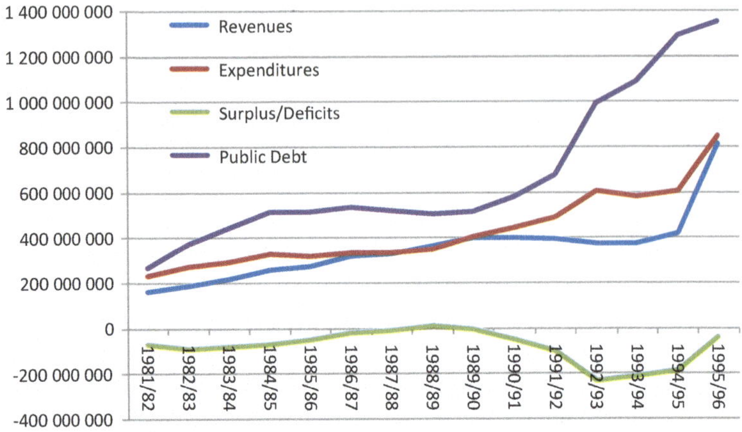

Fig. 3.6 State finances, 1982–1997 (1000's SEK) (Fregert and Gustafsson 2008, pp. 68–76)

25,100 MSEK that was paid out as equity to (the now state owned) Gota Bank in order to aid its liability holders.[54]

As shown in Fig. 3.6 the impact of the crisis on the state's finances is clear, the 73,000 MSEK is of less relative importance in comparison to the 400,000 MSEK revenues of the state than what was the case in the crisis in 1857/58, but the roles of the state was fundamentally different at the two times. Evident is the increase in state expenditures in relation to the crisis while the revenues are staying the same. The impact on the state's debt from the program to save the banks is thus as expected. Moreover, this debt was entirely imported from abroad while the above conclusion that this was one direct reason for the abandonment of the fixed currency holds. Arguably, with the crisis, including the extensive program to save the banks, many parts of the welfare program had to give into the need to correct the state deficit.

3.4 Concluding Discussion on Banking Crises and Crisis Management in Swedish History—Some Stylized Facts

To sum up some of the experiences of banking crises and their management in Sweden we can conclude that the traditional way of providing liquidity by lender of last resort will quickly be broadened to a more elaborated scheme including the tax payers. This is due to the fact that the central bank is more constrained due to its

[54]Englund (1999), Prop (1991/92: 21), Prop (1991/92: 63), Prop (1991/92: 135), Prop (1991/92: 168).

obligation to the currency. Bank bailouts are thus not constrained by resources the same way. The pattern of dividing the work between providing liquidity directly by discounting or buying assets and the more long term bank bailout schemes funded by importing fresh capital is a theme which goes through all crises. Another is the fact that in terms of the state's finances the bailout schemes are large commitments for tax payers. Supervision seems in larger crises to not be able to stem the development of a crisis. And the question is why this is the case—is it is due to lack of enforcement or because the magnitudes of the crises are of such importance.

What is striking is that it is the banks to be saved that to a large extent design the saving schemes. They are calling attention to their own difficulties and drawing up the lines for their salvation. The ideology of the government plays no role at all; when the pressure mounts the government will step in. It also means that the representatives of the banks assume that they will be saved—and this is as is commonly known tied to their size. Smaller banks making the same mistakes as large banks, putting too many eggs in the same portfolio, will have to pay the price of bankruptcy, but this is not the case for the main banks. In fact these seem to strengthen their positions after crises, a question which deserves to be more deeply studied (as well as what would be the causes for this).

It is clear however that the networks of these bank's representatives plays an important role. Historically bank representatives in Sweden have close ties to each other as well as to politicians (and it is not only historical, today's chairman of *Svenska Bankförenigen* [the Swedish Banker's association] is none other than the former Social Democratic minister of finance Thomas Östros). This may also explain why the state is not prepared to let the market rule and let banks fail. A consequence of this is that today's Swedish banking system contains banks that have been saved at least once but most of them several times over.

Finally, it can be concluded, somewhat surprisingly, that neither the size of banks or in what way the ownership is structured seem to make any difference for banks when it comes to risk taking and possibility of falling into crises. Banks of unlimited liability, limited liability, and foundations were all subject to bailouts. And clearly that larger banks have larger possibilities for diversifying their assets and liabilities does not mean that they are prepared to do so.

References

Riksdagstryck [Parliamentary Publications]

BaU—Bankoutskottet [Standing Committee on Banking] 1922: 25, 1932: 22.
MoAK Motion andra kammaren [Motion second chamber] 1932: 346, 509.
RdAK Riksdagen andra kammaren [Parliamentary proceedings Second chamber] 1922: 23.
RdFK Riksdagen första kammaren [Parliamentary proceedings first chamber] 1922: 20.

Kprop—Kunglig proposition [Royal proposition] 1879: 29, 1922: 149, 1932: 248.
Prop—Proposition 1991/92: 21, 63, 153, 168, 1992/93: 50, 135.
RdRB—Revisionsberättelser 2: a Samlingen 1: a Afdelningen. Riksdagens revisorers berättelse angående Riksbanken 1874—1881 [The Parliamentary Auditors' Reports Concerning the Riksbank].
RdSkr—Riksdagens Underdåniga Skrifvelser [Parliamentary Resolutions] RdS 1922: 78.

Sources at the National Archive of Sweden

Bankkommittén 1881—ÄK No 394 Vol. 1—5 [Temporary Committee on Banking 1881].
Finanskommittén 1858—ÄK No 496 Vol. 1–4 [Temporary Committee on Finance 1858].
RbDA—Riksbanken Depositionsafdelningen Huvudbok 1858. Rb No 4348–4352 [The Riksbank. Department of Deposits, General Ledger].
RbFP—Riksbanken Fullmäktige Protokoll 1856–1859, 1869–1881. Rb No 150–153, 163–175 [Minutes of the Board of the Riksbank].
RbFSP—Riksbanken Fullmäktige Särskilda Protokoll 1869–1881. Rb No 249–257 [Minutes of the Board of the Riksbank in Special Matters].
RbR—Riksbankens Registratur Konceptböcker 1869–1881. Rb No 428–430 [Letters of the Board of the Riksbank, Concepts].
RbSLF—Riksbanken Statslånefonden 1858–1864. Rb No 4812–4816 [The State Loan Fund—administered by the Riksbank].
RbSLFH—Riksbanken Statslånefonden Huvudbok 1858–1864. Rb No 4817–4821 [General Ledger, the State Loan Fund—administered by the Riksbank].
RGKJHFH—Jernvägshypoteksfonden Hufvudbok 1879–1894. RGK No 7893–7907 [General Ledger, the Railroad Mortgage Fund—administered by the National Debt Office].
RGKJHFL—Jernvägshypoteksfonden Lånediarium. RGK No 4851 [Loan Diary, the Railroad Mortgage Fund—administered by the National Debt Office].
RGKJHFM—Järnväghypoteksfonden Memorialbok. RGK No 8514 [Memorial book, the Railroad Mortgage Fund—administered by the National Debt Office].
RGKLKO—Riksgäldskontoret Lånekontrakt Original 1858–1879. RGK No 9061 [National Debt Office Borrowing Contracts, Original].
RGKLKT—Riksgäldskontoret Lånekontrakt Tryckta 1858–1872. RGK No 9060 [National Debt Office Borrowing Contracts, Printed].
RGKLP—Låneprotokoll Riksgälsdskontoret 1879–1880. RGK No 4462–4463 [Lending Minutes of the National Debt Office].

Secondary Literature

Bagehot, W. 1866. What a Panic is and How it Might be Mitigated. In *Central Banking in History*, vol. 1, ed. M. Collins. Cambridge, UK: Edward Elgar.
Bagehot, W. 1916. Lombard Street. In *Central Banking in History*, vol. 1, ed. M. Collins. Cambridge, UK: Edward Elgar.
Bank of England (N/A) "Quantitative Easing Explained" Pamphlet ISBN 1 85730 114 5 (Print and on-line).
Beck, T., D. Coyle, M. Dewatripont, X. Freixas, and P. Seabright. 2010. Bailing out the Banks: Reconciling Stability and Competition. An Analysis of State-Supported Schemes for Financial Institutions. Centre for Economic Policy Research (CEPR).
Bignon, V., M. Flandreau, and S. Ugolini. 2009. Bagehot for Beginners: The Making of Lending of Last Resort Operations in the Mid-19th Century. Working Paper Norges Bank's Bicentenary project 2009: 22.

Bordo, M. D. 1989. The Lender of Last Resort: Some Historical Insights. NBER Working Paper No 3011.

Bordo, M. D. 1998. Currency Crisis (and banking crisis) in Historical Perspective. Research Report No 10. EHF—Institute for Research in Economic History. Stockholm School of Economics, Sweden.

Bordo, M. D., and Schwartz, A. J. 1996. Why Clashes Between Internal and External Stability Goals End in Currency Crises, 1797–1994. NBER Working Paper No 5710.

Bordo, M. D., and Meissner, C. M. 2005. Financial Crises, 1880—1913: The Role of Foreign Currency Debt. NBER Working Paper 11173.

Brisman, S. 1931. Den stora reformperioden 1860–1904. In *Sveriges Riksbank 1668–1924–1931. Bankens tillkomst och verksamhet, part IV*. Sveriges Riksbank. Norstedts. Stockholm, Sweden.

Brisman, S. 1934. *Sveriges affärsbanker*. Stockholm, Sweden: Utvecklingstiden. Svenska bankföreningen. Norstedts.

Capie, F., and G. Wood. 1995. A European Lender of Last Resort? Some Lessons from History. In *International Monetary Systems in Historical Perspectives*, ed. J. Reis. UK: MacMillan Press Ltd.

Chang, R., and A. Velasco. 1998. Financial Crises in Emerging Markets: A Canonical Model. NBER Working Paper No 6606.

Englund, P. 1999. The Swedish Banking Crisis: Roots and Consequences. *Oxford review of economic policy* 15: 3.

Flandreau, M. 2006. Foreign Currency Debt and Currency Crises: When and Why It Should Matter. Paper presented at the ASSA conference in Boston, MA, January 7, 2006.

Flodström, I. 1912. *Finansstatistiska utredningar utgivna genom Kungl. Finansdepartementet V. Sveriges Nationalförmögenhet omkring år 1908 och dess utveckling sedan midten av 1880-talet*. Beckmans. Stockholm, Sweden.

Fischer, S. 1999. On the Need for an International Lender of Last Resort. *Journal of Economic Perspectives* 13: 85–104.

Fregert, K., and R. Gustafsson. 2005. Fiscal statistics for Sweden 1719–2003. *Research in Economic History* 25: 169–224.

Freixas, X., G. Curzio, G. Hoggarth, and F. Soussa. 2000. Lender of Last Resort: What Have We Learned Since Bagehot? *Journal of Financial Services Research* 18: 63–84.

Gasslander, O. 1962. *History of Stockholm Enskilda Bank to 1914*. Stockholm, Sweden: Esselte AB.

Goodhart, C. A. E. 1987. Why Do Banks Need a Central Bank? In *The Central Bank and the Economic System*, ed. C. A. E. Goodhart (1995). Cambridge, Mass: MIT Press.

Goodhart, C.A.E. 1999. Myths About the Lender of Last Resort. *International Finance* 2: 339–360.

Hagberg, A. (2007) *Bankkrishantering. Aktörer, marknad och stat*. Doctoral thesis, Stockholm School of Economics.

Kindleberger, C. P., and R. Z. Aliber. 2005. *Manias, Panics, and Crashes A History of Financial Crises Fifth edition*. Wiley & Sons.

Kock, K. 1931. *Skånska Privatbanken. Minnesskrift*. Stockholm, Sweden: Norstedts.

Larsson, M. 1998. *Staten och kapitalet*. Stockholm: SNS.

Lönnborg, M., A. Ögren, and M. Rafferty. 2011. Banks and Swedish Financial Crises in the 1920s and 1930s. *Business History* 53 (2): 230–248.

McGouldrick, P. 1984. Operations of the German Central Bank, and the Rules of the Game, 1879–1913. In *A Retrospective on the Classical Gold Standard, 1821–1931*, ed. M. Bordo, and A. Scwartz. The University of Chicago Press, US.

McKinnon, R.I. 1993. The Rules of the Game: International Money in Historical Perspective. *Journal of Economic Literature* 31: 1–44.

Meltzer, A. 1986. Financial Failures and Financial Policies. In *Deregulating Financial Services: Public Policy in Flux*, ed. G. G. Kaufman, and R. C. Kormendi. Ballinger Publishing Company, Cambridge.

Nilsson, G. B. 1989. *André Oscar Wallenberg. II. Gyllene tider 1856–1866.* Norstedts. Stockholm, Sweden.
Ögren, A. 2007. Lender of Last Resort in a Peripheral Economy with a Fixed Exchange Rate: Financial Crises and Monetary Policy in Sweden under the Silver and Gold Standards, 1834–1913. In *Centers and Peripheries in Banking: The Historical Development of Financial Markets*, ed. P. Cottrell, E. Lange, and U. Olsson, 225–252. Ashgate.
Ögren, A. 2012. Central Banking and Monetary Policy in Sweden During the Long Nineteenth Century. In *The Gold Standard Peripheries—Monetary Policy, Adjustment and Flexibility in a Global Setting*, ed. A. Ögren, and L-F. Øksendal. London: Palgrave Macmillan Publishers.
Reinhart, C. M., and K. S. Rogoff. 2009. This time is different. *Eight Centuries of Financial Follies*. Princeton University Press.
Rockoff, H. 1986. Walter Bagehot and the Theory of Central Banking. In *Financial Crises and the World Banking System*, ed. F. Capie, and G.E. Wood. UK: The Macmillan Press.
Sayers, R. S. 1976. *The Bank of England 1891–1944,* vol. 1. UK: Cambridge University Press.
Schön, L. 2000. *En modern svensk ekonomisk historia. Tillväxt och omvandling under två sekel.* Stockholm, Sweden: SNS.
Söderlund, E. 1964. *Skandinaviska Banken 1864–1914*. Stockholm, Sweden: Esselte.
Talia, K. 2001. *Monetary Integration and Disintegration: Studies in the Scandinavian Currency Union, 1873–1924.* Licentiate thesis, Stockholm School of Economics, Sweden.
Tilly, R.H. 1986. German Banking, 1850–1914: Development Assistance for the Strong. *Journal of European Economic History* 15: 189–209.
Wood, G.E. 2000. The Lender of Last Resort Reconsidered. *Journal of Financial Services Research* 18: 203–227.

Author Biography

Anders Ögren is an associate professor in the Department of Economic History, Lund University in Sweden. He is the author of many papers on monetary history and history of economic thought. His most recent publication is "A neglected contribution to monetary theory in the eighteenth century: Anders Wappengren on paper money, floating exchange rates, and purchasing power parity," *European Journal of the History of Economic Thought.*

Chapter 4
It is Always the Shadow Banks: The Regulatory Status of the Banks that Failed and Ignited America's Greatest Financial Panics

Hugh Rockoff

Abstract This paper surveys the failures that ignited major financial panics in the United States. It starts with the Panic of 1819 and covers 11 others through the Panic of 2008. This sample covers all of the "great" panics to judge from the consensus of financial historians. Several generalizations about the regulatory status of these banks stand out. (1) Panics typically were ignited by a sequence of failures. (2) Typically, the sequence included institutions from different parts of the country and different parts of the financial system, contributing to the fear that the entire financial system was at risk. (3) Typically, shadow banks (unregulated or lightly regulated banks) were an important component of the sequence, and often were the culminating failure in the sequence that triggered the panic. Big trouble following the failure of shadow banks is not a new problem that emerged in the twenty-first century, but rather a persistent problem that began in the nineteenth century.

Keywords Shadow banks · Panics · Walter bagehot · Bank of united states
Lender of last resort · Federal reserve

4.1 Some Questions and Definitions

The failure of a famous financial firm features prominently in the narrative histories of most U.S. financial panics. The most recent panic is typical: Lehman brothers failed on September 15, 2008: and … all hell broke loose. Future historians, we can be sure, will dwell on the failure of Lehman Brothers when they write the history of the panic. Many of these failures, although not all, have been examined by economic and social historians who have written detailed case studies. But there has not been, as far as I am aware, a systematic attempt to compare and contrast these

H. Rockoff (✉)
Department of Economics, Rutgers University, 75 Hamilton Street, New Brunswick
NJ 08901, USA
e-mail: Rockoff@econ.rutgers.edu

© Springer Nature Singapore Pte Ltd. 2018

H. Rockoff and I. Suto (eds.), *Coping with Financial Crises*,
Studies in Economic History, https://doi.org/10.1007/978-981-10-6196-7_4

cases, and extract some general conclusions. Here I survey these failures, focusing on their regulatory status. It seems to be a common assumption that the failure of Lehman brothers was something new, a panic started by the failure of a shadow bank.

In a speech given at Princeton University Ben Bernanke (2010) noted that the standard view of earlier had slowed the response to the crisis in 2008.

> Because the runs on the shadow banking system occurred in a historically unfamiliar context, outside the commercial banking system, both the private sector and the regulators insufficiently anticipated the risk that such runs might occur. However, once the threat became apparent, two centuries of economic thinking on runs and panics were available to inform the diagnosis and the policy response.

Here I re-examine the role of shadow banks in earlier crises. As it turns out, failures of shadow banks that demoralize financial markets are nothing new; they were an important factor in almost all of the major panics of the nineteenth and twentieth centuries. We are unlikely to repeat the exact mistakes made during the most recent financial crisis. But a better understanding of the role of shadow banks in past financial crises may make it easier to avoid mistakes in the future when the financial system looks different from the system that collapsed in 2008.

Before turning to the historical record it is necessary to define three terms that recur repeatedly in what follows: panic, shadow bank, and failure.

A panic is, as Walter Bagehot explained in *Lombard Street* (1924 [1873], 118) simply "a sudden demand for cash." It's a fundamentally different state of financial markets in which almost everyone is trying to protect themselves by turning their assets into cash.

Although there are a few debatable cases, the term shadow bank is also reasonably clear. A shadow bank is first of all a bank: a financial intermediary that relies heavily on short-term liabilities for funding. But it is a bank that is not subject to close scrutiny and regulation by a government authority. Often shadow banks were private institutions not subject to any form of regulation. In other cases, however, they were nominally subject to regulation, but given free rein in practice. For some purposes it is sufficient to define state chartered banks and trust companies as shadow banks. But in other cases it is better to put them in an intermediary category. Another aspect of shadow banks, one that undoubtedly contributed to the ready acceptance of the term is that they are not well known to the public; not hidden, but in the shadows. And this was true of many of the banks identified here as shadow banks. Brokers and investment banks may be well-known to financial professionals, but unknown to the average person.

My definition corresponds to current usage. Lehman Brothers is generally referred to as a shadow bank. It fulfills both of my conditions. It relied heavily on short-term repo loans. And although was nominally regulated by the Securities and Exchange Commission, it was given free rein in practice. As an operational matter, I classify national banks, the First and Second Banks of the United States, and the Federal Reserve as regulated banks. Unregulated private bill brokers, investment banks and the like, as shadow banks; and state chartered banks and trust companies as an intermediate category of shadowy banks.

I use the term failure to refer to a bank that has suddenly stopped payment on its short-term obligations, or is thought likely to do so, and created a sudden fear that it may never be able to make good on its obligations. In some cases the offending firm did not fail in the sense that its assets were liquidated by a court appointed official; it merely suspended payment of its obligations for a time, or was in trouble but was rescued in some way, etc. I have made these distinctions as necessary, but have used the term "failure" to cover these cases because my main concern here is with events that produced panics. When a bank stopped payment, depositors often assumed that it was bankrupt and that it would be a long time before it redeemed any of it's deposits. It was the fear of this outcome that created panics. The press often referred to these banks as failures, although in some cases they were able to reopen.

In Sect. 4.2 I will briefly outline the relationship between this paper's stress on major failures and other ideas about the origin of financial panics. Section 4.3 identifies the panics that are examined here and explains why some episodes which sometimes have been labeled panics, are excluded. Section 4.4 explains why one would expect a sequence of failures that crossed regional and institutional boundaries. Section 4.5 explains why shadow banks were likely to be important links in the chain of failures that sparked panics. Section 4.6 discusses each panic separately. And Sect. 4.7 summarizes the main conclusions and draws some implications.

4.2 Famous Failures and Alternative Theories

It is conceivable that failures of trusted firms by themselves accounted for the financial crises that have periodically disrupted the American financial system. A financial panic in this view is like a panic in a crowded auditorium when a crazy person shouts fire and there is a mad rush for the exit. Diamond and Dybvig (1983) were the first to provide a formal model of a fragile banking system prone to runs, although the idea that a fractional reserve banking system is inherently fragile is, of course, much older. They analyzed the case of a "sunspot" that leads to a sudden run on banks. Perhaps the unexpected failure of a shadow bank can be thought of as the sunspot that quickly leads to the bad equilibrium.

A considerable body of research, on the other hand, argues that panics arose when distortions built up in the financial system. Some examples are Calomiris and Gorton (1991), Schularick and Taylor (2012), or to take an older example, Mitchell (1941).

A full explanation of panics, I believe, will include the underlying fragility of the banking system, the forces that produce stresses in the financial system, and the failures that turned anxiety into panic. In *Lombard Street* Bagehot discusses "incipient panics," periods of elevated anxiety about the financial system when an accidental event, such as the unexpected failure of a great banking firm, is more likely to ignite a panic.

The idea that famous failures played a causal role in panics is related to the idea that there are "systemically important" banks. The idea is that there are certain banks whose can be safely ignored by central banks because they would be ignored by financial markets, but that there are other banks that because of their size and their interconnectedness with other financial institutions must be bailed out because ignoring them would ignite a panic.[1] Hopefully, a study of the failures that ignited past panics will help identify the markers of "systemically important banks."

4.3 Twelve Major Financial Panics

This paper examines the failures (or in two cases, suspensions of cash payments) that precipitated twelve major financial panics in the United States. The chronology of the panics is shown in Table 4.1. It was constructed by looking at the classic financial and general economic histories of the United States—Sprague's *History of Crises under the National Banking System*, Friedman and Schwartz's *A Monetary History of the United States*, Studenski and Krooss's *Financial History of the United States*, and so on—as well as more recent studies.[2]

I included panics that drew the attention of several writers, about a half dozen depending on the period covered. I put some weight on textbooks about American economic history because, as is well known, the authors of those books possess an unusually broad yet nuanced understanding of American economic history. The most notable events occasionally referred to as panics that I excluded, and the reasons for doing so, are summarized in Table 4.2 I excluded panics that were associated with wars, such as the panic of 1914, that appeared to be confined to the stock market, such as the rich man's panic of 1903, or that were the result of monetary policy actions by the central bank, such as the severe contraction of 1920–1921. From the Great Depression I included only what Friedman and Schwartz (1963, 308–332) described as the "First Banking Crisis" which they date as beginning October 1930. Friedman and Schwartz also identify a Second Banking Crisis beginning in March 1931, a major deterioration of financial conditions

[1]I have used a variety of terms—caused, ignited, triggered, precipitated—merely to achieve some variation. The meaning in each case is the same.

[2]The sources consulted to construct the list included Abramovitz (1959), Bogart (1930), Bordo et al. (2002), Calomiris and Gorton (1991), Coman (1910), Dewey (1931), Friedman and Schwartz (1963), Glasner (1997), Jalil (2013), Kemmerer (1910), Kindleberger (1989), Lebergott (1964), Miron (1986), Myers (1970), Shultz and Caine (1937), Sobel (1999), Sprague (1910), Studenski and Krooss (1963), Thorp et al. (1926), Walton and Rockoff (2014), Wicker (1996), and Wicker (2000).

Table 4.1 The failures that ignited America's most important financial crises

Year of panic	Level of panic	Name and location	Type of institution
1819	**A**	Western and southern branches of the Second Bank of the United States	Federal charter
		Bank of the State of Kentucky	*State Bank*
1837	**A**	J.L. & S. Josephs, Co. (New York)	**Investment Bank**
		Hermann, Briggs & Co. (New Orleans)	**Cotton factor (broker)**
1839	**A**	The United States Bank of Pennsylvania (Philadelphia)	**Investment Bank**
		Morris Canal and Banking Company (New Jersey)	*Commercial Bank*
1854	**B**	Ellis & Sturges, Goodman & Co. (Cincinnati)	**Private Bank**
		Smead and Co. (Cincinnati)	**Private Bank**
		Ohio Savings Bank (Cincinnati)	*Savings bank*
		Kentucky Trust Company	*Trust company*
1857	**A**	Ohio Life Insurance and Trust Company (Ohio and New York)	*Trust company*
1873	**A**	Jay Cooke and Company (Philadelphia)	**Investment Bank**
		First National Bank of Washington	National Bank
		National Bank of Commonwealth of New York	National Bank
1884	**B**	Metropolitan National (New York)	National Bank
		Second National Bank	National Bank
		Marine National (New York)	National Bank
		Grant & Ward (New York)	**Broker**
1890	**B**	Baring Brothers (London)	**Investment Bank**
		Charles M. Whitney (Boston)	**Broker**
		Decker Howell and Company (New York)	**Broker**
1893	**A**	Wisconsin Marine and Fire Insurance Company Bank (Milwaukee)	**Private Bank**
		Herman Schaffner and Company (Chicago)	**Private Bank**
		United States Loan and Trust Company (Chicago)	**Trust Company**
		Columbia National Bank (Chicago)	National Bank
		Capital National Bank (Indianapolis)	National Bank
		Chemical National Bank (Chicago)	National Bank
1907	**A**	Knickerbocker Trust Company (New York)	*Trust Company*
		Mercantile National Bank (New York)	National Bank
1930	**A**	Bank of United States (New York)	*State Bank*
		Caldwell and Company (Nashville)	**Investment Bank**
2008	**A**	Lehman Brothers (New York)	**Investment Bank**
		Bear Stearns (New York)	**Investment Bank**

(continued)

Table 4.1 (continued)

Year of panic	Level of panic	Name and location	Type of institution
		Fannie Mae and Freddie Mac (Washington DC)	Government sponsored mortgage insurers
		Countrywide Financial (Calabasas, CA)	**Mortgage Bank**

Note: In several cases the financial institution did not fail in the sense that it passed into bankruptcy. In the case of Bear Stearns, for example, a sale of the firm was arranged. But in each case there was a widespread fear that investors would suffer substantial losses.

Table 4.2 Some excluded panics

Year	Reason for exclusion
1730	Colonial
1763	Colonial
1772	Colonial
1792	Mainly stock market?
1812	War of 1812
1825	Important in Europe; Seldom identified as a major U.S. panic
1833	Contraction due to monetary policy
1860	Civil War. Mainly the South
1861	Civil War. National in scope
1878	Confined mainly to building and loans??
1896	Seldom mentioned by financial historians
1901	Stock market panic
1903	"Rich Man's Panic." Mainly stock market
1914	World War I
1920–1921	Contraction due to monetary policy
1929	Mainly stock market
1931	Partially a continuation of the initial banking crisis which began in late 1930
1933	Partially a continuation of the initial banking crisis which began in late 1930
1937–1938	Contraction due to monetary and fiscal policy

associated with Britain's departure from the gold standard in September 1931, and a Final Banking Crisis beginning in January 1933. Wicker (1996, Chap. 3) provides somewhat different starting dates for the First and Second Banking Crises, refers explicitly to the developments in the American banking system associated with Britain's departure from gold as a banking crisis, and distinguishes between regional and national panics. But I excluded the banking crises following 1930 because they seem to be surges of fear within an ongoing process.[3]

[3]A preliminary look suggests that the Second Banking Crisis fits the mold. This crisis was centered in Chicago and inaugurated by the failure of the Foreman Group of Banks. Foreman was a Savings

I divided the panics into two categories as shown in column 2 of Table 4.1. The A level panics are discussed in almost all financial and economic histories and left obvious imprints on time series such as the stock of money and real GDP. The B level panics were regional affairs that are sometimes omitted in U.S. financial histories and left imprints on the time series that are harder to see with the naked eye.

Recently, Jalil (2013) went back to the financial press and identified seven major banking panics and 20 non-major panics during the period 1825–1929. My list of major panics during this period agrees with his except that Jalil identifies a major panic in 1833–1834. And I include only 2 of his 20 non-major banking crises. The difference in coverage, however, is not as great as it first appears. As indicated above I excluded several war related crises and several severe contractions precipitated by monetary and fiscal policy. The latter consideration explains my exclusion of 1833–1834. And Jalil includes a number of panics of restricted geographic impact. These include a panic in December 1905 that according to Jalil affected only Chicago, a panic in 1908 in New York City, a panic in 1920 in Boston, a panic in 1920–1921 in North Dakota, and panics in 1927 and 1929 in Florida. Had I included them, I would have labeled them C level panics. It would be fruitful test of this paper's generalizations to see whether they hold in these additional cases.

4.4 A Sequence of Failures

The third column of Table 4.1 lists the failures that contemporary observers and financial historians have identified as the key failures in each panic. The failures are listed in chronological order. The failure listed next to the panic year is the one that occurred closest in time to the panic; earlier failures are listed below with the first failure at the bottom of the list. In one case, 1857, there seems to have been only one important failure, although this case could be debated since a few sources mention additional failures.

A sequence of failures makes sense. An initial failure puts people on high alert; ready for fight or flight. A subsequent failure or failures then ignites a full blown panic. The first failure, after all, might mean that an individual firm had made a bad mistake: the prudent stance would be watchful waiting. Subsequent failures would prove that the problem was systemic: at some point prudence becomes "run for the hills."

One can view the process as one of Bayesian updating of the expectation of the probability that the financial system as a whole had become illiquid or bankrupt.

(Footnote 3 continued)

and Trust Company, not a commercial bank, and was heavily invested in suburban real estate (Postal-Vinay 2015).

The Panic of 1907 provides a good example. Several national banks came under pressure, and resort was had to Clearing House loan certificates, a form of privately issued emergency credit. These banks did not fail, but as Sprague (1910, 249) pointed out these difficulties "doubtless gave rise to a vague feeling of distrust." Then the run on the Knickerbocker Trust Company unleashed a full blown panic. In some cases the sequence was small, two or three firms, but in a few cases the sequence was longer.

Typically, a sequence included firms from different parts of the country and/or different parts of the financial system. Again, this makes sense. A failure in just one part of the country or one part of the financial system might be addressed by shifting funds to a safer region or safer type of financial institution. But once failures had leaped these boundaries the natural inference would be that wealth wasn't safe in any kind of financial intermediary; only cash or government bonds would do. To reiterate, we can think of the process as Bayesian updating of the probability of an illiquid bankrupt financial system. Initially, the probability that the financial system is bankrupt appears to be extremely low. But as more information arrives, the estimate of the probability that the system is bankrupt rises until wealth holders feel they must act to save their wealth.

In 1930 the important failures were of shadow banks in Nashville (an investment bank) and New York (a state chartered commercial bank). An economic contraction had begun in August 1929 and had been accelerated by the stock market crash. But the failures at the end of 1930 appear to have added a financial panic to a severe contraction.

4.5 Typically, They Were Shadow Banks

Unregulated or lightly regulated financial institutions, what today we would call shadow banks—or perhaps following Michener and Richardson (2013) with reference to the lightly regulated state chartered commercial banks, "shadowy banks"—have always been an important part of the financial system. The classic descriptions of the private banking sector in the nineteenth century are Redlich (1968, part II, Chap. xiv, 60–84) and Sylla (1976). Column 4 of Table 4.1 shows the regulatory status of the firms that started the financial panics. Banks that were regulated at the federal level are printed in ordinary type. Banks that were regulated at the state level are printed in italics and banks that were unregulated are printed in bold. For the 2008 crisis, however, I followed conventional definitions. Lehman Brothers is shown as a shadow bank even though it was nominally regulated by the Securities and Exchange Commission.

The ink tells the story: shadow banks played a prominent role in precipitating almost all of the panics. The New York office of a firm chartered by Ohio was the problem in 1857. The failure of an unregulated investment bank, Jay Cooke and

Company, was the trigger for the panic of 1873. An unregulated brokerage, today it might be called a hedge fund, Grant & Ward, triggered the panic of 1884. Unregulated brokerages were part of the sequence that produced the panic of 1890. The failure of national banks figured prominently in the run-up to the Panic of 1893, but so did the failure of unregulated private banks. Again in 1907 troubles at national banks were important, but suspension of cash payments by a lightly regulated trust company triggered the panic.

Why were shadow banks so important in the United States? Shadow banking was encouraged by several factors. One was that state chartering of commercial banks produced a geographically fragmented banking system. Branching across state lines was prohibited through most of America's history. Commercial banks, therefore, were often small, geographically limited affairs that could not provide capital for industrial firms.[4] The stock and bond markets expanded to fill the gap, and these markets required brokerages and investment banks which could morph into shadow banks. Another factor making for shadow banking was reliance on the real bills doctrine as a basis for regulating chartered banks—reflected for example in prohibitions against real estate lending—that created gaps in the financial system for private institutions to fill. Perhaps a legal ethos in the United States that held that what was not forbidden was permitted played a role as well.

4.6 The Evidence: Case by Case

In this section I tell the story of shadow banks in each of the great financial panics.

4.6.1 The Panic of 1819

The first major banking panic in the United States was the only one where federally regulated institutions played the lead role. After the establishment of the Second Bank of the United States in 1816 the West had been caught up in real estate speculation. Much of the land was still held by the federal government, but was being purchased rapidly from federal land offices. Many of the mortgages to purchase this land were provided by state chartered banks and private banks. But the western and southern branches of the Second Bank were major suppliers of loanable funds. The Second Bank had initially adopted the policy that notes issued by one branch should be redeemed at every other branch. The idea was to create a currency acceptable nationwide while giving all regions access to the seigniorage produced by creating money. But this policy was not accompanied by any restrictions on the total amount of notes that an individual branch could issue. This

[4]This point is developed in detail by Calomiris and Haber (2014).

allowed the western branches—Cincinnati, Chillicothe, Lexington, and Pittsburgh —to make large loans in a currency that other branches were responsible for redeeming. There were also problems at the Baltimore branch with speculation in stock of the Second Bank and insider loans. To a degree, the western and southern branches of the Second Bank behaved much like Fannie Mae and Freddie Mac in the run-up to the panic of 2008: borrowing short-term from other financial institutions and making reckless loans ultimately collateralized by real estate while insufficiently restrained by regulation.

In 1818, for this and other reasons, the Second Bank found itself dangerously overexposed.[5] In July 1818 the directors of the Second Bank demanded that the Cincinnati branch begin collecting debts owed by the private banks in Cincinnati. In August it ordered branches to refuse to redeem the notes of other branches. The effects in the West were dramatic. The federal Land Office added to the pressure on the western banks by ruling that Federal land could be sold only for specie or notes issued by the Second Bank; not for notes issued by local banks. Like the more famous "specie circular" issued by Andrew Jackson, this policy helped end the boom in land sales. In November three private chartered banks in Cincinnati suspended and in November the Bank of the State of Kentucky (Huntington 1915, 292).[6] A similar story was playing out in western Pennsylvania where the Pittsburgh branch was taking actions to restrict credit (Blackson 1978, 341–366). A national banking panic was underway.

The real estate boom in the West, of course, came to a screeching halt. In the end the Second Bank would own a great deal of western real estate. Westerners were understandably outraged by this sequence of events, even as they were partly responsible. William Jones, the President of the Second Bank was forced out, and in March 1819 Langdon Cheves, a conservative southern politician became president. Cheves continued the contractionary policy of his predecessor.[7] The Cincinnati branch of the Second Bank was closed in October 1820, a participant in and victim of the crisis (Caterall 1903, 79–80). All of the other western banks besides the branches of the Second Bank were small state chartered or private banks. They were shadow banks by my definition.

---

[5]According to the statistics for the Bank as a whole in Historical Statistics, Table Cj189-200, the Bank had total assets of $57 million in 1818 which had fallen to $48 million by 1820. The reserve ratio (specie to short-term liabilities) had increased from 0.11 to 0.27 and leverage (short-term liabilities to capital) had fallen from 0.6 to 0.4. No real estate is recorded on the official balance sheet.

[6]There was also a private bank in Cincinnati, John H. Piatt & Co., but it is not clear whether it suspended with the others. In the fall of 1819 some merchants in Cincinnati announced that they would accept only Piatt's notes. But in February 1820 twenty-one leading merchants announced that they would no longer accept the notes. Piatt then gave up banking, returned to his grocery business, and redeemed most of his notes with merchandise (Rowe 1912, 175–178).

[7]Traditionally many historians followed Ralf Cattrall (1903) who viewed Cheves as the savior of the bank. But others such as Fritz Redlich (1968, 106–110) and Edwin Perkins (1984) argued that it was a mistake for Cheves to follow a policy of austerity as the economy fell into a recession.

4.6.2 The Panic of 1837

Several candidates have been brought forward to explain the Panic of 1837. Some of the earlier writing blamed Andrew Jackson's "specie circular" issued on July 11, 1837, This order required the U.S. Land Office to accept only specie (gold or silver) for federal land. The goal was stop or least slowdown the western and southern real estate booms that were being financed by banknotes issued by state banks. Presumably, this led to a wave of western bank failures, beginning the unravelling of the banking system that led to the suspension of payments by the New York banking system in May of 1837. Later writers, such as Hammond and Temin stressed the role of the Bank of England. More recently, Peter Rousseau has argued persuasively that the "Distribution of the Surplus" was the crucial blow.

This panic was triggered by two failures: Hermann, Briggs and Company, a New Orleans Cotton factor (broker) and J.L. and S. Joseph a broker and investment bank in New York City. The two failures were linked; the Josephs had accepted a large amount of paper endorsed by Hermann Briggs. This panic therefore clearly illustrates the crossing of regional boundaries. Other factors were important in raising the level of anxiety in financial markets, but these failures were the catalysts for the panic.

4.6.3 The Panic of 1839

This Panic was triggered by suspension of specie payments by the United States Bank of Pennsylvania in October 1839. This Bank was the successor to the Second Bank of the United States. After Andrew Jackson vetoed the bill re-chartering the Second Bank, the President, Nicholas Biddle had been able to secure a charter from Pennsylvania and continue operations. After the suspension the Bank continued to struggle, but went bankrupt in 1841, adding to the depth of the ongoing depression. The United States Bank of Pennsylvania had abandoned the real bills model and became an investment bank and hedge fund. Although it had obtained a charter issued by the State of Pennsylvania it was pretty much free to follow its own investment policy, and clearly qualifies as a shadow bank.

The United States Bank of Pennsylvania was preceded in death by the Morris Canal and Banking Company, a state chartered institution. Although the failure of the Second Bank was undoubtedly the key event, the failure the Morris Canal and Banking Company also sent a message to financial markets that even banks that were connected to apparently sound infrastructure investments could fail, undermining confidence in the system as a whole.

4.6.4 The Panic of 1854

The Panic of 1854, like the Panic of 1819, was most severe in the West. Cincinnati was the epicenter. The year 1853 was marked by railway construction in Ohio that "turned into a mania" (Berry 1943, 513). The railroads were unable to raise the cash they needed by borrowing in the eastern United States or Europe, so they turned to local banks. These were, according to Berry, private banks that lent to the railroads who offered equity as collateral; shadow banks in today's lexicon. It was a classic case of violating real bills. Interest rates rose substantially in the latter part of 1853 in response to the growing desperation of the railroads for funds. And then the western financial system was hit by a series of bank failures.

Several failures occurred almost simultaneously. The Kentucky Trust Company of Covington failed, and that led to a run on the Ohio Savings Bank in Cincinnati which had the same president. A private bank, P.B. Manchester also failed, and Ellis and Sturges, another private bank suspended. In November Ellis and Sturges and two other private banks closed.[8] All would be shadow banks in today's lexicon.

On December 1, 1854, according to Berry (1943, 514) "the merchants and manufacturers found no bank accommodations whatsoever." And according to Smith and Cole (1935, 128) the price of Cincinnati exchange in New York went from a normal discount of 1–1½ percent to 2¼–2½ in the autumn, and to 3½–3¾ in December. There were also financial troubles in New York (Ó Gráda and White 2003). Berry (1943, 516) describes the situation in the latter half of 1854 as one in which "trouble shot back and forth between New York and the Interior."

The economy recovered from the Panic of 1854 during the next two years, but then it was hit by a new and more severe crisis.[9]

4.6.5 The Panic of 1857

This panic is an outlier among American financial panics because it is usually traced to a single failure, that of the Ohio Life Insurance and Trust Company at the end of August 1857, rather than to a series of failures. Hugh McCulloch, a well-regarded western banker who later served as the first Comptroller of the Currency and as Secretary of the Treasury, wrote (1888, 132) that "It was a bolt from a cloudless sky." This case brings to mind, in other words, the image of a lone individual causing a panic by shouting "fire" in a crowded auditorium.

---

[8]The run on Ellis & Sturges was sparked by a rumor that Ellis had died, but the revelation that he was merely very very ill did not save the bank.

[9]Although the Panic of 1857 was more severe than the Panic of 1854, and began with the failure of an Ohio shadow bank, Chabot and Mour (2014) find that the commercial banks in Ohio recovered faster after the Panic of 1857 than did the commercial banks in Indiana after the Panic of 1854.

Although it had been chartered as a insurance and trust company Ohio Life had actually engaged in issuing bank notes and had invested heavily—one can say recklessly—in local railroads. The bankruptcy proceedings revealed that 73% of its surviving assets consisted of bonds and shares issued by railroads. Most were issued by railroads in Ohio and Indiana, and several of the railroads were closely tied to one another (Riddiough and Thompson 2012, 35; Spiegelman 1948). The bank, especially the New York Office, had also made many personal loans.

It was, in other words, a shadow bank.[10] Usually the crossing of regional boundaries in the failures leading up to a panic is accomplished by the failure of independent firms in different regions. In this case it was accomplished by the failure of a single firm with branches in the Midwest and New York.

4.6.6 The Panic of 1873

This panic was sparked by the failure of Jay Cooke and Company on September 18, 1873. At the time Jay Cooke and Company failed, Cooke was the most trusted living American financier; surely the only one who enjoyed as much prestige on Main Street as on Wall Street. Cooke had helped finance the Civil War by establishing a network of agents throughout the North to sell the bonds to middle class investors. After the war these investors turned to Cooke and his agents for financial advice and to his bank for a safe place to put their savings. When Cooke's firm closed its doors, the shock was palpable.

> Like a thunderclap in a clear sky," said the Philadelphia Press. No one could have been more surprised, said the Philadelphia Inquirer, if snow had fallen amid the sunshine of a summer noon" (Oberholtzer 1907, 423).

Cooke was an investment banker who had gone all in on the Northern Pacific Railroad. His bank was supplying cash for construction to the Northern Pacific in exchange for long-term bonds, He relied partly on small deposits from people of modest means, attracted to his bank because of his role in helping to finance the Union. One source of funds, although a minor one, was the Freedman's Savings Bank; the bank set up after the Civil War to help former slaves save. Osthaus (1976, 153–155) identifies two direct connections with Cooke. Five hundred thousand of the Freedman's Bank's reserves were deposited in the First National Bank of Washington, Henry Cooke President. And Jay Cooke and Company received a $50,000 loan secured by Northern Pacific bonds. The loan was callable and had to be repaid in 5 days. Thus, it was similar to the repo loans that Lehman Brothers relied on. In this case, however, there was a relatively happy ending. Conservative trustees forced Jay Cooke and Company to return the loan in February 1872, and

---

[10] Riddiough and Thompson (2012) explicitly refer to the Ohio Life as a shadow bank and draw a parallel between the Ohio Life and the firms that failed and precipitated the panic of 2008.

the bank lost only $200.[11] Jay Cooke and Company, in other words, bears a strong family resemblance to Lehman Brothers; it was clearly a shadow bank by today's definition.

4.6.7 *The Panic of 1884*

The Panic of 1884 was produced by a tightly packed cluster of failures. On May 6, the Marine National Bank suspended because of a worthless loan of $750,000 to Grant and Ward a brokerage, whose bankruptcy was revealed on May 8.[12] On the 13th, the Second National Bank suspended, and on the 14th the Metropolitan. Looking back, Alexander Noyes (1909, 100) concluded that

> "When it is considered that the performances of John C. Eno (a bank president accused of fraud), Grant & Ward, the Marine Bank, and Metropolitan Bank, all came to public knowledge within a single week in the same community, the shock to financial confidence is not hard to understand."

Although the failures of several National Banks were an important part of the story, the foundational failure appears to have been Grant and Ward, a firm that might be mistaken for a hedge fund, but in fact was simply a Ponzi scheme. Ferdinand Ward told potential investors that he was winning highly profitable government contracts—for flour, blankets, etc.—in which they could invest. He could win these contracts, he suggested because his partner was Ulysses S. Grant, savior of the Union and twice president of the United States. But there were no contracts. Ward was simply robbing Peter to pay Paul. He had lured Grant into a partnership by first offering a position to Grant's son. Ulysses Grant was ruined by his association with Ward. However you look at it, Grant and Ward was clearly a shadow bank.

4.6.8 *The Panic of 1890*

The Panic of 1890, like the Panic of 1884, was mild. Sprague (1910, 124) refers to it as a "financial stringency" rather than a panic; Wicker (2000) refers to it as "banking unrest." Like the Panic of 1837 it was strongly shaped by events abroad. Indeed, Sprague (1910, 128) thought that there would have been no panic in the United States if it had not been for the Baring Crisis in Britain. Barings was an

[11]Henry Cooke resigned from the Freedman's bank's board of trustees shortly afterwards, but it appears that Henry Cooke was responsible for many of the bad investments made by the Freedman's bank, the relatively successful outcome in this case notwithstanding.

[12]This would be about $200 million today (2015) using nominal GDP per capita as the inflator; about $1.14 billion using GDP as the inflator. From https://www.measuringworth.com.

investment bank, and therefore by American usage a shadow bank, although it was a very prominent bank, and cast a very long shadow.

There were, however, important failures in the United States before news of the Baring crisis crossed the Atlantic. On November 7, 1890 the Bank of England advanced its discount rate from 5% to 6% signaling increased tension in the world's leading financial center. The U.S. stock market swooned, a result triggered, according to Wicker (2000, 45) by the failure of "the large and well-respected brokerage firm of Decker, Howell and Co" on November 11. Another well-respected brokerage, Charles M. Whitney & Co. also failed. The news of the embarrassment of Baring Brothers reached the U.S. on November 15. Some commercial banks such as the Bank of North America were involved in the panic, but center stage clearly belonged to the shadow banks.

4.6.9 The Crisis of 1893

While the events of 1890 were relatively mild and short lived, the crisis of 1893 and proved to be the start of a major economic depression, possibly the most severe before the Great Depression.

Sprague (1910, Chap. iv) distinguishes three stages in the Panic, The first runs from January through April 1893. Sprague tells us that there was no distrust of the banking system during this stage, but there was a slump on the stock market, and a general slowing of economic activity. The failure of the Philadelphia and Reading Railroad in late February and National Cordage Company in early May were key events in the stock market slide.

Sprague's second stage runs from early May to mid-July. During this period there were many failures of financial institutions in the Midwest, Pacific Coast, and the South. The distrust of the solvency of the banks in these regions in turn produced a drain of cash from New York.[13]

The most important failures during this phase were in Chicago. Frank Cyril James (1938, 580–591) provides a detailed description of the banking panic. On Monday, May 8, 1893 the Chemical National Bank of Chicago suspended and soon went into receivership. Shortly thereafter the Capital National Bank of Indianapolis, which was closely associated with the Chemical National, and the Evanston National Bank, also went into receivership. The Chemical National was widely regarded as an unsound institution by Chicago bankers, many of the loans being notes of insiders and the Clearing House refused to aid the bank.

As things turned out, however, some of the bank's depositors were protected. The Chemical National had won the right to have a branch at the Chicago World's

[13]Friedman and Schwartz (1963, 107–109) maintained that the banking system suffered from both an internal drain of gold produced by the bank failures discussed here, and an external drain produced by uncertainty over continued maintenance of the gold standard.

Fair (World's Columbian Exposition).[14] The branch had $100,000 in deposits, many from foreign exhibitors, and so a committee of wealthy Chicagoans was formed to guarantee the deposits. The managers of the Fair did "not desire an exhibition of a failed national bank among the interesting collection on the Midway Pleasance" (James 1938, 582).

A few days later the Columbia National Bank and United States Loan and Trust Company with which it was intimately connected closed their doors. The Columbia National and the United States Loan and Trust were both controlled by Zimri Dwiggins who had, according to James, created a financial house of cards. The base was the Trust Company which issued bonds, the proceeds from which he used to purchase stock in country banks. When Dwiggins' banks failed, the country banks went with them. Again, the Chicago Clearing House refused to aid the Bank. Some of Dwiggins holdings were mainstream banks, but the Loan and Trust Company could fairly be described as a shadow bank.

With banks in Chicago and rural Illinois and Indiana failing, the panic seemed to be well underway. The public, however, retained some confidence in the Chicago banks, despite the failures of the Chemical National, Evanston National, and Columbia National. The reason was probably that these failures were quickly framed as the work of imprudent bankers, in particular the president of the Columbia National, Zimri Dwiggins.

But then on Saturday June 3, Herman Schaffner and Company broke. The firm initially had specialized in commercial paper, but had been drawn into financing local businesses including speculators in street-railway stocks and real estate developers (Judy 2013). Herman Schaffner and Company might be described as a bill broker or in its later stages an investment bank or hedge fund. In any case, it would be a shadow bank by today's definitions. In the end it turned out to be a tragic story. Schaffner hired a boat and rowed into Lake Michigan from which his body was later recovered. Following Schaffner's failure a panic, concentrated among the savings banks, took hold. While the *New York Times* had concluded that the failure of the empire of small banks built by Zimri Dwiggins was understandable, the failure of Herman Schaffner & Company was a different story. "Schaffner & Co. always stood well in the regard of New-Yorkers, and their failure caused a good deal of surprise" (*New York Times* June 4, 1893, 1). It is said that 35,000 depositors in the Illinois Trust and Savings Bank demanded their cash. For a time the banks in Chicago once more seemed to be on the mend. But then panic took hold again. On Monday July 17, The Missouri National Bank failed, bringing with it a string of failures.

Sprague's (1910, 175) third phase of the crisis begins in the third week of July. The coup de grâce was the failure on July 25 in Milwaukee of the Wisconsin Marine and Fire Insurance Bank. Again it was a shadow bank. The Wisconsin

[14]The Chemical National had paid $20,000 for the right to the branch. Having a branch required special permission from Congress because Illinois was a unit banking state. National banks were required to follow state law on this issue.

Marine had been founded in 1839 by George Smith, a young Scottish immigrant. The charter permitted Smith to write insurance and do some banking. He had no authority to issue bank notes, but he did so anyway. He issued "certificates of deposit" in convenient denominations payable to bearer—effectively bank notes—that circulated widely in the Midwest (Farwell 1905; Smith 1966). Smith's early years in the Midwest have been celebrated by a number of writers for whom "George Smith's money," as it came to be known, was a brilliant example of how an unregulated bank could supply currency successfully. The role of the bank in the crisis of 1893, however, has received less attention.

George Smith retired at a relatively young age and returned to Britain. His deputy, Alexander Mitchell, a fellow Scott, continued to run the bank successfully for many years. Later, Mitchell's son, U.S. senator John L. Mitchell, became president. Under his leadership the Bank abandoned its prudent ways. The younger Mitchell invested heavily in the debt of Ferdinand Schlesinger, a "plunger" in the vocabulary of the time, who had been borrowing heavily from several sources to finance an ambitious plan to dominate Great Lakes iron ore production. The bank also lent heavily to insiders including Senator Mitchell. The bank's suspension was a shock. According to Cyril James (1938, 593):

> saddest of all [the failures in 1893], the Wisconsin Marine and Fire Insurance Bank, inheritor of the glorious mantle of George Smith, went into the hands of a receiver. It was [quoting the *Chicago Tribune*] 'an institution which everyone thought was rock-rooted and solid as the eternal hills.'[15]

To describe the height of the crisis in 1893 Sprague turned to a long extract from the *Commercial and Financial Chronicle*, as he did with other financial crises, to describe the most intense phase of the crisis. The *Chronicle* told the story this way.

> Our markets have been more disturbed and excited this week than at any time this year… Monday and Tuesday an unusual number of failures among our banks and private firms were reported in various parts of the country, but especially in the West, some of them being concerns of long standing and held in high repute. … The demand for currency for shipment to the West, stimulated by the failure of the "Mitchell" bank at Milwaukee and of banks at Louisville and Indianapolis was urgent on Tuesday … (Sprague 1910, 176; quoting the *Commercial and Financial Chronicle*, July 29, 1893, p. 162).

The *Chronicle* was not alone in describing the shock produced by the downfall of the "Mitchell" bank. On July 25, 1893 *The New York Times* told its readers that "The Wisconsin Marine & Fire Insurance Co. was founded by Alexander Mitchell and was considered the strongest bank in Milwaukee." On July 29 the *Wall Street*

---

[15]However, there was redemption. The shareholders were personally liable under an 1880 law and Senator Mitchell, the largest shareholder, lost heavily (*New York Times*, November 16, 1893, 4), but the firm was reorganized and reopened. Years later the Wisconsin Marine and Fire was merged with another pioneer bank to form the Marine National Exchange Bank of Milwaukee (Smith 1966, 177–178). More acquisitions and mergers followed, and today George Smith's Bank can be found in the DNA of JPMorgan Chase & Co.

Journal (1893, 4) reprinted an extract from a market newsletter that began as follows.

> This has been the worst week the writer has ever known in Wall Street and that by a long way. The failure of the Wisconsin Marine & Fire Insurance Bank of Milwaukee was of course a shock to Wall Street. It was not only that the Bank was an old one in high credit, but that the big owners have a lot of stock of Northwest and St. Paul which had been coming on the market to provide funds.[16]

The shocking fall of the Wisconsin Marine and Fire Insurance Bank was reported throughout the country. The *Fort Worth Daily Gazette*, July 26, 1893, 4, for example, reported that …

> Many persons had become so imbued with the idea that this bank – "the old Mitchell bank" – was a Gibraltar of finance, that they could not credit the report that it had closed. There was a general belief that when all other banking institutions had disappeared from the face of the earth, that the Mitchell bank would continue to do business. It was this firm faith in the bank's stability that made the shock so great."

The story that the "Gibraltar of finance" had fallen was picked up by a number of papers around the country. The *Los Angeles Herald* (July 26, 1893, 1) ran the story under the headline: "The Financial Gibraltar of the Cream City Collapses." The New Orleans *Times-Picayune* (July 26, 1893, 7) also used the phase. It reported on several bank failures in the Midwest, but designated the "Milwaukee Failure the most serious." The reason: "it was this firm faith in the bank's stability that made the shock to the public confidence so great." The Rochester *Democrat and Chronicle* (July 27, 1893, 12) told its readers that

> the tumble in stocks for two days past has been in part attributed to the suspension of the Wisconsin Marine and Fire Insurance Bank, better known as Mitchell's bank of Milwaukee. The failure is significant, as the institution was founded in 1843, and was considered the mainstay of finance in the Northwest.

After the fact, there were experts who claimed that they knew it was a problem all along. On July 26, 1893, p. 3 the *Chicago Daily Tribune* described the failure of the Wisconsin Marine at length, describing it as "the oldest bank in the West", and telling the story of how it provided needed currency after the Panic of 1837. But the *Tribune* also reported that "a prominent and well-informed Chicago banker" claimed that while the failure was a "startling incident" … "it need cause no anxiety to other banks, except perhaps in Milwaukee." The Bank, the expert claimed, "was always run on short reserves." The question that must have occurred to many readers, however, is why one should believe the expert after all that had happened.

The failures and panic in the interior of the country led to a drain of specie from the big New York banks. Some writers have also stressed the fear that the United

[16]Investment in railroads were part of the problem, but its troubles stemmed mainly from loans to Ferdinand Schlesinger who was trying to dominate Great Lakes iron ore production and shipping and personal loans to Senator John L. Mitchell, the son of one of the early principals of the bank and now the president of the bank.

States would not be able to maintain a parity between Friedman and Schwartz (1963, 107–109) maintained that the banking system suffered from both an internal drain of gold produced by the bank failures discussed here and an external drain produced by uncertainty over continued maintenance of the gold standard. In any event, the New York banks suspended specie payments early in August and gold went to a premium. Within six weeks, however, the banking panic had calmed down. People seemed to have realized that they had over-reacted and that their deposits were generally safe, and the Congress had addressed the external drain by repealing the Silver Purchase Act. Nevertheless, the economic contraction set in motion by the panic proved to be long and painful.

The panic of 1893 witnessed failures of national banks, investment banks, state banks and trust companies, and brokers. This panic is therefore a particularly clear example of the proposition that a financial panic in which the precipitating failures come from all corners of the financial system is likely to be a bad one. After all, if one is afraid simply of savings banks or building and loans one can shift one's funds to another sector. But what if all sectors are under threat? Then only cash will do.

4.6.10 The Panic of 1907

Sprague's (1910, 246–256) account of this panic is especially important because it was fresh in his mind when he began his classic history of financial panics. According to Sprague (1910, 246) the precipitating event was a "copper gamble," a failed attempt to corner the copper market. F. Augustus Heinze who was behind the copper speculations had gained control of the Mercantile National Bank. This led to withdrawals by depositors concerned about Heinze's solvency. The bank requested assistance from the New York Clearing House which was granted on the condition that Heinze and his board resign. The Bank was able to open under these conditions, but was closed in January 1908. In the wake of the troubles at the Mercantile National, the Clearing House was called upon to aid a number of other banks that had suffered withdrawals because of their actual or rumored relationships with Heinze. The aid provided by the Clearing House was successful. There was no panic, but Sprague (1910, 249) adds that these difficulties "doubtless gave rise to a vague feeling of distrust."

Attention then turned to the Knickerbocker Trust, the third largest Trust in New York. The Knickerbocker, like other Trusts, did a banking business under a state charter, and competed aggressively with the national banks in New York. The trusts were not allowed to issue bank notes, but in general they were less regulated than the national banks. Some underwrote security issues, but they also wrote mortgages and invested directly in real estate, a field where the participation of National banks was limited. The Trust companies had expanded rapidly in the period leading up to the Panic of 1907 and were major competition for the more highly regulated state and national banks (Neal 1971). They were, in short, shadow banks.

The problem for the Knickerbocker was the ties of its President, Charles T. Barney to Charles W. Morse, a financier in turn tied to Heinze and the latter's attempt to corner the copper market. On Monday October 21, Barney was forced out at a directors meeting closely watched by J.P. Morgan (Tallman and Moen 1995; *Washington Post*, October 22, 1907, 3). At about the same time, one of the New York national banks announced that it would not clear for the Knickerbocker. A heavy run forced the Knickerbocker to suspend on Tuesday. From there the panic spread rapidly throughout the banking system, although the heaviest damage was done to the Trust Companies (Moen and Tallman 2000). The Knickerbocker was able to resume in March 1908.

Again in 1907 troubles at national banks were important, but suspension of cash payments by a lightly regulated trust company triggered the panic. Frydman et al. (2015) refer to the trust companies explicitly as shadow banks because they were subject to fewer restrictions than the state or federally chartered commercial banks and discuss some of the effects of the collapse of many of the trust companies. Its always the shadow banks.

4.6.11 The Panic of 1930

Two failures have been identified as the catalysts for the Panic of 1930. Elmus Wicker argued that the key failure was Caldwell and Company, an investment bank located in Nashville Tennessee. Friedman and Schwartz argued that the key failure was The Bank of United States, a state chartered bank in New York City. The reputation of Caldwell and Company, which failed in November 1930, was excellent. According to John McFerrin (1969, 117–119), the historian of Caldwell and Company, by the late 1920s the bank "had so increased in size and built up such prestige in financial circles that it was referred to as the 'Morgan of the South.'"

Caldwell and Company, whose failure in November 1930 sparked runs in the South, was an investment bank that got into trouble through classic violations of the real bills doctrine. It was heavily leveraged: On June 30, 1926 capital was 10.1% of total assets; by the end of 1929 it was 4.7%. To finance its operations it relied heavily on deposits, particularly from municipalities obtained as part of deals for help in marketing their bonds, and deposits from Caldwell controlled companies. The largest category of its assets included common stocks of the companies it controlled. These would not have been liquid even in the best of times because controlling interests in unlisted regional firms could not be disposed of on short notice (McFerrin 1969, 119–120). Caldwell and Company, obviously was similar in some ways to Lehman Brothers, and was a shadow bank by today's definitions.

The reputation of the Bank of the United States is best characterized as mixed. Joseph S. Marcus was the founder of the Bank of United States. An immigrant from what is now Lithuania, in 1906 he helped found the Public Bank to cater to Jewish immigrants, many of them in the garment trade, on the lower East Side of New

York. The Panic of 1907 wiped out many small banks on the Lower East Side, but the Public Bank survived and prospered in the years following based on its "reputation for integrity" (Werner 2009 [1933], 3). In 1913 after a quarrel with a partner, Marcus helped found a new bank, also on the Lower East Side, the Bank of United States. This bank also prospered in part because of Marcus's "reputation for shrewdness and honesty" (Werner 2009 [1933], 7). In July 1927 Joseph S. Marcus died and his son, Bernard K. Marcus, took over.

But under his son the bank expanded rapidly through mergers and acquisitions establishing branches throughout the city, and began an aggressive program of investments in stocks and real estate made by two affiliates: City Financial Corporation and the Bankus Corporation (Bank plus Marcus?), set up to evade legal restrictions on mortgage lending. According to Peter Temin (1976, 92) most of the bank's impaired loans were the result of "direct or indirect claims on real estate."

The reputation of the Bank of United States at its failure in December 1930 varied among different sectors of the public. That it was the largest failure in U.S. history to that point—although at the time it was the twenty-eighth largest bank in the United States (O'Brien and Trescott 1992, 384)—that its name suggested a special relationship to the government, and that it was a bank in New York City, the nation's financial center may have led unsophisticated investors to think that a fundamental pillar of the financial system had collapsed (Friedman and Schwartz 1963, 309–311; Kennedy 1973, 1). That the bank was not a government bank was widely explained in the papers in the immediate aftermath of the failure, so the damage done by its misleading name was limited. But the name may have attracted depositors among the immigrants that the bank catered to, and the subsequent lack of support of the bank from the government may have increased their sense of betrayal. On the other hand, the failure to bail out depositors as discussed below, and the revelation that a bank based on small deposits of individuals engaged in the garment trade had been heavily engaged in real estate speculation must have been unnerving for similar depositors in similar institutions.[17]

The narrative that gained circulation in the immediate aftermath of the failure was that the bank had been prudently managed by its founder Joseph S. Marcus, but that unbeknownst to the public it had gone badly awry after his son had taken over in 1927; wise father, prodigal son. The *Brooklyn Daily Eagle* (December 28, 1930, 12) claimed that "banking opinion has always looked on the works of the late Joseph S. Marcus, particularly in planting his bank branches in "gold mine" centers, as those of a banking genius". The *St. Louis Post-Dispatch* (February 20, 1931, 24) claimed that during his lifetime Joseph "enjoyed a high reputation as a banker and as a scrupulously honest man." The story of the Bank of United States in 1930 is reminiscent of the story of the Wisconsin Marine and Fire Insurance Company Bank which failed in 1893 and of Overend, Gurney, the English bank that failed in 1866. In all three cases the reputation of bank was based on the reputation of one of

---

[17] A number of Clearing House banks offered to lend cash at 5% on the security of up to 50% of deposits in the bank.

the early founders of the bank, a reputation that endured even as newer managers began to make speculative long-term investments. These failures taught the public that established reputations for soundness and acumen might prove to be hollow: not a good omen for financial stability.

One could argue about which of these two failures, Caldwell and Company or Bank of United States, was the "real" trigger for the panic. But the two failures (and a contemporaneous wave of smaller failures) probably reinforced one another. The implication of having two large financial institutions in different parts of the country and from different sectors of the financial system failing one after the other was to raise the probability that money really wasn't safe in any financial intermediary. This is reminiscent of the twin failures in 1837, one in New Orleans and one in New York. The banks that failed in 1930 evidently failed for the same balance-sheet reasons that banks had failed in the late 1920s (White 1984). An extensive debate has proceeded on whether the failures in the 1930s were the result of illiquidity or insolvency. A recent paper by Bordo and Landon-Lane (2010) argues that the problem was mainly illiquidity and surveys the earlier literature.

In any case, it is clear that doubts about the safety of the banking system took a turn for the worse after the failures of Caldwell and Company and Bank of United States. Friedman and Schwartz (1963, 311) looked at currency held by the public and bank reserves, both of which show upward trends starting at the end of 1930. A related piece of evidence is shown in Fig. 4.1 which plots postal savings monthly from January 1929 to December 1932. It is a classic "hockey stick" with the inflection point in November 1930.

There was a debate at the time about whether the Bank of United States should have been bailed out. An arrangement was close to being worked out, but at the last moment the New York Clearing House banks, the largest in the City, withdrew from the rescue plan, and the bank was closed. Jackson Reynolds, the President of the First National Bank and of the Clearing House Association, maintained that closing the bank would have only local effects (Friedman and Schwartz 1963, 310n). He might have put his point into today's language by claiming that the bank was not "systemically important."

The possibility that anti-Semitism played a role in the decision not to bailout the Bank of United States has been a matter of intense controversy. The Bank of United States dealt, at least when it began, mainly with Jewish customers. In an article in *Business Week* and in his TV program "Free to Choose," Milton Friedman suggested that anti-Semitism played a role in the decision not to bail out the bank.[18] In this respect there is a strong parallel with the Panic of 1837. In 1837 both precipitants of the crisis were led by German Jews. It does not seem that this caused much of a problem for them before they failed, but anti-Semitism does seem to have influenced the way some observers thought about the failures afterwards (Lepler 2013, *passim*). Friedman's contention about anti-Semitism was vigorously

[18]Friedman and Friedman (1980) is the volume based on the TV series. The episodes are available on youtube.

challenged by Joseph Lucia (1985), whose argument was criticized in turn by Friedman and Schwartz (1986), and they in turn were in turn criticized by and Anthony Patrick O'Brien (1992) and O'Brien and Paul B. Trescott (1992). In any case, whether the Clearing House banks thought that the failure of the Bank of United States could be ignored because only local businesses and depositors would be affected or because only local Jewish businesses and Jewish depositors would be affected, and whether the Clearing House banks were concerned about real estate investments or Jewish real estate investments, it is clear that the failure of the Bank of the United States was viewed by some influential bankers as a failure that would not start a panic. The mistake was failing to recognize that an institution that was considered unimportant by the financial cognoscenti might be considered very important by the general public, especially in the context of news about deteriorating economic and financial conditions.[19]

4.6.12 The Panic of 2008

The most recent crisis is another example of the rule that it is the failure of trusted firms that start panics. Lehman Brothers' stock had been falling for some months before it filed for bankruptcy protection on September 15, 2008. But dial the clock back to 2007. In March *Fortune Magazine* released its annual list of "America's Most Admired Companies" based on surveys of corporate executives and Wall Street analysts. Lehman Brothers Holdings was ranked number one among securities firms in 2007 ahead of Goldman Sachs, Morgan Stanley, Merrill Lynch, etc. Which firm was number two? Bear Stearns! True, by March 2008 the two had fallen a bit. Lehman Brothers was now ranked third among securities firms and Bear Stearns, which was only two months away from its government-aided acquisition by JPMorgan, was ranked eighth. Other firms that would play a role in the panic also did well in the 2007 rankings. American International Group ranked seventh in the property and casualty group ahead of State Farm and Nationwide. Countrywide Financial ranked third among Mortgage Service companies, IndyMac Bancorp ranked seventh, and Freddie Mac ranked ninth.[20]

The failure of a firm with Lehman Brother's reputation would have been unsettling at any time. But it was particularly demoralizing in 2008 because of the events that had proceeded it. As suggested by Anna Schwartz investors were especially alarmed by the failure of Lehman Brothers because they were expecting a bailout along the lines of the Federal Reserve's assisted purchase of Bear Stearns (Ryssdal 2009; Sorkin 2009, epilogue, Kindle locations 10281–10335).

---

[19]The failure of the Bank of United States caused some concern in London. But the damage was limited because it was quickly realized that the bank "did not stand in the front row of American Institutions." Special Cable to THE NEW YORK TIMES. (1930, Dec 12). MARKETS ABROAD AFFECTED. *New York Times (1923-Current File).*

[20]Fannie Mae did not make the top 10.

4.7 Summary and Conclusions

We have surveyed the narrative histories of 12 financial panics in the United States that were started by the failure of financial institutions. This list includes all of the major panics. Excluded are panics sparked by wars, minor regional panics, and panics confined mainly to the stock market. What generalizations follow? Typically, panics were sparked by a sequence of failures that included firms from different parts of the country and different parts of the financial system. Of the 12 cases examined here, only one, the panic of 1857, is generally attributed to a single failure. The prevalence of sequences makes sense from a Bayesian perspective. Each failure raised the subjective probability that the system as a whole was illiquid. Shadow banks played a prominent role. In the thirteen cases examined here, there were only two in which the final failure was not a shadow bank.

Why was it the shadow banks that were, so often, the cause of havoc? In part, it was because unregulated or poorly regulated shadow banks could decide to go in for a strategy of concentration on a narrow range of risky long-term assets, a strategy barred to regulated banks. More fundamentally, the fragmentation of the American commercial banking system meant that American industrialists had to turn to a largely unregulated network of stock and bond markets, investment banks, and private investors for capital. Fragmentation of American commercial bank regulation goes back to the fundamental constitutional conflict over state versus federal power, and was reinforced at times by Populist opposition to control of banking by Wall Street (Calomiris and Haber 2014). The result was an abundant supply of capital to American industry, but an environment in which shadow banks could thrive.

Why, given the high frequency of panics in the nineteenth and early twentieth centuries did we go so long without a crisis after the banking panics of the early 1930s? One factor that has been cited repeatedly, and undoubtedly played a role, was the increased regulation of banking that came with the New Deal. Deposit insurance, importantly, mitigated the tendency of people to run to their bank and demand cash at the first sign of trouble. But this survey suggests that there was another important factor: the presence after World War II of a central bank that was both able (in part because of the abandonment of the gold standard) and willing (in part because it had learned the costs of inaction during the Great Depression) to act as lender of last resort. The United States had two central banks in the 19th century and during the time they were in operation the United States was able, for the most part, to avoid financial crises. The exceptions were the panic of 1819 and the panic (or financial stringency) of 1833–1834. Both panics seem to have begun with contractionary policies adopted by the Bank itself.[21] The First and Second Banks, however, faced considerable opposition. State chartered banks and the governments that chartered them were jealous of their federal competitor. Revelations about corruption hurt the Banks. And the North-South divide—Southerners did not want

[21]On 1833–1834 see Meerman (1963).

a central bank headquartered in a Northern city—combined to undermine support for the First and Second Banks. There ensued a long period without a central bank (1837–1913) marked by frequent banking panics.

The creation of the Federal Reserve in 1913 produced an institution with the power to act as lender of last resort. For a number of reasons it did not act in that capacity during the 1930s. The story was different, however, after World War II. There were a number of events in the postwar period—prominently, the credit crunch of 1966, and the failures of Continental Illinois in 1984 and Long-Term Capital Management in 1998—that prior to 1945 might well have precipitated a financial crisis, but these events were prevented from doing so by the timely intervention of the Federal Reserve. In 2008 the Federal Reserve almost pulled off another save, but the decision to let Lehman Brothers go, although perhaps required by legal constraints, provoked an old-school financial panic.

The Dodd-Frank Act hopes to prevent another financial panic by identifying "systemically important" financial institutions. The assumption seems to be that these institutions can be identified by looking at balance sheets: simply identifying institutions with large balance sheets and with important counterparties should get the job done. But the history U.S. financial panics suggest that identifying systemically important financial institutions will be a fraught task. The failures that sparked America's financial panics were often shadow banks, not intermediaries on the radar screen of regulators. Sometimes they were to be found in New York, but on other occasions they were to be found in regional financial centers.

Acknowledgements This paper had its origin in a conversation with Albrecht Ritschl who asked me a number of searching questions about the history of U.S. banking panics some of which I finally answer here. A previous draft was presented at a conference in October 2014 at Indiana University celebrating the research contributions of Elmus Wicker. I thank the participants in that conference, especially my discussant Richard Sylla for helpful comments. It was also presented at a meeting of the Chicago friends of economic history in May 2015. Farley Grubb also provided some insightful comments. My Rutgers colleagues, Michael Bordo and Eugene White, as always, provided insightful comments and encouragement. The remaining errors are mine.

References

Abramovitz, Moses. 1959. Employment, Growth, and Price Levels. Part 2: Historical and Comparative Rates of Production, Productivity, and Prices: Hearing of the Joint Economic Committee. Testimony of Moses Abramovitz. 86th congress, first session.

America's most admired companies. Various Years. In *Fortune Magazine* [database online]. Available from http://money.cnn.com/magazines/fortune/mostadmired/2007/full_list/F.html. Accessed May 23, 2013.

Bagehot, Walter. 1924 [1873]. *Lombard Street: A description of the Money Market*, 14th ed. London: William Clowes and Sons, Limited.

Bernanke, Ben S. 2010. On the Implications of the Financial Crisis for Economics. Remarks by Ben S. Bernanke. In *Conference co-sponsored by the Blenheim center for finance and the center for economic policy studies*. Princeton, NJ.

Berry, Thomas Senior. 1943. *Western Prices Before 1861; A Study of The Cincinnati Market*. Harvard economic studies, vol. LXXIV. Cambridge, Mass: Harvard University Press.

Blackson, Robert Markle. 1978. The Panic of 1819 in Pennsylvania. Ph.D. dissertation, Pennsylvania State University.

Bogart, Ernest Ludlow. 1930. *Economic History of the American People*. New York and London.: Longmans, Green and Co.

Bordo, Michael D., Michael J. Dueker, and David C. Wheelock. 2002. Aggregate Price Shocks and Financial Instability: A Historical Analysis. *Economic Inquiry* 40 (4) (10): 521–538.

Bordo, Michael, and John Landon-Lane. 2010. The Banking Panics in the United States in the 1930s: Some Lessons for Today. *Oxford Review of Economic Policy* 26 (3): 486–509.

Bruner, Robert F., and Sean D. Carr. 2007. *The Panic of 1907: Lessons Learned From the Market's Perfect Storm*. Hoboken, NJ: Wiley.

Calomiris, Charles W., and Gary Gorton. 1991. The Origins of Banking Panics: Models, Facts, and Bank Regulation. In *Financial Markets and Financial Crises.*, ed. R. Glenn Hubbard, 109–173. A National Bureau of Economic Research Project Report. Chicago and London: University of Chicago Press.

Calomiris, Charles W., and Larry Schweikart. 1991. The Panic of 1857: Origins, Transmission, and Containment. *The Journal of Economic History* 51 (4): 807–834.

Calomiris, Charles W., and Joseph R. Mason. 1997. Contagion and Bank Failures During the Great Depression: The June 1932 Chicago Banking Panic. *The American Economic Review* 87 (5): 863–883.

Calomiris, Charles W., & Stephen H. Haber. 2014. *Fragile by Design: The Political Origins of Banking Crises and Scarce Credit*. Series: The Princeton Economic History of the Western World, Series ed. Joel Mokyr. Princeton and Oxford: Princeton University Press.

Carter Susan et al. (eds.). 2006. Historical *Statistics of the United States: Earliest Times to the Present*. Millennial ed., 5 Vols. New York: Cambridge University Press.

Catterall, Ralph C. H., 1903. *The Second Bank of the United States*. The Decennial Publications of the University of Chicago [2d ser., vol. 2]. Chicago: University of Chicago Press.

Chabot, Benjamin, and Charles C. Moul. 2014. Bank Panics, Government Guarantees, and the Long-Run Size of the Financial Sector: Evidence from Free-Banking America. *Journal of Money, Credit, and Banking*, August, 46 (5): 961–997.

Coman, Katharine. 1910. *The Industrial History of the United States*. New York: The Macmillan Company.

Dewey, Davis Rich. 1931. *Financial History of the United States*. American Citizens Series, 11th ed. New York: Longmans, Green and Co.

Diamond, Douglas W., and Philip H. Dybvig. 1983. Bank Runs, Deposit Insurance, and Liquidity. *Journal of Political Economy* 91 (3): 401–419.

Esbitt, Milton. 1986. Bank Portfolios and Bank Failures during the Great Depression: Chicago. *The Journal of Economic History*, 46, (2) (The Tasks of Economic History): 455–462.

Farwell, John V. 1905. George Smith's Bank. *Journal of Political Economy* 13 (4): 590–593.

Friedman, Milton, and Rose D. Friedman. 1980. *Free to Choose: A Personal Statement*, 1st ed. New York: Harcourt Brace Jovanovich.

Friedman, Milton, and Anna J. Schwartz. 1963. *A Monetary History of the United States, 1867–1960*. National Bureau of Economic Research. Studies in Business Cycles, vol. 12. Princeton: Princeton University Press.

Friedman, Milton, and Anna J. Schwartz. 1970. *Monetary Statistics of the United States: Estimates, Sources, Methods*. National Bureau of Economic Research. Studies in Business Cycles, vol. 20. New York: National Bureau of Economic Research.

Friedman, Milton, and Anna J. Schwartz. 1986. The Failure of the Bank of United States: A Reappraisal: A reply [A monetary history]. *Explorations in Economic History* 23 (2) (04): 199–204.

Frydman, Carola, Eric Hilt, and Lily Y. Zhou. 2015. "Economic Effects of Runs on Early 'Shadow Banks': Trust Companies and the Impact of the Panic of 1907." *Journal of Political Economy*, 123 (4): 902–940.

Glasner, David. 1997. *Business Cycles and Depressions: An Encyclopedia*. New York and London: Garland Publishing Inc.

Gorton, Gary. 2010. *Slapped by the Invisible Hand: The Panic of 2007*. Financial Management Association Survey and Synthesis Series. New York: Oxford University Press.

Ó Gráda, Cormac, and Eugene N. White. 2003. The Panics of 1854 and 1857: A View From the Emigrant Industrial Savings Bank. *The Journal of Economic History* 63 (1): 213–240.

Haeger, John Denis. 1979. Eastern Financiers and Institutional Change: The Origins of the New York Life Insurance and Trust Company and The Ohio Life Insurance and Trust Company. *The Journal of Economic History* 39 (1, The Tasks of Economic History): 259–273.

Hamilton, David E. 1985. The Causes of the Banking Panic of 1930: Another View. *The Journal of Southern History* 51 (4): 581–608.

Hammond, Bray. 1948. Banking in the Early West: Monopoly, Prohibition, and Laissez Faire. *The Journal of Economic History* 8 (1): 1–25.

Huntington, C. C. 1915. *A History of Banking and Currency in Ohio Before the Civil War*. Columbus, Ohio: Heer.

Jalil, Andrew J. 2013. A New History of Banking Panics in the United States, 1825:1929: Construction and Implications. Mimeo.

James, Frank Cyril. 1938. *The Growth of Chicago banks*. New York; London: Harper & Brothers.

Judy, Paul R. 2013. *Chronicle of the History of A.G. Becker & Co.*, Insolvency of Herman Schaffner & Co. Available from http://agbecker.us/. Accessed Nov 20, 2014.

Kemmerer, Edwin Walter, and United States. National Monetary Commission. 1910. *Seasonal Variations in the Relative Demand for Money and Capital in the United States; A Statistical Study*. [United States] 61st cong., 2d sess. senate. doc. vol. 588. Washington: Govt. Print. Off.

Kennedy, Susan Estabrook. 1973. *The Banking Crisis of 1933*. University Press of Kentucky.

Kindleberger, Charles Poor. 1989. *Manias, Panics, and Crashes: A History of Financial Crises*, Rev ed. New York: Basic Books.

Knox, John Jay, Bradford Rhodes, and Elmer Haskell Youngman. 1903. *A History of Banking in the United States*. New York: B. Rhodes & Co.

Larson, Henrietta Melia. 1936. *Jay Cooke, Private Banker*. Harvard Studies in Business History, vol. II. Cambridge, Mass: Harvard University Press.

Lebergott, Stanley. 1964. *Manpower in Economic Growth; The American Record Since 1800*. Economics Handbook Series. New York: McGraw-Hill.

Lepler, Jessica M. 2013. *The Many Panics of 1837: People, Politics and the Creation of a Transatlantic Financial Crisis*. New York: Cambridge University Press.

Lucia, Joseph L. 1985. The Failure of the Bank of United States: A Reappraisal. *Explorations in Economic History* 22 (4) (10): 402–416.

McCulloch, Hugh. 1888. *Men and Measures of Half a Century; Sketches and Comments*. New York: C. Scribner's Sons.

McFerrin, John Berry. 1969. *Caldwell and Company; A Southern Financial Empire*. Nashville, Tenn.: Vanderbilt University Press.

Meerman, Jacob P. 1963. The Climax of the Bank War: Biddle's Contraction, 1833–34. *Journal of Political Economy* 71 (4): 378–388.

Miron, Jeffrey A. 1986. Financial Panics, the Seasonality of the Nominal Interest Rate, and the Founding of the Fed. *The American Economic Review* 76 (1): 125–140.

Mitchell, Wesley C. 1941. *Business Cycles and Their Causes*. A New Edition of Mitchell's Business Cycles: Part III ed. Berkley and Los Angeles: University of California Press.

Mitchener, Kris James, and Gary Richardson. 2013. Shadowy Banks and Financial Contagion During the Great Depression: A Retrospective on Friedman and Schwartz. *American Economic Review* 103 (3) (05): 73–8.

Moen, Jon R., and Ellis W. Tallman. 1992. The Bank Panic of 1907: The Role of Trust Companies. *The Journal of Economic History* 52 (3): 611–630.

Moen, Jon R., and Ellis W. Tallman. 2000. Clearing House Membership and Deposit Contraction During the Panic of 1907. *The Journal of Economic History* 60 (1): 145–163.

Myers, Margaret G. 1970. *A Financial History of the United States*. New York: Columbia University Press.

Neal, Larry. 1971. Trust Companies and Financial Innovation, 1897–1914. *The Business History Review* 45 (1): 35–51.

Noyes, Alexander Dana. 1909. *Forty Years of American Finance: A Short Financial History of the Government And People of the United States Since the Civil War, 1865–1907*. New York: G. P. Putnam's sons.

O'Brien, Anthony Patrick. 1992. The Failure of the Bank of the United States: A Defense of Joseph Lucia: A Note. *Journal of Money, Credit, and Banking* 24 (3) (08): 374–84.

Oberholtzer, Ellis Paxson. 1907. *Jay Cooke, Financier of the Civil War*. Philadelphia: G.W. Jacobs.

Osthaus, Carl R. 1976. *Freedmen, Philanthropy and Fraud: A History of the Freedman's Savings Bank*. Urbana, IL: University of Illinois Press.

Paganelli, Maria Pia. 2006. Vanity and the Daedalian Wings of Paper Money in Adam Smith. In *New Voices on Adam Smith.*, ed. Eric Schlieser, Leonidas Montes. London and New York: Routledge.

Perkins, Edwin J. 1984. Langdon Cheves and the Panic of 1819: A Reassessment. *The Journal of Economic History* 44 (2, The Tasks of Economic History): 455–461.

Postel-Vinay, Natacha. 2015. What Caused Chicago Bank Failures in the Great Depression? A Look at the 1920s. Cambride Working Papers in Economic and Social History. Working Paper No. 22-2015.

Redlich, Fritz. 1968; 1951. *The Molding of American Banking: Men and Ideas*. History of American Economy [History of American Business Leaders.] New York: Johnson Reprint Corp.

Reinhart, Carmen M., and Kenneth S. Rogoff. 2009. *This Time is Different: Eight Centuries of Financial Folly*. Princeton and Oxford: Princeton University Press.

Riddiough, Timothy J., and Howard E. Thompson. 2012. *Déjà vu all Over Again: Agency, Uncertainty, Leverage and the Panic of 1857*. Hong Kong Institute for Monetary Research. Working Paper No. 10/2012.

Rockoff, Hugh. 2011. Upon Daedalian Wings of Paper Money: Adam Smith and the Crisis of 1772. In *The Adam Smith Review*, ed. Fonna Forman-Barzilai, vol. 6, 237–268.

Rousseau, Peter L. 2002. Jacksonian Monetary Policy, Specie Flows, and the Panic of 1837. *The Journal of Economic History* 62 (2): 457–488.

Rowe, John J. 1912. Banks and Bankers. In *Cincinnati the Queen City*, ed. Charles Frederic Goss, vol. 2, 171–214.

Ryssdal, Kai. 2009. Interview with Anna J. Schwartz. In Marketplace, Taking Stock: Lessons from History. June 9. [database online]. Available from http://www.marketplace.org/topics/business/taking-stock/taking-stock-lessons-history. Accessed May 29, 2013.

Schularick, Moritz, and Alan M. Taylor. 2012. Credit Booms Gone Bust: Monetary Policy, Leverage Cycles, and Financial Crises, 1870–2008. *American Economic Review* 102 (2) (04): 1029–1061.

Shin, Hyun Song. 2009. Reflections on Northern Rock: The Bank Run that Heralded the Global Financial Crisis. *The Journal of Economic Perspectives* 23 (1): 101–120.

Shultz, William J., and M.R. Caine. 1937. *Financial Development of the United States*. New York, NY: Prentice-Hall Inc.

Smith, Alice E. 1966. *George Smith's Money; A Scottish Investor in America*. Madison: State Historical Society of Wisconsin.

Smith, Adam. 1976 [1776]. *An Inquiry into the Nature and Causes of the Wealth of Nations*. The Glasgow Edition of the Works and Correspondence of Adam Smith., ed. by R. H. Campbell, Andrew S. Skinner, and William B. Todd, vol. 2. Oxford: Clarendon Press.

Smith, Walter Buckingham, and Arthur Harrison Cole. 1935. *Fluctuations in American Business, 1790–1860*. Harvard Economic Studies. Cambridge: Harvard University Press.
Sobel, Robert. 1999; 1968. *Panic on Wall Street: A History of America's Financial Disasters*. Washington, DC: Beard Books.
Sorkin, Andrew Ross. 2009. *Too Big to Fail: The Inside Story of How Wall Street and Washington Fought to Save the Financial System from Crisis–and Themselves*. New York: Viking.
Spiegelman, Mortimer. 1948. The Failure of Ohio Life Insurance and Trust Company, 1857. *Ohio State Archaeological and Historical Quarterly* 57: 247–265.
Sprague, O. M. W. 1910. *History of Crises Under the National Banking System*. U. S. 61st cong., 2d sess. senate. doc. 538. Washington: Govt. Print. Off.
Studenski, Paul, and Herman Edward Krooss. 1963. *Financial History of the United States: Fiscal, Monetary, Banking, and Tariff, Including Financial Administration and State and Local Finance*, 2d ed. New York: McGraw-Hill.
Sylla, Richard. 1976. Forgotten Men of Money: Private Bankers in Early U.S. History. *The Journal of Economic History* 36 (1, The Tasks of Economic History): 173–188.
Tallman, Ellis W., and Jon R. Moen. 1990. Lessons from the Panic of 1907. *Federal Reserve Bank of Atlanta Economic Review* 75 (3): 2–13.
Tallman, Ellis W., and Jon R. Moen. 1995. Private Sector Responses to the Panic of 1907: A Comparison of New York and Chicago. *Federal Reserve Bank of Atlanta Economic Review* 80 (2): 1–9.
Temin, Peter. 1976. *Did Monetary Forces Cause the Great Depression?*, 1st ed. New York: Norton.
Temin, Peter. 1969. *The Jacksonian Economy*. The Norton Essays in American History, 1st ed. New York: Norton.
Temin, Peter. 1975. The Panic of 1857. *Intermountain Economic Review* 6 (1)1–12.
Thorp, Willard Long, Hildegarde E. Thorp, and Wesley C. Mitchell. 1926. *Business Annals*. New York: National Bureau of Economic Research, inc.
Trescott, Paul B. 1992. The Failure of the Bank of the United States, 1930: A Rejoinder. *Journal of Money, Credit, and Banking* 24 (3) (08): 384–99.
Wallis, John Joseph. 2001. *What Caused the Crisis of 1839?* NBER Working Paper Series on Historical Factors in Long Run Growth. NBER Historical Working Paper No. 133. Cambridge, MA.
Walton, Gary, and Hugh Rockoff. 2014. *History of the American Economy*, 12th ed. Mason, Ohio: South-Western, Cengage Learning.
Weber, Warren E. Accessed October 2014. Pre-1861 United States Banking Information. The Federal Reserve Bank of Minnesota. http://www.minneapolisfed.org/research/economic_research/bankarchive/.
Werner, Morris Robert. 2009. *Little Napoleons and Dummy Directors: Being the Narrative of the Bank of United States*. Yardley PA: Westholme Publishing, LLC. Originally published, New York and London, Harper & Brothers, 1933.
White, Eugene Nelson. 1984. A Reinterpretation of the Banking Crisis of 1930. *The Journal of Economic History* 44 (1): 119–38.
Wicker, Elmus. 1980. A Reconsideration of the Causes of the Banking Panic of 1930. *The Journal of Economic History* 40 (3): 571–583.
Wicker, Elmus. 1996. *The Banking Panics of the Great Depression*. Studies in Monetary and Financial History. New York: Cambridge University Press.
Wicker, Elmus. 2000. *Banking Panics of the Gilded Age*. Studies in Macroeconomic History. Cambridge, UK; New York: Cambridge University Press.

Author Biography

Hugh Rockoff is a Distinguished Professor of Economics at Rutgers University in New Brunswick New Jersey and a research associate of the National Bureau of Economic Research. He received his A.B. from Earlham College in 1967 and his Ph.D. from Chicago in 1972. He has written many articles and several books on banking and monetary history and wartime economic controls. His most recent paper is "War and Inflation in the United States from the Revolution to the Persian Gulf War." In *Economic History of Warfare and State Formation*, eds. Jari Eloranta, Eric Golson, Andre Markevich, and Nikolaus Wolf. His recent working papers can be found at www.nber.org.

Chapter 5
Milton Friedman and Anna J. Schwartz on the Inherent Instability of Fractional Reserve Banking

Hugh Rockoff

Abstract Throughout their long collaboration Milton Friedman and Anna J. Schwartz consistently argued that fractional reserve banking was "inherently unstable." This paper traces the evolution of their ideas, the policies that they advocated to reduce the problems created by the inherent instability, and the implications of their views for current attempts to strengthen the banking system. Recent attempts to reform banking have incorporated some of the ideas that they advocated, but in some cases have moved in a different direction.

Keywords Banking panics · Crises · Milton Friedman · Anna J. Schwartz
Free banking · Lender of last resort

5.1 Introduction

Milton Friedman and Anna J. Schwartz believed that Laissez Faire was the best general rule for guiding economic policy. But when it came to banking, they advocated government interventions designed to mitigate the "inherent instability" of fractional reserve banking. To be sure, they thought it was possible to separate the role of banks as providers of the payments mechanism, which needed government involvement, from the role of banks as intermediaries in the market for savings and investments, which was better left to the market. But the consistency of their advocacy of government intervention in banking may come as a surprise to people who are familiar with them as forceful advocates of free markets but unfamiliar with their work on banking.

Typically, of course, historians of thought trace the views of one economist at a time. But this is not a typical case. Milton Friedman and Anna J. Schwartz were brilliant, independent minded economists, but their masterwork was a

---

H. Rockoff (✉)
Department of Economics, Rutgers University, 75 Hamilton Street,
New Brunswick, NJ 08901, USA
e-mail: Rockoff@econ.rutgers.edu

© Springer Nature Singapore Pte Ltd. 2018

H. Rockoff and I. Suto (eds.), *Coping with Financial Crises*,
Studies in Economic History, https://doi.org/10.1007/978-981-10-6196-7_5

trilogy, *A Monetary History of the United States* (1963), *Monetary Statistics of the United States* (1970), and *Monetary Trends in the United States and the United Kingdom* (1982), the product of a collaboration that spanned decades. After finishing this great work they remained close friends and professional collaborators and confidants over the remainder of their lives. Friedman and Schwartz were, in my opinion, the most important duo in economics since Marx and Engels, and it is appropriate, indeed necessary to consider their oeuvre on this issue as a whole.

The phrase "inherent instability" has be used in many contexts. Nathaniel Hawthorne, for example, referred to "the inherent instability of human affairs" in the *House of Seven Gables*. The phrase, to judge from JSTOR, first came into common use among economists in the 1930s and 1940s when it was used as a possible description of the economic system as a whole, or as a description of various sectors such as agriculture or banking (as did its opposite "inherent stability.") R.G. Hawtrey seems to have been one of the first influential economists to popularize the term. He used the phrase "the inherent instability of credit" repeatedly in the *Art of Central Banking* (1932). Oscar Morgenstern (1943, 299), to take a later example, referred to the "inherent instability of the monetary and banking system" in the course of his attempt to explain the international diffusion of the business cycle. Friedman and Schwartz used the phrase repeatedly to refer to the potential fluctuations in the stock of money that were possible with a fractional reserve banking system.

5.2 The Inherent Instability of Fractional Reserve Banking

As far as his major work is concerned, Friedman first developed the reasons for the inherent instability of banking in detail in "Commodity-reserve currency" (1951, 212–213).[1] Here he followed the economist's traditional method of starting with a very simple monetary economy and then adding complications. It was a stylized history grounded in fact, but leavened with imagination. He began his story with a pure commodity standard, like a pure gold standard, in which only the monetary commodity circulated as money. He then explained why banks would be formed that would issue claims to the monetary commodity which would also circulate as money. He then went on to explain why banks, institutions that borrowed short term and lent long-term, would be tempted to make their short-term instruments close substitutes for the monetary commodity which could then circulate as money.

[1]Friedman (1950, 477) used the phrase in the course of pointing out that Wesley C. Mitchell rejected the idea that the economic system as a whole was inherently unstable. The term was also mentioned in DePres et al. (1950), a report by a committee of the American Economic Association which included Friedman.

Fractional reserve banking would then be "inherently unstable" because attempts to convert claims to money into the monetary commodity would produce changes in the total quantity of money.

Friedman, of course, was basically restating the conventional economic wisdom. Paul Samuelson in the first edition of his textbook (1948, 320), for example, explains the "fundamental fact that *fractional reserve banking* [his italics] is essentially an unstable "fair-weather" business." One difference is that the story that Samuelson tells is what was then the traditional, possibly apocryphal, story of the goldsmiths. The goldsmiths, according to this story, started out by simply warehousing gold and then discovered that they could get away with lending part of the gold out at interest. Friedman on the other hand, starts with investment bankers who were borrowing short-term, lending long term, who discover that they could make their liabilities more attractive by giving them properties that allowed them to circulate as money.

Granted that the balance sheet of a fractional reserve bank suggests that a fractional reserve system might be unstable, how do we know that it would be? The answer for Friedman and Schwartz is that banking history is replete with banking crises. Both Friedman and Schwartz had experienced the banking crises of the Great Depression at first hand. And banking crises are the standard fare of banking histories. Indeed, one of Schwartz's first published papers (1947) describes a run on a bank in Philadelphia.

5.3 Removing Gold from Circulation as a Partial Remedy

In "Commodity-reserve Currency" Friedman (1951, 212) wrote that

> One way to eliminate this inherent instability is to prohibit the use of currency commodity as a circulating medium, restrict its use to reserves, and make reserve requirements uniform for all types of currency. The first two steps were taken with gold in the United States after 1933, though without eliminating inherent instability because of the failure to take the third step.

In a footnote he explained that the problem was that the ultimate gold reserve behind Federal Reserve notes and bank deposits, both of which circulated as money after 1933, were different. There was more gold behind notes (although it couldn't be taken possession of !) than behind deposits. In a panic people might want to convert deposits into notes. It would have been better, Friedman thought, if the reserve ratios were equal.

Friedman didn't say exactly how he wanted to accomplish this, but it would have been necessary to raise the gold cover of bank reserves at the Federal Reserve and/or lower the gold cover behind notes sufficiently to equalize the gold cover for each asset. Friedman's recommendation would have eliminated instability deriving from one source, different perceived gold covers, but if Federal Reserve notes were regarded as safer than bank deposits for other reasons, say because Federal Reserve notes were a legal tender, then some instability would remain.

There were still national bank notes (privately issued paper money) in circulation when gold was prohibited from circulating from hand to hand. But they were retired in 1935. Another way of reducing inherent instability would have been to eliminate Federal Reserve notes, eliminate the bond backing requirement for notes issued by commercial banks, and allow both privately issued national bank notes and deposits to be issued on the same basis—for example, with the same required reserve ratio. This would have further reduced instability. Even in this case, however, depositors would have an incentive to convert deposits into notes in troubled times because noteholders ranked ahead of depositors in bankruptcy proceedings. The reason is straightforward. When one of the parties to a transaction accepts notes in payment, the individual's only contract, for practical purposes is with the bank that issued the notes. Should the bank fail, the note holder will not be able to go back to the person that originally tendered the note for a valid payment. When one accepts a check, however, the contract with the writer of the check remains intact, morally and legally, even after it is revealed that the bank on which the check was written has failed. It would be possible, then, to further reduce the inherent instability of the banking system by equalizing notes and deposits in bankruptcy proceedings.

When Friedman and Schwartz turned to the events that spelled the end of the gold standard in *A Monetary History* (1963, 462–483) their focus was on international repercussions rather than on the effects on confidence in the banking system, perhaps because the faith in the gold standard as the guarantor of a sound financial system had already begun to wane.

5.4 One Hundred Percent Reserves as a Remedy

The straightforward way of eliminating the inherent instability caused by fractional reserve banking is to simply eliminate fractional reserve banking. Make it a law that all deposits or privately issued bank notes must be backed dollar for dollar by reserves. Although it might sound implausible on first hearing—how would banks make any money?—100% reserves is a feasible system. Banks would have to charge for the service of warehousing cash and providing other services. And any loans or investments they made would have to be financed by issuing stock or long-term bonds. But it could be done, and bank panics would be impossible because any demand from depositors for cash could be met.

This was the famous proposal of Henry Simons (1948a [1934]), a professor of economics at Chicago in the 1930s who is often regarded as the founder of the Chicago school of economics. One hundred percent reserves were also advocated by Simons's colleague, Lloyd Mints (1950), a distinguished historian of monetary doctrines. Although Simons was one of the best known advocates of 100% reserves in the 1930s, to the point where the idea came to be known as the "Chicago Plan" for banking reform, he was by no means the only originator of the idea, nor the only major advocate. Irving Fisher, for one, got in on the act. Albert G. Hart (1935) discusses Simons's plan along with some of the other plans for 100% reserves that arose independently, and reports that "from conversations with various American economists I am convinced that the same notion occurred to economists at several other centres of economics at the same time, although their findings have not happened to be published." Evidently, as Hart notes, 100% reserves was an obvious plan given the meltdown of the banking system in the early 1930s. Hansen (1941) chided Simons for failing to cite Frederick Soddy as the inventor of 100% reserves. There was more than a drop of acid in this remark because Soddy, a Nobel-prize winning chemist (1921), was an amateur economist who had a reputation as a monetary crank. In a review of Hansen's book, Simons (1939) acknowledged Soddy as a forerunner, but argued that there were times when ignoring predecessors was justified, and that once started there was, in any case, no need to stop with Soddy!

In what would become his most famous essay published two years after his 100% reserve proposal, "Rules Versus Authorities in Monetary Policy" (1936), Simons returned to the 100% reserve proposal. But his thinking had progressed and he now argued that in the absence of more fundamental reforms adopting 100% reserves would lead merely to the proliferation of near monies. In a footnote (1948b, 329) Simons wrote that

> The so-called "100 percent" scheme of banking reform can easily be defended only as the proper first step toward reconstruction of our whole financial organization. Standing by itself, as an isolated measure, it would promise little but evasion—small effects at the price of serious disturbance—and would deserve classification as merely another crank scheme.

What Simons now thought was necessary was the elimination of all short-term borrowing. Capital investments should be financed by equity or very long-term debt. It would simply be impossible in such a world to set up a corporation that would issue debt that would mimic the properties of bank deposits or notes. In retrospect we can see Simons warning us about the dangers of shadow banking.

Friedman endorsed 100% reserves in his *Program for Monetary Stability* (1959, 65–75), although not the more radical elimination of all short-term borrowing advocated by Simons in "Rules versus Authorities." Indeed, Friedman claimed that he would change nothing in Simons's plan except to add the requirement that the Federal Reserve pay interest on bank reserves, a reform that was finally achieved in the wake of the Panic of 2008. In 1954 Friedman (1968, 72–76) took note of the large increase in the amount of government bonds held by US banks as a result of World War II. At that time government bonds accounted for more than 50% of the assets of US commercial and savings banks, suggesting that achieving 100% reserves was not as difficult as it might at first appear. He viewed the high proportion of government bonds in bank portfolios as another reason why the U.S. economy was depression-proof. But that was not to last. By 1968 the proportion had fallen to 15%.

Friedman and Schwartz did not ignore the problem of near monies that Simons raised in "Rules versus Authorities." Indeed, in their work on money they concluded that the best definition of money was M2, which included time deposits (savings deposits) at commercial banks. At the time, some economists were arguing that only demand deposits should be counted as part of the money supply, because only cash and demand deposits could be used as a means of payment. And Friedman and Schwartz (1970) presented estimates of M3 which included deposits at mutual savings banks and the postal savings system, and M4 which included in addition shares in savings and loan associations as alternative candidates for "the stock of money." Nevertheless, it appears that Friedman and Schwartz saw less danger, at least in the short run, from the development of money substitutes than did Simons.[2] It was an empirical judgment. Additional support for this judgment was provided by Cagan and Schwartz (1975). They explored the interest elasticity of the demand for money econometrically and found that the elasticity had remained the same or declined in the postwar period. This finding suggested that the growth of money substitutes had not reduced the effectiveness of monetary policy.

5.5 Higher Reserves as a Remedy

In principle any increase in required reserves would help to stabilize the stock of money in the face of an attempt by the public to convert deposits into currency. But neither Friedman nor Schwartz, as far as I am aware, ever advocated a policy of increases in the required reserve ratio, taxes on low reserve ratios, or other partial measures. It may be that the gains in stability from partial measures did not appear substantial, at least until they were carried to the point that 100% reserves would be as nearly as easy to achieve.

Some examples of the possible advantages of raising required reserve ratios based on the Great Contraction are shown in Table 5.1. The first panel shows what actually happened. Between October 1929 (the stock market crash) and April 1933 (just before Roosevelt took office) the stock of money fell 48%. The second panel shows what would have happened under 100% reserves. Since the amount of high-powered money rose, the stock of money would have increased 9.5%. The third panel shows what would have happened had the initial reserve ratio been 50% and then risen by the same percentage that it actually rose. In this case, there would have still been a major decline in the stock of money, but it would have been only 60% as large as it actually was.[3]

[2]My interpretation of Simons is that he expected evasion to arise quickly once 100% reserves were put in place, but he doesn't discuss explicitly how long this would take.

[3]In both of the counterfactual examples the initial stocks of money would have been lower. We can imagine that the economy had adjusted to these lower amounts through lower prices, and that what mattered was the change from 1929 to 1933.

Table 5.1 The great contraction with alternative reserve rules

	Money (M2)	High-powered money	Reserve ratio of the banking system (%)	Currency-deposit ratio (%)
Actual changes				
Oct-29	48,167	7.345	0.079	0.086
Apr-33	29,756	8.074	0.117	0.212
Percent change	−48.16	9.46	38.94	89.66
100% reserves				
Oct-29	7.345	7.345	1.000	0.086
Apr-33	8.074	8.074	1.000	0.212
	9.46	9.46	0.00	89.66
High (50%) reserves				
Oct-29	13,607	7.345	0.50	0.086
Apr-33	10,302	8.074	0.74	0.212
	−27.84	9.46	38.94	89.66

Conceivably, also, a high required reserve ratio could be lowered or suspended during a financial crisis, instantly providing banks with funds they could use to meet withdrawals. That changes in required reserve ratios could have a potent effect is indicated by Friedman and Schwartz's discussion of the negative effects of increases in required reserves mandated by the Federal Reserve during the 1930s, but as far as I know, they never advocated manipulation of required reserve ratios as a policy instrument.

5.6 The Clearing House as a Remedy

A Monetary History covered the years 1867 to 1960. The Federal Reserve was established in 1913. So during roughly half the years they studied there was no central bank in the United States to alleviate banking crises. There were, in fact, five banking panics during the period 1867–1913: in 1873, 1884, 1890, 1893, and 1907. The panics of 1884 and 1890 were somewhat less severe. O.M.W. Sprague (1910), the leading historian of America's banking crises during this era, describes 1890 as a mere "financial stringency." There was no central bank that could serve as lender of last resort during this era, but there was an institution that could play the part of a central bank: the Clearing House. There were Clearing Houses in most major cities; the most important was in New York. In essence they were what their name suggests: an institution that allowed banks to clear obligations by simply settling net balances. If, for example, Bank A owed $50 to bank B, Bank B owed $50 to Bank C, and Bank C owed $100 to Bank A, a simple payment of $50 from C to A would clear all the debts. There would be no need to ship cash from A to B to C.

If a panic was threatened the Clearing House could help in several ways. First, the Clearing House could issue what were called Clearing House Loan Certificates to members who put up adequate collateral. The loan certificates could then be used by the banks in lieu of cash to settle their accounts. In our example, if Bank C experienced a run and didn't have the cash to pay the $50 it owed to Bank A it could provide a Clearinghouse Loan Certificate. Second, suppose the main problem was that members were being drained of cash by the public. In that case the Clearing House could issue low denomination Clearinghouse Certificates that the banks could offer their depositors in lieu of cash. Finally, the Clearing House could undertake investigations of banks that were in trouble and report its findings to its members and, depending on the likely effect, to the general public. Perhaps a positive report would allay the fears that were producing runs.

The Clearing Houses did good work (at times) in addressing the post-Civil War panics. And a number of scholars have studied them in part because they are a private-enterprise solution to the problem of inherent instability. O.M.W. Sprague's *History of Crises under the National Banking System* (1910) was the first detailed survey of their role in the crises, and remains an important source of information. Friedman and Schwartz, it appears, relied heavily on Sprague when they described the role of the Clearing Houses. Sprague recognized the value of Clearing Houses, but was also highly critical of their responses to the panics. One of his key criticisms turned on the idea of "pooling reserves." In the crises of 1860, 1861, and 1873, but not in later crises, the members of the New York Clearing House had agreed to treat their gold reserves as a common pool that any of the members could draw on as needed. When this was done the New York Clearing House had, in Sprague's view, effectively turned itself into a central bank. One of the main purposes of Sprague's book was to convince the New York Clearing House banks to pool reserves, and do so in a timely fashion, in all incipient panics. Recent research by Gorton (1985), Gorton and Mullineaux (1987), Moen and Tallman (1998, 2000, 2012, 2014), and other scholars has uncovered considerable amounts of new information, both quantitative and qualitative, about the role the Clearing Houses played in financial panics, and has strengthened the view that they reduced the severity of the panics.

It remains true, however, that while the actions taken by the Clearing Houses ameliorated the effects of the panics, they were not a cure. The panic of 1907 is a good example of the limits of the Clearing Houses. In October 1907 there were runs on a number of banks in New York, and the Clearing House provided assistance which calmed depositors. But when the Knickerbocker Trust Company, a large institution that was not a member of the Clearing House experienced a run, aid was not forthcoming, the Knickerbocker suspended, and this precipitated a banking panic. Part of the problem was that the New York Trust Companies were less tightly regulated than the banks that were members of the Clearing House and for that reason, resented. Friedman and Schwartz (1963, 159) concluded that had the Knickerbocker been a member of the Clearing House, it probably would have been helped, and that the crisis might have been prevented. Real GDP fell 11% between

1907 and 1908. It took until 1911 for real GDP to recover the level reached in 1906.[4]

In the wake of the 1907 crisis Congress established the National Monetary Commission which recommended establishing the Federal Reserve. As an interim measure, however, it provided for an emergency currency. If a panic was threatened before the Federal Reserve was set up, national banks would be allowed to form associations that would issue currency to members of the association on the basis of collateral they provided. The banks in turn could pay out the emergency currency to worried customers. The Aldrich-Vreeland currency as it was known after the enabling legislation resembled the Clearing House approach in that it was the product of a collaboration of private banks, but solved the membership issue that had undermined the response of the New York Clearing House in 1907. The public was used to national bank notes which were secured by government bonds. The national banks could not easily secure additional bonds in an emergency. The Aldrich-Vreeland Currency was almost identical in appearance to the national bank notes, but the amount could be expanded because it was based on a wide array of collateral.

The Aldrich-Vreeland currency was used in 1914. A stock market and banking panic seemed to be in the offing when World War I erupted. There was widespread fear that Europeans would liquidate their American securities and take their gold back to Europe. As a result the stock market was closed and the Aldrich-Vreeland currency was issued. Most students of the episode, including Friedman and Schwartz, agree that the issue of the Aldrich-Vreeland currency nipped a potential panic in the bud.[5] Friedman and Schwartz (1963, 172) put it this way:

> to judge by that one episode, the Aldrich-Vreeland Act provided an effective device for solving a threatened interconvertibility crisis without monetary contraction or widespread bank failures.

And they go on to suggest that the issue of Aldrich-Vreeland Currency would have been “equally effective” in meeting the banking crisis of 1930. Of course, as Friedman and Schwartz are careful to note, there is only one observation. And it was an unusual observation: an external threat that potentially affected all of the banks, a situation in other words, conducive to collective action. In some respects the panic of 1914 was similar to the banking panics that followed the outbreak of the Civil War. And on that occasion the New York Banks did agree to pool their gold reserves, something that they were able to do on only one postwar occasion. The United States, moreover, soon learned that neutrality while Europe was at war would be a highly profitable. The situation in 1930 was different, a banking panic after a sobering stock market crash and in the midst of an already severe economic contraction.

---

[4]Data from www.measuringworth.com.

[5]Silber (2007) provides a detailed treatment of the episode and reaches a similar conclusion.

5.7 Restriction of Convertibility as a Remedy

When a bank's or a banking system's reserves are exhausted it has to restrict the convertibility of its deposits into cash. The payments mechanism is severely disrupted and economic activity will be harmed. Restriction, however, was not the end of all banking. Checks could still be written, money could still be deposited in banks, sometimes in special accounts backed by 100% reserves. If restriction came before reserves were completely exhausted, banks could adopt rules permitting gradual withdrawals. They could also make exceptions: for individuals dealing with emergencies, for example, or firms needing cash to meet payrolls.

Restriction, moreover, might have had what Friedman and Schwartz (1963, 165–167) labeled a "therapeutic" effect. Depositors could no longer hope to improve their position by running down to the bank and demanding cash. The restriction would give people time to calm down and for the panic to "wear off." Perhaps there is an intrusion of "behavioral economics" here. Friedman and Schwartz appear to be suggesting that people can get into an emotional state, a panic, which distorts their ability to make purely rational decisions. Friedman and Schwartz (1963, 329), I should hasten to add, did not think that restriction was an optimal solution to the problem of banking panics. But they did think it was superior to what actually transpired in 1930–1933, a panic that seemed to wax and wane, but never disappeared.

Runs are possible when deposits are by custom or law convertible on demand into cash. This is not always the case. Many banks, savings banks, and building and loan societies issued time deposits that contained an option which the bank could exercise to delay payment. The bank could say that the deposits would be redeemed in, say 60 or 90 days. These options were exercised during panics and were generally effective in protecting the institutions that relied on them. In the Great Depression many savings banks and building and loan societies were able to protect themselves by invoking time-to-pay options.[6] It's also possible to have bank notes that can be converted into short-term obligations in an emergency. Many banks in Scotland in the nineteenth century, for example, issued notes with "option clauses" that explained to note holders that their notes could be converted, at the discretion of the bank, into short-term interest bearing securities. Option clauses, however, were not generally permitted in the United States. National bank notes had to be redeemed on demand.

5.8 Deposit Insurance as a Remedy

Deposit insurance is another method for reducing the danger of bank runs and panics. If depositors know that their deposits are insured, they have less reason in an emergency to run to their bank to try to be first in line to convert their deposits

[6]George Bailey (Jimmy Stewart) might have considered this option in "It's a Wonderful Life" rather than using the money Mary (Donna Reed) saved for their honeymoon.

into cash. Friedman and Schwartz, famously, praised deposit insurance in *A Monetary History* (1963, 440).

> Adopted as a result of the widespread losses imposed by bank failures in the early 1930's, federal deposit insurance, to 1960 at least, has succeeded in achieving what had been a major objective of banking reform for at least a century, namely the prevention of banking panics.

It was a matter of both logic and experience. Deposit insurance removed the reason for bank runs, and in fact bank failures were rare for a long time after deposit insurance went into effect. Even in the prosperous 1920s there were hundreds of bank suspensions each year. The lowest number from 1921 to 1929 was 366 in 1922. The highest number from 1945 to 1960 was 9 in 1958 (Friedman and Schwartz 1963, 438). Friedman and Schwartz were not alone, of course, in seeing the benefits of deposit insurance.

This view was also shared, not surprisingly, by liberal economists. Paul Samuelson in the First Edition of his textbook (1948, 323) told the reader that

> the importance of this measure [Federal deposit insurance] can scarcely be exaggerated. It would be absolutely wrong to say that bank bankruptcy is no longer a danger. But certainly, there need never again be universal bank runs.

In later years Friedman and Schwartz continued to support deposit insurance. Friedman returned to deposit insurance in "Why the American Economy is Depression-Proof" (1968) based on a lecture originally delivered in 1954. There Friedman extolled the virtues of deposit insurance, which he claimed was a more basic change in the American banking system than the Federal Reserve because it had "made bank failures almost a thing of the past" (Friedman 1968, 75).

What about moral hazard? Would bank depositors have any reason to monitor their bank if the government was insuring their deposits? Wouldn't risky, badly managed banking proliferate? Friedman and Schwartz recognized, of course, that deposit insurance reduced the incentive for depositors to monitor banks, and that as a result banks would be prone to take larger risks, but they thought that the benefits of deposit insurance outweighed the costs. That statement, of course, is made holding constant the existing set of institutions and policies. Since deposit insurance created a moral hazard problem, the inevitable result was that government would become more involved in supervising and regulating banks, something that Friedman opposed. He put it this way in *A Program for Monetary Stability* (p. 67 of the 1992 reprint) that "This amelioration of one defect of fractional reserve banking [instability] was attained, however, only by exacerbating the other; federal insurance of deposits involves a substantial increase in government intervention into the lending and investment process."

At the time he wrote *A Program for Monetary Stability* moral hazard was mainly a theoretical concern. Once the savings and loan crisis erupted, however, concerns about the moral hazard created by government sponsored deposit insurance moved to the front of the class. Friedman, however, rejected the view that deposit insurance was the main culprit behind the savings and loan collapse. True, deposit insurance had been conducted in such a way that depositor had "nothing to lose" if a bank ran into trouble. But shareholders or managers of mutual savings banks did have something to lose.

The savings and loan crisis erupted, he argued, when inflation erased the equity of the savings and loans. Once the equity cushion was gone there was no constraint on risky behavior. It hit the balance sheets of savings and loans especially hard because, by law, they were heavily invested in fixed rate, long-term mortgages. The rates on these assets could not rise with inflation, but the rates savings and loans had to pay on deposits were under competitive pressures to go higher. Here is his bottom line. "Had monetary growth been restrained from 1970 on, the accelerating inflation would have been avoided, and the number of annual bank and savings and loan failures would still be in single digits, despite the defects in insurance arrangements" (Friedman 1992, 251n).

Schwartz (1979) spoke to the moral hazard dilemma when she discussed a paper by Homer Jones (1979) on New Deal financial market regulation.[7] Jones had argued that a good reform for deposit insurance would be to tie deposit insurance premiums to bank capital. Banks with higher ratios of capital to assets would pay lower deposit insurance premiums. An even better solution, Jones argued, would be to eliminate deposit insurance altogether. As long as monetary policy was good, there was in his judgment, no need for deposit insurance. Schwartz (1979, 94–95) disagreed completely with Jones's idea of eliminating deposit insurance. To the contrary, she regarded deposit insurance "as indispensable to the stability of our economy" and a "beneficial legacy of the New Deal period." It could, however, be reformed. The main problem, as Schwartz saw it, was that the Federal Deposit Insurance Corporation was keeping banks in operation in order to protect the insurance fund. The right solution, in her view, was to give the Federal Deposit Insurance Corporation an "unlimited claim on the Treasury." Bad banks should be shut down, insured depositors should be paid even if it means going to the Treasury for funds, and uninsured creditors such as depositors who hold deposits in excess of the insurance maximums and shareholders should absorb the losses.

Another potential problem with deposit insurance was the development of near monies. Deposit insurance imposed costs on financial institutions that issued deposits subject to Federal insurance: an annual fee for belonging to the Federal Deposit Insurance system and the costs of additional supervision and regulation. Those costs encouraged the growth of financial intermediaries based on near monies that were not subject to deposit insurance. While some shadow banking was in evidence during the years when Friedman and Schwartz were most active, the full dimensions of the growth of a large shadow banking system that relied on near monies could not be perceived in those years.

[7]Homer Jones was Friedman's professor at Rutgers University. Jones went on to head the research department of the St. Louis Federal Reserve which became known for its monetarist views.

5.9 A Lender of Last Resort as a Remedy

The classic view of the Lender of Last Resort is to be found in Bagehot's *Lombard Street* (1924 [1873], 187–188).

"It [the Bank of England] must in time of panic do what all other similar banks must do; that in time of panic it must advance freely and vigorously to the public out of the reserve."

The idea was simple, once people saw that they were able to get the cash they needed, the panic would subside. Experience, for example the experience of the Bank of England in the crisis of 1825, proved that free and vigorous lending worked. The rule that the Bank should lend freely in a panic was, however, subject to two qualifications.

"First. That these loans should only be made at a very high rate of interest. This will operate as a heavy fine on unreasonable timidity, and will prevent the greatest number of applications by persons who do not require it."

As I will show below Friedman and Schwartz rejected this stricture when they came to criticize the Federal Reserve's policy during the Great Contraction (1929–1933). The reason, perhaps, is that while Bagehot had to worry about protecting the Bank of England's normally limited gold reserve, the Federal Reserve had an abundance of gold in the 1930s, and could in any case have moved to a fiat standard, as the U.S. soon did, without creating the emotional reaction that such a move would have had in 19th century Britain, where preservation of the gold standard was an article of faith.

Even more problematic was Bagehot's second qualification.

> Secondly. That at this rate these advances should be made on all good banking securities, and as largely as the public ask for them. … No advances indeed need be made by which the Bank will ultimately lose (Bagehot 1924, 188).

Capie (2002, 310) describes how, in theory, Bagehot's rule would work.

> The mechanism can be thought of as the central bank with a discount window that is of frosted glass and is raised just a few inches. Representatives of institutions could therefore appear at the window and push through the paper they wanted discounted. The central bankers would return the appropriate amount of cash, reflecting the going interest rate. The central banker does not know, nor does he care, who is on the other side of the window. He simply discounts good quality paper or lends on the basis of good collateral.

What about a bank that did not have enough good assets to get the cash it needed to stave off a run? It would have to throw up its hands and to enter the bankruptcy process. Bagehot thought that normally there were so few bad assets floating around that his good-collateral-only policy would not hamstring the Bank of England, because most of the collateral circulating in the market would be good in the long run.

But in practice central banks have often aided institutions that might prove insolvent because of the fear that if they were allowed to fail a panic might be ignited, or if one was already underway, might be intensified. Even the Bank of

England, itself, had not followed Bagehot's good-quality-only rule. In 1801 the Bank lent to Hibberts, Fuhr, & Purrier on guarantees from 13 firms including Baring Brothers & Co. In 1836-37 the Bank loaned to several firms that had run into difficulties while financing trade with the United States. Aid was provided to Sir James Esdaile, Esdaile, Grenfell, Thomas & Co. on the guarantee of several private bankers. Aid was also provided to the three W's—Wiggin, Wildes, and Wilson—for a time, although they were eventually allowed to fail. And aid was provided to W. & J. Brown & Co., which received a total of almost £2,000,000, about £5.6 billion in today's money using GDP as the inflator (www.measuring-worth.com). The most famous use of firm-specific aid was in 1890. The house of Barings had gotten into trouble by investing heavily in Argentine and Bolivian bonds. With a pledge of help from the government, the Bank of England organized a guarantee fund. When the public learned about the trouble that Barings had gotten into they also learned about the guarantee fund, and no run ensued. It was an example of successful central banking, but not of Bagehot's rule.

In *A Monetary History* Friedman and Schwartz argued that during what they dubbed the "Great Contraction" (1929–1933) the Federal Reserve followed a disastrous policy of non-intervention and that following Bagehot's rule would have been a far better policy.

> The actions required to prevent monetary collapse [in the early 1930s] did not call for a level of knowledge of the operation of the banking system or of the workings of monetary forces or of economic fluctuations which was developed only later and was not available to the Reserve System. On the contrary, as we have pointed out earlier, pursuit of the policies outlined by the System itself in the 1920's, or for that matter by Bagehot in 1873, would have prevented the catastrophe. (Friedman and Schwartz 1963, 407).

But that does not mean that they thought that Bagehot's policy was optimal. To the contrary, they argued that the best policy was to maintain the stock of money by creating enough high-powered money to offset the downward pressure on the stock of money produced by the increase in the currency-deposit ratio of the public and the increase in the reserve-deposit ratio of the banks as both the public and the banks struggled to remain liquid. High-powered money could be created by lending to banks, and here a low rate to encourage borrowing was to be preferred to Bagehot's high rate. And high-powered money (the monetary base) could be increased simply by Federal Reserve purchases of bonds, what was then called open market operations, and what would now be called quantitative easing. This comes out clearly in their criticism of Federal Reserve policy in 1931 and 1932.

> … in October [1931], it [the Federal Reserve] permitted its discounts and its bills bought to rise sharply. But this was at the initiative of the member banks, in spite of sharp rises in the rates on both, and was a result of the desperate situation of member banks because of the double drain [of cash abroad and internally]. As we have seen, even after the height of the crisis, the New York Bank reduced bill buying rates only gradually and kept them above market rates, so bills bought declined rapidly. The System took no active measures to ease the internal drain, as it could have done through open market purchases. (Friedman and Schwartz 1963, 395).

5.10 Free Banking as a Remedy

The United States is uniquely prone to banking crises. Systems in other advanced economies have done much better. The United States has had many banking panics, but Canada, for example, has had none (Bordo et al. 2015). And it is not simply a matter of having an effective central bank. The basic problem has been that the U.S. banking system was fragmented. Until recent years, banking stopped at the state line. And in unit banking states it might stop at the border of the local town or village. People had little confidence in the strength of these banks and would withdraw their cash at the first sign of trouble. These banks in turn would draw down their reserves in large correspondent banks transmitting the pressure, or the anticipated pressure, to large financial institutions. The origins of this system were complex, but the roots were the conflict between the states and the federal government for power and the opposition of Populist farmers to control and exploitation, as they saw it, from bankers in Eastern financial centers (Calomiris and Haber 2014).

The experience of Canada and other banking systems that have avoided financial panics, even in the absence formal lenders of last resort, has led to a number of writers of the "free banking school" to argue that an unregulated banking system could be stable. In "Does the government have any role in money" Friedman and Schwartz (1986b) rejected that view. They focused particularly on the case of Scotland in the first half of the nineteenth century. Scotland had a relatively unregulated banking system, branch banking was the norm, and no significant crises. Friedman and Schwartz, however, maintained that there were several special factors. Most importantly, perhaps, the large Scottish banks, the Bank of Scotland and the Royal Bank of Scotland, provided aid for the Scottish banking system in times of stress, relying as circumstances demanded on London financial market and the Bank of England.

5.11 Bailouts as a Remedy

A central bank could follow Bagehot's policy of lending on good collateral. But what about the policy of aiding systemically important financial institutions which are on the brink of failure, as the Bank of England and its partners did in the Barings Crisis, or the more extreme policy of simply bailing out failed banks?

Much can be learned about Friedman and Schwartz's attitude toward bailouts from their discussion in *A Monetary History* of the failure of the Bank of United States in December 1930. This failure, they argue, was of special importance because it was the first large bank in New York City to fail during the Great Contraction, and possibly because its name misled some people into believing that it was sponsored by the federal government, although in fact it was an ordinary commercial bank chartered by the state of New York. The aggregate deposit-currency ratio began to fall after this failure, showing that it had significant macro-economic consequences. In a long footnote in *A Monetary History* Friedman and Schwartz (1963, 309–310n9) described the efforts to save the bank. The plan was to merge it with several others in New York and to inject $30 million provided by the clearing house banks. It would not have been the sort of emergency lending described by Bagehot in *Lombard Street*, but it would have been similar to the rescue organized by the Bank of England in the Baring crisis and in earlier crises. In *A Monetary History* Friedman and Schwartz provide only hints as to why the plan fell apart. They report a recollection by one of the participants, Jackson Reynolds, the President of First National Bank and of the Clearing House Association, who thought that the effects of the closure would be "local." And they report the recollection of another participant that the representatives of the Clearing House were concerned about the Bank of United States' real estate investments. In modern parlance the beliefs were that the bank was not "systemically important" and not solvent.

In some of his popular writings and in his 1980 TV series, "Free to Choose," Friedman went further in pointing to the failure of the Bank of United States as the trigger for the crisis and in identifying the reasons why it was allowed to close. He began Episode Three, "Anatomy of a Crisis," his story of the Great Depression, with scenes in which he is filmed looking up at the building that was the former home of the Bank of United States.[8] This was where the crucial event occurred, Friedman tells the viewer, which turned a recession that was already severe because of the stock market crash into a crisis.[9] He goes on to explain that the bank served mainly Jewish merchants on the Lower East Side of New York, the famous starting point for many poor Jewish immigrants. Anti-Semitism, Friedman suggested, was one of the reasons why the Clearing House failed to rescue of the Bank of United States. Rumors fueled by anti-Semitism, he added may even have contributed to the runs on the bank that had so weakened it that a rescue was necessary. This was undoubtedly done to increase the visual drama for the sake of the television audience, but nevertheless it helped to make the failure of the Bank of United States an important component of the understanding that most economic historians have of the Friedman-and-Schwartz interpretation of the Depression. In the end, in the *A Monetary History* Friedman and Schwartz (1963, 311) noted that the Bank paid 83.5% of its adjusted deposits after it was liquidated during the depression. That fact and other evidence (Friedman and Schwartz 1963, 355) suggested the Bank was probably a good candidate for a rescue. Evidently, Friedman and Schwartz's criteria for a rescue, perhaps like the Bank of England's in the Barings crisis, is that aid makes sense if an important bank is not clearly insolvent.

The references in *A Monetary History* to the Bank of United States (and the reference in the television show?) stirred up an energetically contested debate about

[8]http://www.youtube.com/watch?v=SWVoPrntBso.

[9]The book that accompanied the television series, Friedman and Friedman (1980, 80–82), also gives a starring role to the failure of the Bank of United States.

the solvency of the Bank of the United States and the reasons why it was not assisted (Temin 1976, 90–93, Lucia 1985, Friedman and Schwartz 1986a, O'Brien 1992, and Trescott 1992). Joseph Lucia (1985) in particular took Friedman and Schwartz to task for exaggerating both the importance and the solvency of the Bank of United States. Friedman and Schwartz (1986a) responded on a number of issues, but their main point was that even though the failure of the Bank of United States had a major impact, the stock of money could have been maintained in 1930–1933 with open market operations, and that this would have been an effective response even if many banks, such as the Bank of United States, had been deemed insolvent and allowed to fail. Indeed, they seem to suggest that the right policy would have been to allow it to fail if it was clearly insolvent.

On other occasions, however, Friedman and Schwartz suggested that aiding banks that appeared to be insolvent would not be such a bad thing. In discussing the Reconstruction Finance Corporation Friedman and Schwartz (1963, 330–331) suggested that Reconstruction Finance Corporations funds in the form of capital would have helped the banking system in 1932 and that the Corporation's policy of demanding the bank's best assets as collateral for its loans was a mistake.

More decisively in "Why the American economy is depression-proof (1968)" in which, as I noted above Friedman extolled the virtues of deposit insurance, he added that it was not merely deposit insurance that got the job done, it was also the way in which bank failures were handled by the Federal Deposit Insurance Corporation.

> A bank no longer fails when it has been badly managed and its assets fall short of its liabilities. The F.D.I.C. takes over its bad assets, or assumes responsibility for them, and arranges a merger of the "bad" bank with a "good" bank (Friedman 1968, 75)

Friedman went on to compare this approach, favorably, with the approach of the Federal Reserve which

> was never more than a "lender of last resort."; it gave depositors no protection against bad banking, and partly as a consequence, was unable even to perform its proper function of protecting them against bad central banking. The F.D.I.C. has in effect converted all deposit liabilities of private banks into a Federal Liability. It has thus eliminated the basic cause for runs on banks of the kind that occurred in 1931 to 1933 as well as earlier periods (Friedman 1968, 75).

There is no logical contradiction between this view and the one expressed in reply to Lucia. Nevertheless, here Friedman came much closer to endorsing the positive benefits of government bailouts for insolvent banks.

In June 1970 the Penn Central Railroad declared bankruptcy. There was a widespread fear that the failure of Penn Central to make good on its borrowings in the commercial paper market would ignite a panic. The Federal Reserve then took several actions designed to prevent a panic including open market purchases to increase the stock of money. What about bailing out Penn Central itself? Friedman (1970) was critical of the need for a rescue operation. In his view, there was little danger of a banking panic. Failures of industrial firms were distinctly different from failures of financial firms, and only the latter could precipitate a panic. As long as the payments system was protected by the Federal Reserve and deposit insurance there was no need, in his view, to bail out an industrial firm.

In 1984, however, Continental Illinois, the nation's eighth largest bank failed because of losses on investments in energy loans made by Penn Square Bank of Oklahoma. The Federal Reserve and Federal Deposit Insurance Company cooperated in creating a bailout plan that included replacement of the bank's management. Friedman and Schwartz (1986a) thought that the bailout had been handled well, and used it as an example of the ongoing danger of contagion that created a need for government involvement in banking.

Thus, it would appear that Friedman and Schwartz's usual position was that the social costs of banking panics were so high that it was wise to bail out important financial institutions even if in principle the Federal Reserve could ignore these failures and concentrate simply on increasing high-powered money.[10] Shareholders and administrators should be made to bear the costs of bad decisions, but depositors should be protected.

The defining moment in the most recent crisis was the failure of Lehman Brothers on September 15, 2008. The U.S. economy had already contracted and an atmosphere of near panic prevailed in financial markets. But the failure of Lehman Brothers precipitated a full blown old school financial panic and accelerated the decline in the economy. Why did the failure of Lehman Brothers have major consequences? Other major firms had already gotten into trouble, but had received federal assistance. In March 2008 the Federal Reserve provided financing to help JPMorgan Chase acquire the troubled investment bank, Bear Stearns. In July the Federal Reserve Board and the Treasury authorized lines of credit for the Federal National Mortgage Association (Fannie Mae) and the Federal Home Loan Mortgage Corporation (Freddie Mac). On September 7 Fannie Mae and Freddie Mac were, essentially, nationalized. But on September 15 Lehman Brothers, a troubled investment bank—a very large and well regarded investment bank—was simply allowed to fail, while at the same time American International Group, an insurance company, which had sold credit protection against a large volume of now toxic assets, was bailed out by the Federal Reserve in return for a nearly 80% share in the company. These apparently contradictory decisions raised questions about the willingness or the ability of the government to act as lender of last resort, and that may well have been the final precipitant of the panic.

There has been some debate about why Lehman Brothers was allowed to fail. The Federal Reserve has maintained that it lacked the legal authority to rescue Lehman Brothers because Lehman was clearly insolvent; Lehman Brothers simply lacked securities that could adequately collateralize sufficient loans. On the other hand, more than a few observers have suggested that political considerations also played a role. As the crisis progressed the government came under increasing pressure to end what appeared to the public to be simply handouts to the richest

[10]See Nelson (2013) for a broader discussion of the extent to which Friedman's ideas about monetary and banking policy were implemented after the crisis in 2008.

Americans. Shortly before the collapse of Lehman Brothers, Treasury Secretary Henry Paulson purportedly told Ben Bernanke and Timothy Geithner at the Federal Reserve: "I can't be Mr. Bailout" (Sorkin 2009, locations 5055–10 of 13,296).[11]

In an interview with National Public Radio in June 2009 Anna J. Schwartz, in one of her last comments on public affairs, took a relatively hard position on bailouts. There she argued that the best policy would have been for the Federal Reserve to state clearly: "We will help a bank, which basically is solvent. We will not do that for a bank, which is on the verge of bankruptcy." But hadn't that been tried with Lehman Brothers? No, she argued, the drastic effect of the failure of Lehman Brothers was the result of an inconsistent policy. "… when Lehman Brothers was permitted to fail, the market was simply bewildered. Because here you had treated Bear Stearns in this kindly fashion, and what reason was there not to do the same when Lehman Brothers arose?" Ryssdal (2009).

Andrew Ross Sorkin (2009, locations 10,283–91, of 13,296) reached a similar conclusion in his detailed history of the financial crisis.

> They offered a safety net to Bear Stearns and backstopped Fannie Mae and Freddie Mac but allowed Lehman to fall into chapter 11, only to rescue AIG soon after. What was the pattern? What were the rules? There didn't appear to be any, and when investors grew confused – wondering whether a given firm might be saved, allowed to fail, or even nationalized – they not surprisingly began to panic.

5.12 What Would Milton and Anna Say?

Having reviewed the evolution of Friedman and Schwartz's views on the regulation of banking, it is tempting to say that in the present circumstances Friedman and Schwartz would recommend ____. But, of course, we can't complete the sentence. Friedman and Schwartz would analyze the myriad of current trends and institutional constraints and come up with good ideas, but we don't possess the same analytical skills. We can't "channel" Friedman and Schwartz or design a computer to replace them. We can study all the games of world chess champion Magnus Carlsen, but we cannot play as well as he does. But knowing their basic principles we can perhaps

[11]That said, the first version of the bailout bill that Paulson sent to Congress which was 840 words long, would have authorized $700 billion for buying toxic assets, and made the Secretary of the Treasury immune from oversight by the courts or Congress. The text of the proposal read, in part, "Decisions by the Secretary pursuant to the authority of this Act are non-reviewable and committed to agency discretion, and may not be reviewed by any court of law or any administrative agency." http://www.nytimes.com/2008/09/21/business/21draftcnd.html?_r=1.

see the broad outline of where their thinking would take them. These principles, I believe, can be summed up as follows, although one could cite individual passages where Friedman and Schwartz seemed to head in a different direction.

(1) Fractional reserve banking is inherently unstable. And for that reason requires some form of government regulation or intervention. Laissez Faire is a good general rule, but there is a role for government in banking.
(2) The radical solution to the problem of inherent instability is 100% reserves. But alternative measures such as deposit insurance, branch banking, or a central bank acting as lender of last resort may also be effective in some circumstances.
(3) Policies should be evaluated by comparing them with credible alternatives. A policy with respect to banking might be unnecessary or counter-productive given an optimal policy with respect to the growth of the stock of money, yet might be highly desirable given a less than optimal monetary policy.
(4) Provided the stock of money is being maintained at appropriate levels through open market operations the best policy for a central bank is Bagehot's rule, to lend freely on good collateral to solvent banks.
(5) If the central bank cannot be trusted to follow an optimal monetary policy, there may be a case for bailouts in which insolvent banks receive government aid in some fashion. Perhaps the central bank or the Federal Deposit Insurance Corporation could take over the bank's bad assets and merge the remainder of the insolvent bank with a solvent bank.
(6) Regulations and policies should be clearly stated and apply to all depository institutions. The radical solution, 100% reserves, is a good example.

Recent reform efforts have fallen in with the idea that banking needs strong regulation. But the goal of identifying "systemically important" financial institutions and treating them in a special way would appear to move away from the sort of regulatory framework Friedman and Schwartz favored. Their discussion of the 1930s illustrates the potential problem of trying to prevent panics with special rules for special banks. In 1930 the problem, according to Friedman and Schwartz was a wave of bank failures —many of them small unit banks—in the South and West and the failure of the Bank of United States in New York. The latter, to be sure, was a big bank, and close geographically to major Wall Street banks. But its structure still reflected its roots on New York's lower east side. Would a regulatory system based on the idea of special rules for "systemically important" banks have prevented this catastrophe?

References

Bagehot, Walter. 1924. *Lombard Street: A Description of the Money Market*, 14th ed. London: William Clowes and Sons, Limited. [1873].

Bordo, Michael, Angela Redish, and Hugh Rockoff. 2015. Why Didn't Canada Have a Banking Crisis in 2008 (or in 1930, or 1907, or …)? with Michael Bordo and Angela Redish. *The Economic History Review* 68 (1): 218–243.

Capie, Forrest. 2002. The Bank of England as a Mature Central Bank. *The Political Economy of British Historical Experience, 1688–1914*, ed. Donald Winch and Patrick O'Brien, 295–318. Oxford: Oxford University Press.

Cagan, Phillip, and Anna J. Schwartz. 1975. Has the Growth of Money Substitutes Hindered Monetary Policy? *Journal of Money, Credit and Banking* 7 (2): 137–159.

Calomiris, Charles W., and Stephen H. Haber. 2014. *Fragile by Design: The Political Origins of Banking Crises and Scarce Credit*. Princeton: Princeton University Press.

Despres, Emile, Albert G. Hart, Milton Friedman, Paul A. Samuelson, and Donald H. Wallace. 1950. The Problem of Economic Instability. *The American Economic Review* 40 (4): 501, 503 + 505–538.

Friedman, Milton. 1950. Wesley C. Mitchell as an economic theorist. *Journal of Political Economy* 58 (6): 465–493.

Friedman, Milton. 1951. Commodity-Reserve Currency. *Journal of Political Economy* 59 (3): 203–232.

Friedman, Milton. 1959. *A Program for Monetary Stability*. The Millar Lectures, vol. 3. New York: Fordham University Press.

Friedman, Milton. 1968. Why the American Economy is Depression-Proof. In *Dollars and Deficits: Inflation, Monetary Policy and the Balance of Payments*, 72–96. Englewood Cliffs, New Jersey: Prentice-Hall, Inc.

Friedman, Milton. 1970. *Interview with Milton Friedman, Penn Central Bankruptcy*. Sound Recording 53, ed. Rose D. Friedman, Instructional Dynamics, Online Archive of California.

Friedman, Milton. 1992. *Money Mischief: Episodes in Monetary History*. New York: Harcourt Brace Jovanovich.

Friedman, Milton, and Anna J. Schwartz. 1986a. The Failure of the Bank of United States: A Reappraisal: A Reply. *Explorations in Economic History* 23 (2) (04): 199–204.

Friedman, Milton, and Anna J. Schwartz. 1986b. Has Government Any Role in Money? *Journal of Monetary Economics* 17 (1) (01): 37–62.

Friedman, Milton, and Anna J. Schwartz. 1982. *Monetary Trends in the United States and the United Kingdom: Their Relation to Income, Prices, and Interest Rates, 1867–1975*. National Bureau of Economic Research Monograph. Chicago: University of Chicago Press.

Friedman, Milton, and Anna J. Schwartz. 1970. *Monetary Statistics of the United States: Estimates, Sources, Methods*. National Bureau of Economic Research. Studies in Business Cycles, vol. 20. New York: National Bureau of Economic Research.

Friedman, Milton, and Anna J. Schwartz. 1963. *A Monetary History of the United States, 1867–1960*. National Bureau of Economic research. Studies in Business Cycles, vol. 12. Princeton: Princeton University Press.

Friedman, Milton and Rose Director Friedman. 1980. *Free to Choose: A Personal Statement*. New York: Harcourt Brace Jovanovich.

Gorton, Gary. 1985. Clearinghouses and the Origin of Central Banking in the United States. *Journal of Economic History* 45 (2) (06): 277–83.

Gorton, Gary, and Donald J. Mullineaux. 1987. The Joint Production of Confidence: Endogenous Regulation and Nineteenth Century Commercial-Bank Clearinghouses. *Journal of Money, Credit, and Banking* 19 (4) (11): 457–68.

Hansen, Alvin H. 1941. *Fiscal Policy and Business Cycles*. New York: W.W. Norton & Company inc.

Hart, Albert G. 1935. The "Chicago Plan" for Banking Reform I: A Proposal for Making Monetary Management Effective in the United States. *The Review of Economic Studies* 2 (2): 104–116.

Hawtrey, R.G. 1932. *The Art of Central Banking*. London, New York etc.: Longmans, Green and Co.

Jones, Homer. 1979. Banking Reform in the 1930s. In *Regulatory Change in an Atmosphere of Crisis: Current Implications of the Roosevelt Years*, ed. Gary M. Walton, 79–92. New York: Academic Press.

Lucia, Joseph L. 1985. The Failure of the Bank of United States: A Reappraisal. *Explorations in Economic History* 22 (4): 402–416.

Mints, Lloyd W. 1950. *Monetary Policy for a Competitive Society*. Chicago: University of Chicago Press.

Moen, Jon R., and Ellis W. Tallman. 1998. Gold Shocks, Liquidity, and the United States Economy during the National Banking Era. *Explorations in Economic History* 35 (4): 381–404.

Moen, Jon R and Ellis W. Tallman. 2000. Clearinghouse Membership and Deposit Contraction during the Panic of 1907. *Journal of Economic History* 60 (1) (03): 145–163.

Moen, Jon R., and Ellis W. Tallman. 2012. Liquidity Creation without a Central Bank: Clearing House Loan Certificates in the Banking Panic of 1907. *Journal of Financial Stability* 8 (4): 277–291.

Moen, Jon R., and Ellis W. Tallman. 2014. The Transmission of the Financial Crisis in 1907: An Empirical Investigation. Federal Reserve Bank of Cleveland, Working Paper: 1409.

Morgenstern, Oskar. 1943. On the International Spread of Business Cycles. *Journal of Political Economy* 51 (4): 287–309.

Nelson, Edward. 2013. Friedman's Monetary Economics in Practice. *Journal of International Money and Finance* 38 (11): 59–83.

O'Brien, Anthony Patrick. 1992. The Failure of the Bank of United States: A Defense of Joseph Lucia: A Note. *Journal of Money, Credit, and Banking* 24 (3) (08): 374–84.

Ryssdal, Kai. 2009. Interview with Anna J. Schwartz. In Marketplace, Taking Stock: Lessons from History. June 9. [database online]. Available from http://www.marketplace.org/topics/business/taking-stock/taking-stock-lessons-history. Accessed May 29, 2013.

Samuelson, Paul. 1948. *Economics: An Introductory Analysis*. New York: McGraw-Hill Book Company Inc.

Schwartz, Anna J. 1947. The Beginning of Competitive Banking in Philadelphia, 1782–1809. *Journal of Political Economy* 55 (5): 417–431.

Schwartz, Anna J. 1979. Banking Reform in the 1930s (by Homer Jones): Discussion. In *Regulatory Change in an Atmosphere of Crisis: Current Implications of the Roosevelt Years*, ed. Gary M. Walton, 93–99. New York: Academic Press.

Schwartz, Anna J. 2009. Origins of the Financial Market Crisis of 2008. *Cato Journal* 29 (1): 19–23. (Winter).

Silber, William L. 2007. The Great Financial Crisis of 1914: What Can We Learn from Aldrich-Vreeland Emergency Currency? *American Economic Review* 97 (2) (05): 285–9.

Simons, Henry. 1948a [1934]. A Positive Program for Laissez Faire: Some Proposals for a Liberal Economic Policy. In *Economic Policy for a Free Society*, ed. Henry Simons, 40–77. Chicago: University of Chicago Press.

Simons, Henry. 1948b [1936]. Rules versus Authorities in Monetary Policy. In Henry Simons, *Economic Policy for a Free Society*, 160–183, 325–335. Chicago: University of Chicago Press.

Sorkin, Andrew Ross. 2009. *Too Big to Fail*. New York: Viking Adult.

Sprague, O. M. W. 1910. *History of Crises Under the National Banking System*. U. S. 61st cong., 2d sess. senate. doc. 538. Washington: Govt. Print. Off.

Temin, Peter. 1976. *Did Monetary Forces Cause the Great Depression?*, 1st ed. New York: Norton.

Trescott, Paul B. 1992. The failure of the Bank of the United States, 1930: A Rejoinder. *Journal of Money, Credit, and Banking* 24 (3) (08): 384–99.

Author Biography

Hugh Rockoff is a Distinguished Professor of Economics at Rutgers University in New Brunswick New Jersey and a research associate of the National Bureau of Economic Research. He received his A.B. from Earlham College in 1967 and his Ph.D. from Chicago in 1972. He has written many articles and several books on banking and monetary history and wartime economic controls. His most recent paper is "War and Inflation in the United States from the Revolution to the Persian Gulf War." In *Economic History of Warfare and State Formation*, eds. Jari Eloranta, Eric Golson, Andre Markevich, Nikolaus Wolf. His recent working papers can be found at www.nber.org.

Chapter 6
Financial Crises and the Central Bank: Lessons from Japan During the 1920s

Masato Shizume

Abstract In this chapter, we look at the conduct of prudential policy in Japan during the 1920s. A series of financial crises following a boom during World War I marked the turning point for the emergence of prudential policy in Japan. An economic backlash after the war created mounting bad loans. After the Great Kanto Earthquake in 1923, the Bank of Japan (BOJ) introduced a special treatment facility for the devastated area. The BOJ hoped to rescue solvent but illiquid financial institutions, but the facility was abused by banks that were already in financial distress, paving the way toward a financial crisis. Banking panic spread nationwide in the spring of 1927. In 1928, the authorities introduced new arrangements for prudential policy with mergers and acquisitions, new types of regulations, and dual inspection by the Ministry of Finance and the BOJ. These arrangements restored financial stability while imposing a new constraint on monetary policy.

Keywords Prudential policy · Financial crisis · Central bank · Japan

6.1 Introduction

In this chapter, we look at the conduct of prudential policy in Japan during the 1920s. Japan experienced economic stagnation and financial instability following a boom during and right after World War I (WWI). An economic backlash and the government's attempt to keep economic growth high even after the war created mounting bad loans. Then, the Great Kanto Earthquake hit the Tokyo metropolitan

Masato Shizume would like to thank participants of the Session, "How Financial Networks become Vulnerable to Crises: a Global and Historical Perspective" in XVIIth World Economic History Congress in August 2015, Kyoto for helpful comments, and Seimeikai Foundation for financial support.

M. Shizume (✉)
Faculty of Political Science and Economics, Waseda University, Tokyo, Japan
e-mail: masato.shizume@waseda.jp

© Springer Nature Singapore Pte Ltd. 2018

H. Rockoff and I. Suto (eds.), *Coping with Financial Crises*,
Studies in Economic History, https://doi.org/10.1007/978-981-10-6196-7_6

area in 1923, and the Bank of Japan (BOJ) introduced a special treatment facility for the devastated area. The BOJ's intention ex ante was to rescue solvent but illiquid banks. However, the facility was abused *ex post* by banks already in financial distress, and uncovered the moral hazard problem. In the spring of 1927, financial panic spread nationwide. The crisis accelerated long-awaited reforms. In 1928, the authorities introduced a new scheme of prudential policy encouraging mergers and acquisitions, with new regulations, and dual inspection by the Ministry of Finance (MOF) and the BOJ.

6.2 The Modern Banking System of Japan

Japan has a long tradition of its version of a lightly-regulated financial system. During the Edo Era (1603–1867), money changers supported the national markets of rice and other commodities. They accepted deposits from and extended loans to customers, transferred funds through correspondent networks, and issued paper money. Many moneychangers had their origins in commercial/industrial businesses such as rice trade, metal refining, and textile distribution. And, there was no regulation on concurrent business operations.[1]

After the opening of the treaty ports in 1859 and the following Meiji Restoration in 1868, the new government tried to establish a modern financial system by importing systems from Europe and the United States. In 1872, the government introduced the National Bank Act modeled after the United States. Japanese national banks were privately-run banks as in the United States. Under the initial National Bank Act of 1872, national banks were allowed to engage in the usual banking activities and were also authorized to issue convertible notes. In 1876, the government amended the National Bank Act, making national banknotes inconvertible. Under the new National Bank Act of 1876, national banks were allowed to issue banknotes backed by national bonds. Also in 1876, the government gave a charter to Mitsui Bank, the first private bank (*shiritsu ginko*) in Japan apart from the national banks. After that, a number of private banks were established. These private banks were chartered by the government to engage in the usual banking business, but they were not allowed to issue banknotes. While the origins of these private banks were varied, their operations depended on the managerial skills of moneychangers. At the same time, many moneychangers remained engaged in the de facto banking business without government charters. The Meiji government called such moneychangers quasi-banks.[2]

During the inflationary period after the Seinan Civil War (the last rebellion by former samurai) in 1877, the government became inclined to establishing a central bank as the sole issuer of convertible banknotes. The BOJ was established as the central bank of Japan in 1882, and the right to issue banknotes was taken from the

[1]Shizume and Tsurumi (2016, pp. 3–4).

[2]Shizume and Tsurumi (2016, pp. 4–6).

Table 6.1 Banks in Japan (1876–1925)

	National Banks		Private Banks (excl. National Banks)		Quasi-banks	
Year	Number	Total capital	Number	Total capital	Number	Total capital
1876	5	2	1	2	n.a.	n.a.
1880	151	43	39	6	120	1
1890	134	49	217	19	702	15
	Ordinary Bank		Saving Bank			
Year	Number	Total capital	Number	Total capital		
1900	1801	353	157	32		
1910	1618	437	302	72		
1920	1322	1576	661	548		
1925	1534	2387	133	90		

MOF (1938); Goto (1970); *National Statistical Abstract of the Japanese Empire* (various issues)
Note Total capital is in million yen. *The Fourth Report of the Banking Bureau* (1884) admitted that the coverage of private banks and quasi-banks was incomplete and that the statistics were underestimated

national banks and given to the BOJ alone. In 1893, the government created a savings bank system in order to promote savings among the general public. The transformation from a multiple issuing bank system to a single issuing bank system was completed in 1899. The reform lowered former national banks to the same status as other private banks. After the reform, the private banks became called ordinary banks. The number of private banks kept increasing through the late 19th century along with the development of modern industries in Japan (Table 6.1).[3]

The legacy of the Edo Era was widely utilized in the introduction of a westernized banking system. The regulations on private banks were minimal until the 1920s. At the outset of the modern banking system, there was virtually no specific banking regulation except rules for companies in general. The Bank Act and the Savings Bank Act of 1890 stipulated minimal requirements for bank operations such as limiting big loans to certain borrowers and restricting savings bank assets to safe ones. However, these acts were amended in 1895 to eliminate the limits on big loans and the savings bank asset requirements.[4]

6.3 The World War I Boom (1914–1919)

During and right after WWI, the Japanese economy experienced a boom unprecedented in Japan's modern era. Between 1915 and 1918, the Japanese economy, led by exports, grew by more than 6% annually for the four consecutive

[3]Shizume and Tsurumi (2016, pp. 6–7, 13–14).

[4]Kasuya (2000).

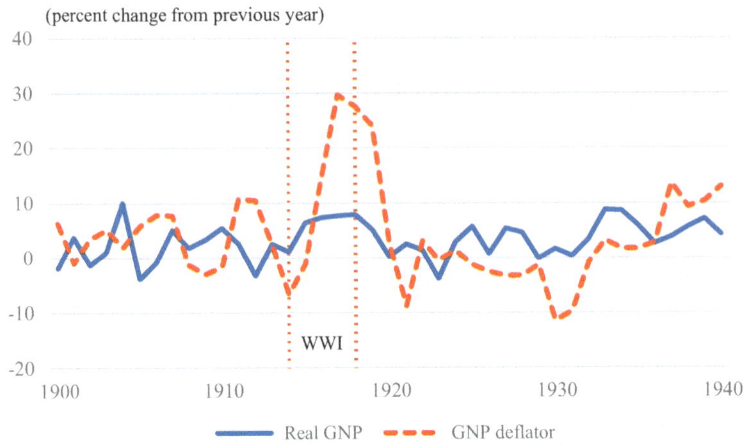

Fig. 6.1 Output and prices. Ohkawa and Shinohara (1979, pp. 256–257, pp. 387–388)

years from 1915 through 1918. In 1919, even though overseas demand shrank, the economy grew by another 5%, led by domestic consumption and supported by government expenditure. The gross national product (GNP) in 1919 was 1.41 times that in 1913. At the same time, prices increased over two-fold in the five years from 1915 through 1919 (Fig. 6.1).

In January 1920, then BOJ Governor Junnosuke Inoue warned about widespread speculation on commodities, company stocks and real estate. He stated, "We have to be cautious of some of the worrisome symptoms accompanying this boom. We see widespread speculation in all the commodities markets… Among new companies, quite a few have been set up only for seeking capital gains without clear strategies or operational plans… Even local farmers are engaged in speculation in real estate and company stocks."[5] He was also worried about the fragility in the banking sector and claimed that "From now on, more banks need to be merged or affiliated with each other."[6]

[5]"Speech by Governor Inoue at the New Year Party of the Tokyo Bills of Exchange," January 27 1920, reprinted in Inoue (1935, pp. 239–240).

[6]"Speech by Governor Inoue at the New Year Party of the Tokyo Bills of Exchange," January 27 1920, reprinted in Inoue (1935, p. 239).

Fig. 6.2 Prices on the Tokyo stock exchange. Data collected by the hypothetic Bank of Japan, archived in Asahi (1930, p. 1089)

6.4 The Postwar Collapse in 1920

With the end of the war boom, prices of commodities, company stocks, and real estate plunged. The average price of company shares listed in the Tokyo Stock Exchange (TSE) peaked at 452 yen (per paid-in capital of 100 yen) in March 1920 and fell by almost a half to 239 yen in August 1920 (Fig. 6.2).

Companies including financial institutions that were involved in speculations suffered from liquidity shortages and/or losses in inventories and other assets. Of these, the Masuda Bill Broker Bank in Osaka failed because of a liquidity shortage in April 1920, triggering bank runs in several regions throughout Japan.[7]

The Masuda Bill Broker Bank was headquartered in Osaka and had branches in the national and regional commercial centers of Tokyo, Nagoya, Kyoto, and Moji. It had been engaged in the intermediation of interbank financial transactions, and its customers had included both local banks and large city banks. Over the four months following the bank's failure, 21 banks suspended their operations either permanently or temporarily.[8]

The BOJ extended various types of "special loans" to ease tensions within financial markets in general and to relieve key industries such as silk and cotton. "Special loans" referred to various kinds of lender of last resort loans extended by the BOJ with special arrangements. They included loans exceeding the credit line per borrower, loans with extended collateral coverage, and loans to borrowers who had no ties to the BOJ as clients at that time. A total of 385-million-yen worth of

[7]Osaka: Asahi Shinbun, April 9, 1920, archived in Kobe University Newspaper Articles Archives, Economic Policy (5–086).

[8]Shizume (2009, p. 2).

"special loans" were approved and, of this, a total of 242-million-yen worth of loans were provided. Virtually all the "special loans" were repaid within a year.[9]

6.5 The Financial Panic of 1922

In 1922, the failure of a local company led to nationwide panic. Ishii Corporation, a lumber company engaged in speculative activities, went bankrupt at the end of February 1922. The failure of Ishii triggered bank runs in Kochi Prefecture (in the southwestern part of Japan) and the Kansai region (Osaka, Kyoto and their environs). This incident indicated how anxious depositors were about the financial soundness of banks in general. Then, from October through December 1922, bank runs spread far across the country, from Kyushu (the westernmost part of Japan) through Kanto (Tokyo and its environs in eastern Japan). In 1922, operations were suspended at 15 banks, either permanently or temporarily. The BOJ extended "special loans" to 20 banks from December 1922 to April 1923.[10]

In the wake of a series of financial crises, the government tightened regulations on smaller savings banks by enacting the Savings Bank Act of 1921, and it initiated reforms in the financial system as a whole, including for the larger ordinary banks. As we will see later, reforming the whole system turned out to need far more political capital than the reform of smaller savings banks.

6.6 The Great Kanto Earthquake and the Earthquake Bill Facility[11]

On September 1, 1923, a severe earthquake hit the central part of Japan, including the cities of Tokyo and Yokohama. According to a survey by the Social Bureau of the Ministry of Home Affairs, the damage to human life and property from the earthquake was as follows: In the seven prefectures of Tokyo, Kanagawa (in which the City of Yokohama located), Chiba, Saitama, Shizuoka, Yamanashi, and Ibaraki, 91,344 people were reported dead, 13,275 were reported missing, and 52,074 were reported to have been injured. The homes of 3,248,205 people were reported to have sustained damages. Twenty-nine percent of the total population of the seven prefectures suffered some form of damage from the earthquake, while 47% of Tokyo residents and 85% of Kanagawa residents suffered such damage.[12]

---

[9]The Bank of Japan (1983, pp. 10–23); Shizume (2009, p. 2, Footnote 5).

[10]Shizume (2009, p. 2).

[11]Shizume and Nanjo (2015) discuss the process and consequences of the introduction of the Earthquake Bill facility in detail.

[12]The Bank of Japan (1933, pp. 749–751).

The Research Department of the BOJ later put the total amount of physical damage at 4.57 billion yen (29.3% of the GNP in 1922), with 343 of the 448 (76.6%) bank head offices and branches located in Tokyo and virtually all of the 42 located in Yokohama having burned down.[13] Depositors feared bank losses and banks feared delays in the repayment of loans.

The government and the BOJ responded quickly. On September 7, the government promulgated an emergency ordinance to impose a moratorium, which allowed for the postponement of payments due from that month onward in the districts affected. As the deadline for payment approached, large numbers of debtors (drawers of bills) were still unable to repay their debts and the banks holding loans to such debtors were concerned about potential runs on their deposits. On September 27, the government promulgated another emergency ordinance that allowed the BOJ to discount bills issued to and/or to be paid by victims of the earthquake. The government would indemnify the BOJ for any losses incurred in the re-discounting of bills and certain other papers payable in the stricken areas (Earthquake Bills, or EBs), to a ceiling of 100 million yen.[14]

Bills eligible as EBs consisted of (i) bills discounted by banks on or before September 1, 1923, to be paid in affected areas (Tokyo, Kanagawa, Saitama, Chiba, and Shizuoka prefectures), (ii) bills discounted by banks on or before September 1, 1923, drawn or payable by parties holding business facilities in the affected areas at the time of the earthquake, (iii) bills renewing any of the above bills, etc., and (iv) bills renewing any of the bills described above and discounted by the BOJ. The BOJ may have discounted the original EBs by March 31, 1924, and the discounted bills may have been renewed.[15]

The discounted bills and renewed bills were to be paid by no later than September 30, 1925. Depositors were relieved by these special measures of the government and the BOJ. By the time the moratorium was lifted in October 1923, financial turbulence had been curbed. Meanwhile, large sums of EBs had yet to be settled.[16]

6.7 The Implementation of the Earthquake Bill Facility

At the onset, the government estimated outstanding EBs at approximately 2.1 billion yen, or the equivalent of 13% of the total of loans held by banks. Of this, 500 million yen was estimated to be discounted by the BOJ, and 100 million yen, or 20% of those bills discounted by the BOJ, were estimated to be unrecoverable and

[13]The Bank of Japan (1933, pp. 751–753).
[14]The Bank of Japan (1983, pp. 50–60).
[15]The Bank of Japan (1983, pp. 59–60).
[16]The Bank of Japan (1983, pp. 60–61); Shizume (2009, pp. 2–3).

would eventually be losses. The estimated loss was more than 80% of the equity of the BOJ.

In 1923, the amount of loans provided by the BOJ to the domestic private sector almost doubled from 344 million yen to 641 million yen. Of this, EBs worth 133 million yen, or 45% of net increase in the BOJ loans, were rediscounted.[17]

The authorities were aware of the potential trade-off between financial stability in the short-run and the prevention of a moral hazard problem in the long-run. To prevent moral hazard, the discount rate of the EBs was set at 8.76, 0.73% higher than the ordinary discount rate on commercial bills (8.03%). By doing so, the government and the BOJ's intention ex ante was to supply liquidity only to solvent parties. However, in reality, it was difficult to evaluate the solvency of related parties in such an emergency. In the course of events, the BOJ needed to take decisive action to avoid turbulence in business conditions, even if it was not convinced that it could properly evaluate the solvency of each bank and debtor. As a result, bills not directly related to the earthquake crept into the EBs discounted by the BOJ.

The biggest moral hazard was the case of the Bank of Taiwan (BOT) and its client, Suzuki and Company. The BOT was a Japanese colonial bank established in 1899. It issued bank notes in Taiwan as well as engaged in the usual banking operations in Taiwan and in mainland Japan. During WWI, it increased lending to companies related to Taiwan, such as Suzuki, a trading house based in Kobe, owning camphor factories and sugar mills, and importing those items from Taiwan. Suzuki did very well during the war but suffered poor business performance after the post-WWI panic in 1920. While the BOT tried to bailout Suzuki, Suzuki resisted retreating from troubled business activities.[18]

The amount of loans to the BOT by the BOJ was relatively modest when the discounting of EBs began in September 1923. However, as the deadline for new discounting approached, the bills brought by the BOT, mainly in connection with the distressed Suzuki, stood out within the total amount of EBs. While the discounting of the EBs from the BOT did not stand out on a daily balance basis, the BOT did stand out in the total amount of the bills presented by the deadline (Table 6.2). Apparently, the BOT had exploited the status of a devastated institution and brought as many bills as issued by its indebted customers to the discount window of the BOJ. Though Suzuki had offices in the Tokyo-Yokohama area, its main office in Kobe was far from "the affected area" and the physical damage it suffered was relatively small.[19]

In April 1924, the BOJ first noticed that the BOT was using the EBs to raise short-term funds. On April 19, 1924, a notice to branch managers from the manager of the BOJ's Supervision Department reports, "The balance discounted under the

---

[17]Shizume and Nanjo (2015).

[18]Shizume and Nanjo (2015).

[19]Shizume and Nanjo (2015).

Table 6.2 Amount of the earthquake bills discounted by the BOJ (September 1923–March 1924)

Bank	Earthquake bills (thousand yen)	Share (percent)
Bank of Taiwan	115,225	26.7
Fujimoto Bill Broker Bank	37,214	8.6
Bank of Chosen	35,987	8.4
Yasuda Bank	25,000	5.8
Murai Bank	20,429	4.7
Total	430,816	100.0

Ehiro (2000, p. 116)

imperial emergency ordinance was 126,180,000 yen at the end of the preceding month, the deadline for new discounting. Collection of the discounted bills are delayed… The amount of the discounted bills continues to increase, even in the middle of the month, mainly due to demands from the BOT for loans having the nature of call loans."[20]

In the course of events, the moral hazard problem became increasingly apparent, and the discounting of the EBs turned out to be a means of relief for insolvent banks contrary to its original purpose (Table 6.3). The BOJ was not able to find an exit from entrenched lending. Settlement did not proceed smoothly, and, due to political pressure, the discount rate of the EBs was lowered to the same level as the ordinary discount rate on commercial bills in December 1924, and the payment deadline was extended twice, once in March 1925 and again in March 1926, and finally set to be September 30, 1927.[21]

6.8 The Financial Crisis of 1927 (the Showa Crisis)

In January 1927, the government incorporated new measures into two legislative bills associated with the disposal of the EBs. In the proposed legislation, the government would issue government bonds of up to 100 million yen to compensate the BOJ for losses resulting from the discounting of the EBs. The government bonds would be lent to banks holding unsettled EBs based on the balance remaining after deducting the BOJ's losses, which is the amount of compensation received from the government. Banks holding EBs would be allowed to apply for the government bond loans only if they had concluded loan agreements for redemption in yearly installments with their debtors. The government bond loans were to be

[20]"Notice from the head of the Supervision Department to branch managers, 19 April 1924," BOJ archive document no. 70,543, *Supervision Department Report*, Oct. 1923–June 1925, cited in Shizume and Nanjo (2015).

[21]The Bank of Japan (1983, pp. 95–102, 106–109).

Table 6.3 Unsettled balance of the earthquake bills (December 1926)

Bank	Discounted by March 1924 (thousand yen)	Share (%)	Unsettled at December 1926 (thousand yen)	Share (%)
Bank of Taiwan	115,225	26.7	100,035	48.4
Fujimoto Bill Broker Bank	37,214	8.6	2181	1.1
Bank of Chosen	35,987	8.4	21,606	10.4
Yasuda Bank	25,000	5.8	0.0	0.0
Murai Bank	20,429	4.7	15,204	7.4
Total	430,816	100.0	206,800	100.0

Ehiro (2000, p. 1160)

paid back with interest rates of 5% or higher and the terms of the loans were not to exceed 10 years.[22]

The two legislative bills related to the resolution of EBs were tabled in the Diet session on January 26, 1927. After passing the House of Representatives (the Lower House) on March 4, they moved on to the House of Peers (the Upper House). On March 12, the supplementary budget for fiscal 1927, which was attached to the legislation, was submitted to the Diet session. Discussion of the legislation got underway as part of the deliberations on the supplementary budget bill. In the deliberations, the legislation ran afoul of attacks by the opposition Seiyu-Kai Party, which charged that the measures amounted to the use of public funds to provide relief for an individual businesses and banks (Suzuki and the BOT). On March 23, the Diet approved the new legislation for the final resolution of the EBs.[23]

Financial panic erupted during these deliberations, triggered by a mistaken remark by Finance Minister Naoharu Kataoka on March 14, in the House of Representatives budget committee. He stated, "As a matter of fact, Watanabe Bank in Tokyo finally went bankrupt around noon today," even though Watanabe Bank had not yet failed.

In the wake of the panic, the Cabinet tried to issue an emergency ordinance authorizing the BOJ to provide relief funds to the BOT, and indemnifying the BOJ for any losses incurred by this action up to a ceiling of 200 million yen. The Privy Council, the body invested with the authority to approve the emergency ordinance, politicized the Cabinet's plan and rejected it on April 17. Then, financial panic spread nationwide. The government declared a moratorium on payments (bank holiday) on April 22 to last until May 13. The BOJ extended its credit from 506 million yen on April 8 to 2096 million yen on April 25. Finally, the panic

[22]The Bank of Japan (1983, pp. 233–234).

[23]The Bank of Japan (1983, p. 169).

Table 6.4 Balances of the BOJ's loans to the private sector and banknotes in circulation (million yen)

Date		BOJ loans	Change	Banknotes	Change
1927/3/14	Monday	228	n.a.	1088	n.a.
1927/3/18	Friday	265	37	1101	13
1927/3/25	Friday	557	292	1325	224
1927/4/1	Friday	516	−41	1324	−1
1927/4/8	Friday	506	−10	1209	−115
1927/4/15	Friday	554	48	1204	−5
1927/4/16	Saturday	581	27	1226	22
1927/4/17	Sunday	–	–	–	–
1927/4/18	Monday	870	289	1497	271
1927/4/19	Tuesday	1002	132	1626	129
1927/4/20	Wednesday	1063	61	1679	53
1927/4/21	Thursday	1665	602	2318	639
1927/4/22	Friday	1671	6	2328	10
1927/4/23	Saturday	1677	6	2334	6
1927/4/24	Sunday	–	–	–	–
1927/4/25	Monday	2096	419	2660	326
1927/4/26	Tuesday	1932	−164	2448	−212
1927/4/27	Wednesday	1693	−239	2216	−232
1927/4/28	Thursday	1559	−134	2081	−135
1927/4/29	Friday (holiday)	–	–	–	–
1927/4/30	Saturday	1484	−75	2037	−44

The Bank of Japan (1983, p. 173, 179)

subsided.[24] Table 6.4 shows the loans made by the BOJ and the banknotes outstanding during the crisis. An increase in the amount of notes in circulation is an indicator that depositors are making withdrawals.

6.9 Acceleration of Financial System Reforms

Major progress towards the resolution of the 1920s financial instability was made in 1927, when structural reforms in the banking sector gained momentum in step with measures to dispose of the bad loans. The new Banking Act was promulgated on March 30, 1927, in the midst of the Showa Financial Crisis, with plans for effectuation on January 1, 1928. The Act stipulated minimum capital requirements for banks and prohibited banks and bank managers from conducting most non-banking businesses.

[24]The Bank of Japan (1983, pp. 169–181); Shizume (2009, p. 3).

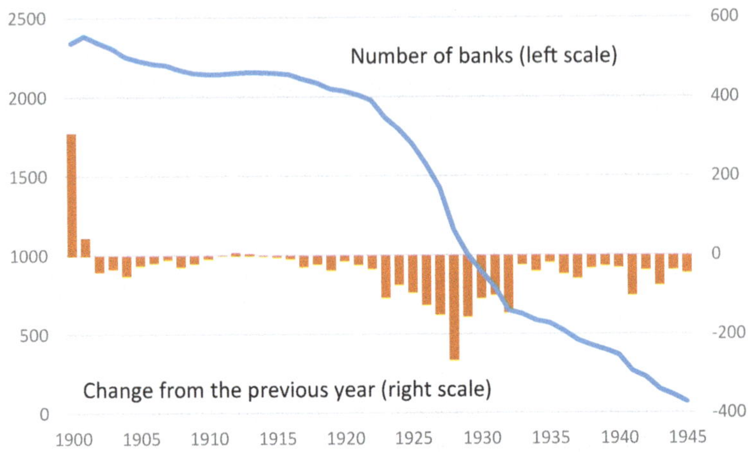

Fig. 6.3 The number of banks in Japan. Goto (1970, pp. 56–58)

Under this Act, the authorities established the prudential policy in a systematic way for the first time, reinforcing bank examination and encouraging the amalgamation of banks to stabilize the financial system as a whole.[25] To this end, the Ministry of Finance established the Bank Examination Division under its Banking Bureau in 1927, and the BOJ established its Supervision Department in 1928.[26]

After the crisis in 1927, mergers and acquisitions accelerated. The number of banks in Japan peaked in 1901 as it reached 2385, and stayed at over 2000 until 1921. Though the number declined steadily through the 1920s, 1577 banks still existed in 1926. The trend accelerated in 1927 with a drastic increase in mergers and acquisitions. The number decreased by 150 in 1927 and by 265 in 1928. In 1932, only 650 banks existed (Fig. 6.3).

At the same time, the Japanese banking system transformed from unit banking to branch banking. In 1900, the average number of offices per ordinary bank was 1.74, meaning that most banks operated only in their head offices and had no branches. The number was 4.76 in 1926 and jumped to 7.06 in 1927. In 1929, it reached to 8.97, meaning that ordinary banks had eight branches on average. This is shown in Table 6.5.

---

[25]Shizume (2009, pp. 3–4).

[26]The Bank of Japan (1983, pp. 286–292).

Table 6.5 Average number of offices per Ordinary Bank

Year	1900	1910	1920	1925	1926	1927	1928	1929
Number	1.74	2.05	3.11	4.49	4.76	7.06	8.12	8.97

Goto (1970, p. 86)

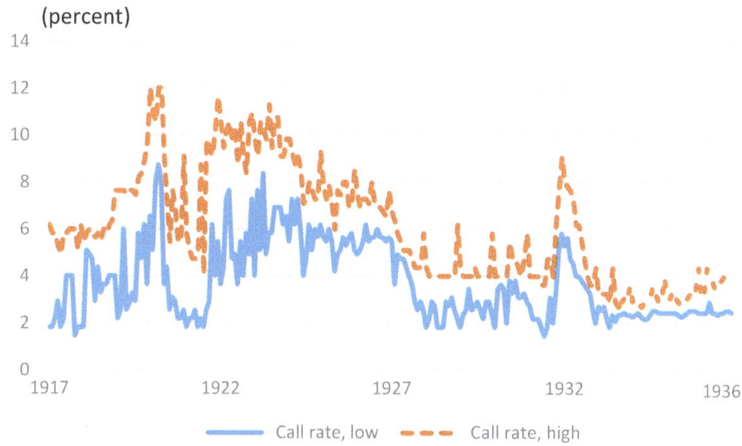

Fig. 6.4 Interbank interest rates. The Ministry of Finance, *reference book of financial matters*, annual editions

6.10 Restored Financial Stability

Supported by the banking reforms and public funding, financial stability was finally restored. Figure 6.4 shows developments in the call rates, the representative interest rates for the short-term interbank transactions. Call rates remained high between the financial panic of 1922 and the Showa Financial Crisis of 1927, reflecting high risk premiums. A number of banks with high risk profiles, such as the BOT, tried to raise funds in the interbank market over that period. Aware of the credit risk of the distressed banks and instability in the financial market in general, lenders required high risk premiums. Call rates decreased substantially in the spring of 1927, as market participants gained confidence from the new Banking Act, the resolution of the financial crisis, and the BOJ's liquidity provisioning.[27,28]

Kamekichi Takahashi, a prominent contemporary economist and ex-editor of *Toyo Keizai Shinpo* (the Oriental Economist) argued that the reforms of the domestic financial system after the financial crisis of 1927 helped Japan respond effectively to the Great Depression in the 1930s:

[27]Shizume (2009, p. 4).

[28]Okazaki (2007) argues that the BOJ carefully selected borrowers in order to avoid the moral hazard problem when extending LLR loans in this occasion.

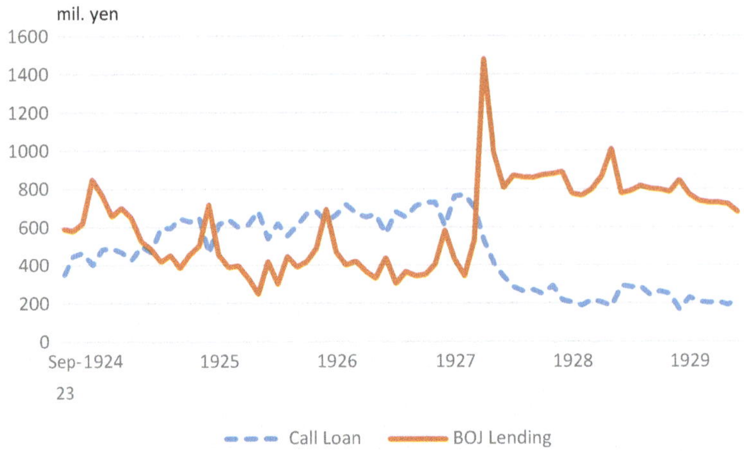

Fig. 6.5 Interbank loans and BOJ credit. The Ministry of Finance, *reference book for financial matters*, various issues

> A number of leading industrial countries suffered from the World Financial Crisis, a financial collapse without precedent, in the third quarter of 1931 (in the case of the United States, the crisis hit in the first quarter of 1933). For many years to follow, the economic activities of these countries were severely disrupted by the financial collapse. Yet Japan remained immune to the financial crisis of the 1930s, enjoying the benefits of the policy changes and the depreciation of the yen… This could be credited to the total restructuring of Japan's banking system in the wake of the financial crisis of 1927.[29]

We should note that the financial stability was also supported by the provision of liquidity by the BOJ. Until the financial crisis of 1927,. the BOJ extended its credit to private banks at the level of around four hundred million yen. It jumped during the crisis and stayed at around eight hundred million yen through the rest of the 1920s, substituting call loans to banks with high risk profiles (Fig. 6.5).

6.11 The Enduring Moral Hazard Problem

Junnosuke Inoue who was the BOJ Governor in 1923, was appointed as the Finance Minister immediately after the Great Kanto Earthquake and played a central role in implementing the EB facility during the initial phase, and was later appointed as the BOJ Governor once again.

Inoue recalled in the meeting of directors and branch managers of the BOJ in May 1928 that the BOJ's efforts for relief finance in the 1920s had gone too far. He said, "From the perspective of the BOJ's policy tradition, there has been much to

[29]Takahashi (1955b, pp. 1315–1316), translated and cited in Shizume (2009, p. 4).

regret about its actions since 1920. The irregular measures after the earthquake in 1923 were a notable example… The attitude of the BOJ during that period was one that should not be tolerated in light of the standards of a central bank."[30]

Eigo Fukai, executive director of the BOJ during the financial crisis of 1927, who later served as Vice Governor and Governor, recalled about the BOJ's experience in the 1920s:

> When we saw the risk of financial distress, we conducted special rescue measures from time to time, stepping into a muddle… When we conducted an individual special accommodation, we saw little cost to dealing with it. We saw little risk of deterioration in monetary conditions. We saw great risk of contagion if the bank failure became open. So, we judged that it was necessary… In retrospect, it was difficult to exit from recurrent cases of special accommodation when the economic conditions changed in such a drastic way. As a result, public sentiment turned to think that the main task of the BOJ should be to rescue businesses through special accommodations.[31]

6.12 Implications for Monetary Policy

The entrenchment of lending by the central bank imposed a new constraint on the operation of monetary policy. After the financial crisis of 1927, most of the lending by the BOJ to the private sector consisted of special loans. Though they were guaranteed by the government, the funds could not be easily removed from the financial markets. The BOJ had to bear the loss of flexibility in its monetary policy operation. This is confirmed in Fig. 6.6 which shows that special loans came to dominate BOJ lending.

Eigo Fukai recalled:

> Loans by the issuing bank should be repaid in the short-term in a prompt manner. If this procedure is secured, the money stock remains stable because when someone invests his/her surplus funds, the investment will eventually be repaid by the deadline. However, if the funds are provided by the issuing bank and the policy is entrenched, there is no way to get the funds repaid. For example, assume Bank A borrows from the issuing bank to repay deposits. The depositors withdraw the funds from Bank A and deposit them in Bank B. If Bank B has borrowed short-term funds from the issuing bank, Bank B may repay its loans borrowed from the issuing bank. Then, even if the money stock remains stable, the short-term lending of the issuing bank to Bank B transforms into an entrenched lending to Bank A in this process. Looking at it from the issuing bank's perspective, a loan to a sound bank turns out to be an entrenched loan to a troubled bank. That is, a bad loan drives out a good loan. If this process continues, in the end, all loans of the issuing bank become entrenched, and the bank has no way to get its loans repaid.[32]

---

[30]BOJ archive document no. 9293, Branch manager conference documents (Spring 1927–fall 1928).

[31]Fukai (1941, pp. 197–198).

[32]Fukai (1928, pp. 442–443).

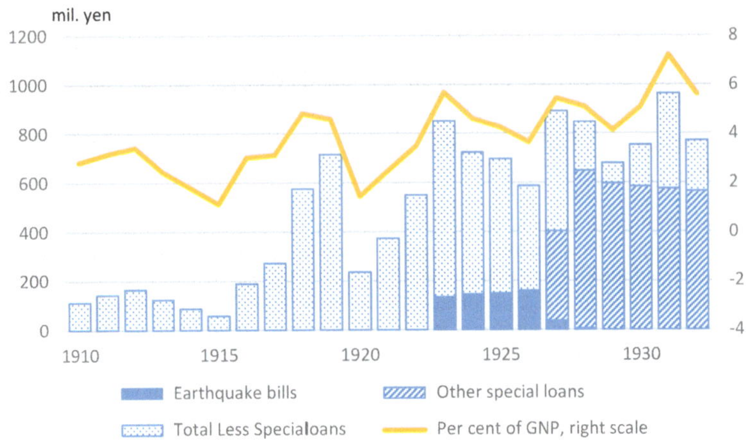

Fig. 6.6 The BOJ's loans to the private sector. The Ministry of Finance, *reference book for financial matters*, various issues

6.13 Lessons for Today

From the experience of Japan in the 1920s we can draw a number of lessons for today's monetary and prudential policies.

First, although the authorities were aware of the bad loan problem caused by inappropriate investments during and right after WWI from the first, the required reforms were postponed due to political difficulties, resulting in the deepening and widening of the problem. Kamekichi Takahashi wrote:

> The fundamental causes of the financial crisis of 1927 were the cumulative mismanagement of cover-ups and halfway measures against earlier flaws dating back to the post-war collapse. These problems were revealed inadvertently during the debate on EBs, igniting the explosion of the financial crisis.[33]

Second, the BOJ's intention *ex ante* was to provide liquidity to solvent financial institutions and to improve the conditions of financial intermediation after the Great Kanto Earthquake. However, it was difficult to evaluate risk profiles of debtors in the midst of an emergency, and the operation of the discounting of EBs resulted in rescuing already insolvent financial institutions. The course of events delayed the disposal of bad loans, exacerbated the moral hazard problem, and paved the way for the financial crisis of 1927.

Third, once the financial crisis erupted, a momentum toward reforms was soon built, and the long-awaited reforms proceeded decisively. In a sense, the crisis accelerated the reforms. Kamekichi Takahashi also wrote, "The unimaginable

[33]Takahashi (1955a, p. 739), translated and cited in Shizume (2009, p. 4).

financial panic induced drastic reforms in the banking system, whether people liked it or not. The panic contributed to many of the reforms that were to follow."[34]

Fourth, even though the central bank could restore the financial stability with its liquidity provisioning, it had to endure lasting constraints on its operation in monetary policy matters. As Eigo Fukai remarked in his book in 1928, prudential policy and monetary policy could not be separated in the operation of central banking.

References

Asahi Shinbun Sha. 1930. *Comprehensive Volume of Japanese Economic Statistics*. Tokyo: Asahi Shinbun Sha (in Japanese).

Ehiro, A. 2000. Financial Crises and the Introduction of Public Funds: Responses to the Financial Crises of the 1920s. In *Financial Crises and Reforms: From History to Present*, ed. by M. Itoh, M. Tsurumi, and Y. Asai. Tokyo: Nihon Keizai Hyoron Sha (in Japanese).

Fukai, E. 1928. *A Treatise of Monetary Control*. Tokyo: Nihon Hyoron Sha. (in Japanese).

Fukai, E. 1941. *Reflections of 70 Years*. Tokyo: Iwanami Shoten. (in Japanese).

Goto, S. 1970. *Japanese Financial Statistics*. Tokyo: Toyo Keizai Shinpo Sha. (in Japanese).

Inoue, J. (1935). *Collections of Writings of Inoue Junnosuke*. Tokyo: The Editorial Committee of Collections of Writings of Inoue Junnosuke (in Japanese).

Kasuya, M. 2000. The Establishment of a Financial System, and the Bank Act and Savings Bank Act. In *Financial Crises and Renovation: From History to Present*, ed. by M. Itoh, M. Tsurumi, & Y. Asai. Tokyo: Nihon Keizai Hyoron Sha (in Japanese).

Ohkawa, K., and M. Shinohara (eds.). 1979. *Patterns of Japanese Economic Development: A Quantitative Appraisal*. New Haven: Yale University Press.

Okazaki, T. 2007. Micro-Aspects of Monetary Policy: Lender of Last Resort and Selection of Banks. *Explorations in Economic History* 44: 657–679.

Shizume, M. 2009. The Japanese Economy During the Interwar Period: Instability in the Financial System and the Impact of the World Depression. *Bank of Japan Review*, 2009-E-2, Reprinted by A. Ögren & L.F. Øksendal. 2012. *The Gold Standard Peripheries: Monetary Policy, Adjustment and Flexibility in a Global Setting*, 211–228. London: Palgrave Macmillan Studies in Banking and Financial Institutions.

Shizume, M., and T. Nanjo. 2015. *Making Credit Policy in Japan: The Earthquake Bills in 1923 and the Aftermath*. Tokyo: Mimeo.

Shizume, M., and M. Tsurumi. 2016. Modernizing the Financial System in Japan During the 19th Century: National Banks in Japan in the Context of Free Banking. WINPEC Working Paper, No. E1607. Tokyo: Waseda University.

Takahashi, K. 1955a. *A History of Economic Fluctuations during Taisho and Showa Eras 2*. Tokyo: Toyo Keizai Shinpo Sha. (in Japanese).

Takahashi, K. 1955b. *A History of Economic Fluctuations during Taisho and Showa Era 3*. Tokyo: Toyo Keizai Shinposha. (in Japanese).

Takahashi, K., and S. Morigaki. 1993. *A History of the Showa Financial Crisis*. Tokyo: Toyo Keizai Shinposha. (in Japanese).

The Bank of Japan. 1933. Japan's Business Sector From the Great Kanto Earthquake Through the Financial Crisis in 1927. In *Historical Materials of Japanese Finance, Meiji and Taisho Eras*,

[34]Takahashi and Morigaki (1993, p. 289), translated and cited in Shizume (2009, p. 4).

Reprinted in the Bank of Japan ed. (1958), vol. 22, 737–1112. Tokyo: Printing Bureau, the Ministry of Finance (in Japanese).
The Bank of Japan. 1983. *The First One Hundred Years*, vol. 3. Tokyo: The Bank of Japan (in Japanese).
The Ministry of Finance. 1938. *Financial History of Meiji-Taisho Era*. Tokyo: Zaisei Keizai Gakkai. (in Japanese).

Author Biography

Masato Shizume is one of the leading experts in Japan on monetary and financial history. Formerly at the Bank of Japan he is now Professor in Faculty of Political Science and Economics, Waseda University. Among his many articles are "Bank of Japan's monetary policy in the 1980s: a view perceived from archived and other materials" written with Masanao Itoh and Ryoji Koike, "Exchange rate adjustment, monetary policy and fiscal stimulus in Japan's escape from the Great Depression" with Masahiko Shibamoto, "Sustainability of public debt: evidence from Japan before the Second World War," and "Why countries adopt the gold standard? Lessons from Japan" with Kris James Mitchener and Marc D. Weidenmier.

Chapter 7
Economic and Social Backgrounds of Top Executives of the Federal Reserve Before and After the Great Depression

Isao Suto

Abstract The main purpose of this study is to survey the processes of governance reform during the Great Depression and their effects on the economic and social backgrounds of the Federal Reserve System's top executives. When confronted by the financial crisis, Congress restructured the Federal Reserve Banks by imposing greater uniformity in structure and control by the Federal Reserve Board in Washington, and Chairman Eccles accomplished a partial purge of the Federal Reserve's management without revision of the Federal Reserve Act by asking Federal Reserve Banks to adhere to the policy regime as set by the Federal Reserve Board. First, we trace the evolution of the governance and membership of the directors and governors/presidents of the Federal Reserve Banks. Second, we observe annual trends in the economic and social backgrounds of the top executive groups of the Federal Reserve from 1915 to 1955 and examine how the Banking Act of 1935 and the partial purge of old-line executives in the mid-1930s affected their backgrounds. We conclude that Eccles' governance reforms had some impact on the executives' ages, levels of education, industrial origins, and lengths of service, and some economic and social networks, including political and religious affiliations, were operating in the Federal Reserve's top executive groups.

Keywords Economic and social backgrounds · Federal reserve
Financial community · Great depression · Panics

I. Suto (✉)
School of Political Science and Economics, Meiji University, 1-1 Kanda-Surugadai,
Chiyoda-Ku, 101-8301 Tokyo, Japan
e-mail: suto@meiji.ac.jp

© Springer Nature Singapore Pte Ltd. 2018

H. Rockoff and I. Suto (eds.), *Coping with Financial Crises*,
Studies in Economic History, https://doi.org/10.1007/978-981-10-6196-7_7

7.1 Introduction[1]

The 2010 Dodd-Frank Wall Street Reform bill attempted to engineer a "fundamental change to the Federal Reserve that would shift power from the Reserve Banks around the country and concentrate it in Washington and New York" (Irwin and Cho 2010, p. A01). The board of directors of the Federal Reserve Bank of New York (New York Bank) would be appointed by the U.S. President. Employees or stockholders of banks would be also prohibited from serving on the board of directors of all the Federal Reserve Bank (Reserve Bank). The Dodd-Frank Act, however, removed every mention of "New York" from the text of Articles, and also excluded Class A directors of the board, who represented leading banks, from voting for the president of any Reserve Bank.[2] This was not the first time that questions have been raised regarding governance of the Federal Reserve System and drastic reforms undertaken. When confronted by the financial crisis in the early 1930s, Congress restructured the Reserve Banks by imposing greater uniformity in structure and control by the Board of Governors of the Federal Reserve System (FRB), and Marriner Eccles, FRB Chairman, accomplished a partial purge of the Reserve Bank management without revision of the Federal Reserve Act. Eccles executed a partial purge of old-line executives in the Reserve Banks as well as the FRB in Washington, asking all executives of the Federal Reserve to adhere to the policy regime as set by the Federal Open Market Committee (FOMC).

Why did Chairman Eccles remove old-line executives from the Federal Reserve System, and why did Congress exclude bankers from voting for Reserve Bank president? To answer these questions, it is first of all necessary to define the persons in whom lawmakers of the original Federal Reserve Act entrusted to lead the Reserve Bank and FRB. It is largely overlooked that the transfer of leadership to the FRB was enforced not by amendment of the original Federal Reserve Act but by extraordinary means. The Banking Act of 1935 admitted that the Reserve Banks' boards of directors will appoint their presidents "with the approval of the FRB" and

[1] I thank Michael Bordo, John A. James, Carolyn Moehling, Hugh Rockoff, Eugene White, and all participants in the Workshop in Money, History and Finance at Rutgers University on November 15, 2010, and 2011 Spring Annual Meeting of the Japan Society of Monetary Economics at Meiji University, for their helpful comments and conversations. I also thanks to the participants in the session "How Financial Networks become Vulnerable to Crises: a Global and Historical Perspective" at the World Economic History Congress (Kyoto, August 3–7, 2015) for their comments and suggestions, and especially to Michael Bordo and Hugh Rockoff for their encouragement to my project. They are not responsible, however, for any remaining errors. And I am grateful to the Japan Society for the Promotion of Science (JSPS) for the 2010–2012 Grant-in-Aid for Scientific Research (C), No. 22530352 and to Gaurav Jain for his excellent research assistance.

[2] See Dodd–Frank Wall Street Reform and Consumer Protection Act of 2010, Title XI, Sect. 1107, which states as following: "The president shall be the chief executive officer of the bank and shall be appointed by the Class B and Class C directors of the bank, with the approval of the Board of Governors of the Federal Reserve System, for a term of 5 years; and all other executive officers and all employees of the bank shall be directly responsible to the president."

have 5 representatives out of the 12 FOMC members, whereas it said nothing about the boards of directors' other powers. The Reserve Bank's board of directors chairpersons could be deprived of their significant power at the FRB's discretion. Chairman Eccles would also wrest leadership from every old-line bankers who controlled the Federal Reserve System so that the FRB headed the FOMC, which was newly constituted by manageable members.

The old-line bankers swept out of office by Eccles had diverse economic and social backgrounds. The Federal Reserve Act as well as rules of both Reserve Banks and FRB required executive officers to have specific economic and social backgrounds. Specifically, some Reserve Bank's directors should have particular industrial backgrounds or experience with the exception of some occupations, and should have a history of residence in their districts. It has often been noted that the FRB members implicitly maintained a balance between political parties. Karl R. Bopp, who joined the Philadelphia Bank as director of personnel and served as Bank president from 1958 to1970, approved the unique composition of the Reserve bank directorates because "an active conflict of interests represented by the several types of directors would yield a sound policy." Then he opined: "central banks are human institutions. As a consequence, mere changes in laws are not always sufficient to produce the changes, which are necessary to achieve designed results. And […] changes in the personnel or in the human elements alone are at times sufficient to produce changes in policy—even without changes in the law."[3]

The purpose of this chapter is to survey the processes of the governance reform during the Great Depression, and these changes' effects on the economic and social backgrounds of the Federal Reserve System's top executive groups. However, we aim not to confirm that these economic and social backgrounds possessed by top executives affected management and policy of the Federal Reserve, even though we are interested in relationship between the Federal Reserve officials' policy orientation and their economic and social backgrounds. Barro and McCleary (2003, 2006) indicate that social background in terms of religion effects economic growth and conversely.

Miller (1961), Brimmer (1972), Havrilesky et al. (1973), and Havrilesky (1986) reported on the backgrounds of some board members and/or other top executives after World War II for the most part.[4] They focused on the directors' backgrounds in terms of possessing unduly narrow diversity for a public institution of the Federal Reserve. The Committee on the History of the Federal Reserve System gathered to write the "Comprehensive History of the Federal Reserve System" in 1954–1955. The Committee (1955) also surveyed the profiles of all 686 Reserve Bank directors

---

[3]Bopp (1935, p. 531). He was a faculty at University of Missouri from 1931 to 1941.

[4]Ervin Miller discussed the occupational backgrounds of the Class C directors, Andrew F. Brimmer, the FRB member, focused on the backgrounds of three classes of directors in 1957, 1967, and 1972. Thomas Havrilesky surveyed the directors' industrial origins during 1950–1970 and 1972–1983.

serving between 1914 and 1955.[5] In this chapter, we separate these individual profiles into annual data so that it is possible to analyze trends in the top executives' economic and social backgrounds, and to compare them with the Reserve Bank presidents and FRB members on a year-to-year basis. We also discuss any change in director's election process and governance of the Reserve Banks and impacts on their governance resulting from the Great Depression, as well as provide a benchmark with which to compare the effectiveness of recent financial reforms.

In Sect. 7.2, we describe how the board of directors of the Reserve Banks were elected or, depending on their status, appointed by the FRB, and how this process changed over time. The board of directors' chairpersons served alongside the governor, who was granted the new title of president in 1936, and this dual leadership sometimes caused confusion in the Reserve Banks' management. We consider, in Sect. 7.3, how the governance of the Reserve Banks was structured, and how directors and chairs exercised their power, and how its governance was restructured by a partial purge of the Reserve Bank management as well as the Banking Act of 1935, which is discussed in Sect. 7.4. Finally, in Sect. 7.5, we observe annual trends in the economic and social backgrounds of top executive groups of the Federal Reserve System in 1915–1955, and offer conclusions regarding how the governance reform affected the boards' economic and social composition.

7.2 Election and Appointment of Reserve Bank Directors

The Federal Reserve Act designed the Federal Reserve System so that both large and small banks would have similar degrees of representation on Reserve Banks' boards of directors as well as have equal responsibility for governance of the Federal Reserve System. According to Owen D. Young, director of the New York Bank, the Act "is like the Constitution of the United States" so that "at best, it can only draw the outline of the picture, and if it had been entirely wisely drawn it would have omitted many details which were inserted."[6] Therefore, in this section, we first describe the election rules for directors, how the election process was amended, and then how directors, including those appointed by the FRB in Washington, were actually elected or appointed. This section discusses basic issues of structure and function because such an overview appears to be absent from the literature.

---

[5]The Committee started as a program supported by the Rockefeller Foundation on January 21, 1954, but stopped substantially because Allan Sproul, chair of the committee, retired as president of New York Bank, and W. Randolph Burgess, who committed to write a history, was appointed as an Undersecretary of the Treasury. In 1956, the project was moved to Brooking Institution, and most documents of the Committee except some, including personal files, were opened to the public on the FRASER website of the St. Louis Bank.

[6]Young to Strong, March 31, 1927, p. 3, Young Papers, Box 263, 463H.

A Reserve Bank is a corporation chartered by the Federal Government for "a period of twenty years from its organization" (Federal Reserve Act, Sect. 4).[7] Member banks own the Reserve Bank's entire capital stock. National banks must be a member of one of the 12 Reserve Banks, while state-chartered banks, including trust companies, can become members if they meet certain conditions.

A Reserve Bank's operations were "conducted under the supervision and control of a board of directors" (Federal Reserve Act, Sect. 4). Because the Reserve Bank had no stockholder meetings under the Federal Reserve Act, director elections offered the only means of control. The directors comprised nine members across three classes. Three Class "A" directors represented stockholding banks while three Class "B" directors, who represented industrial customers, must be "actively engaged in their District in commerce, agriculture, or some other industrial pursuit." The remaining Class "C" directors represented the public interest and were appointed by the FRB. Class B and Class C directors should not "be an officer, director, employee, or stockholder of any bank." One Class C director was designated by the FRB as chair of the board of directors and Federal Reserve agent. Another Class C director was designated by the FRB as deputy chair and deputy Federal Reserve agent, and this director exercised the power of the chair "in case of absence or disability of his principal." Every Class C director must have had "at least two years residence of the District," and the directors who were designated as chair and deputy chair must have had "tested banking experience" All this is summarized in Table 7.1.

Section 7.4 of the Federal Reserve Act laid out detailed instructions regarding director elections. Class A and Class B directors were to be elected by three bank groups, which were classified according to capital and surplus. Each group was allowed to elect one Class A director and one Class B director. Each group contained "as nearly as may be one-third of the aggregate number of the member banks of the district and shall consist, as nearly as may be, of banks of similar capitalization" These requirements are summarized in Table 7.2.

The left column of Table 7.3 shows that member banks of the New York Bank were divided initially into three groups, each comprising 160 or 159 banks. Electors from each bank group could nominate one Class A director and one Class B director and could vote for a first and second choice of director in each class from the candidate list.

The election process was, however, amended by the Act of September 26, 1918. First, voting group classifications were changed so that "each group shall consist as nearly as may be of banks of similar capitalization."[8] According to a statement by the FRB, the original grouping resulted in low voter turnout due to the absence of

[7]However, the Act of February 25, 1927 provided for indeterminate charters. The original Act is in Federal Reserve Board, *Annual Report for 1914*, pp. 25–44.

[8]The full text of this Amendment Act is in *Federal Reserve Bulletin*, October 1918, pp. 947–948.

Table 7.1 Summary of Board of Directors of the Reserve Bank

Class	Class A	Class B	Class C
Number of Directors	3	3	3 (Including chair and deputy chair)
Constituency or Appointer	– Member banks	– Member banks	– FRB
Method of Election or Nomination	– Election	– Election	– Nomination
Representing Interests	– Representative of member banks	– Actively engage in their district in commerce, agriculture, or some other industrial pursuit	– FRB or Public Interest
Ineligible	– No senator nor congressman	No senator nor congressman	– No senator nor congressman
	– Officer or director of more than one member bank shall not be eligible for nomination as a class A director except by banks in the same group as the bank having the largest aggregate resources after 1918	– No officer, director, nor employee of any bank	– No officer, director employee, nor stock-holder of any bank
		– No national bank examiner after 1915*	
		– No officer of insurance company after 1925*	
		– No president of federal savings & loan association after 1939*	
Requirement			– Chair must have at least 2 years residence in the district
			– Chair and deputy chair have "tested banking experience"
		– Have the interest of agriculture, commerce, industry, service, labor, and consumers after 1977	
Term of Service	3 Years, reappointed		

Federal Reserve Bank of New York, *Circular*, No. 2127, October 1, 1940
Note *With advice of the FRB

Table 7.2 Organization of the Reserve Bank's Board of Directors

Class	Director	Voting Group or Appointer
A	A1	Group 1 (Large Banks)
	A2	Group 2 (Medium Banks)
	A3	Group 3 (Small Banks)
B	B1	Group 1 Large Banks)
	B2	Group 2 (Medium Banks)
	B3	Group 3 (Small Banks)
C	C1 (Chair)	FRB
	C2 (Deputy Chair)	FRB
	C3	FRB

Table 7.3 Voting Groups of the New York Bank

	Original Act in 1914		Amendment in 1918		
	Capital and Surplus	Number of Banks	Capital and Surplus	Number of Banks	%
Group 1	Over $185,000	160	Over $1,999,000	55	7.7
Group 2	$70,000–$185,000	159	$201,000–$1,999,000	180	25.2
Group 3	Less than $70,000	159	Less than $201,000	479	67.1

Federal Reserve Board, Annual Reports for 1915, 1918, pp. 172 and 346

"equal representation" for large, medium, and small banks.[9] As a result of the amendment, for instance, member banks of the New York Bank were divided into three groups: (1) banks with capital and surplus in excess of $1,999,000, (2) those with capital and surplus between $201,000 and $1,999,000, and (3) those with capital and surplus less than $201,000. The right column of Table 7.3 shows that this division left 55 banks in Group 1 (large banks), for 7.7% of the total member banks; 299 banks in Group 2 (medium-sized banks), comprising 25.2%; and 354 banks in Group 3 (small banks), making up 67.1% of the membership. Each group was represented by one Class A and Class B director, even though they had different numbers of banks. The same scenario applied to other districts.

Under the original act, Class A directors did not have to belong to the same group as the bank-nominating bank. Occasionally, this led to large banks'

[9]It seems that the Federal Reserve Board believed that the original grouping brought about the dominance of larger banks within all classes of director, for instance James B. Forgan as a Class A director elected by Group 2, and consequently a lower voter turnout. In the election held in 1917, the voting rate was 37.5% in the New York Bank, 41.9% in Richmond, 47.1% in Atlanta, 23.9% in Chicago, 21.6%, in St. Louis, 15.9% in Minneapolis, 7.5% in Dallas, and 39.9% in San Francisco (Federal Reserve Board, *Annual Report for 1917*, pp. 31–32).

employees serving as both Class A and B directors. For instance, in 1914, James B. Forgan of the First National Bank of Chicago, which had $20,731,000 of capital and surplus, was elected as an original director by Group 2 in the Chicago Bank, while George M. Reynolds of Continental & Commercial National Bank of Chicago, which had $30,000,000 of capital and surplus, was elected as a director by Group 1.[10] To prevent the large banks from dominating the directors, the amended Act required a Class A director to be nominated and elected by "the same group as the member bank of which he is an officer or director," and a Class A director "who is an officer or director of more than one member bank" has to be nominated and elected "by banks in the same group as the bank having the largest aggregate resources."[11]

However, it is difficult to conclude that modifying the groupings increased election competitiveness. The first election of directors in 1914 had multiple candidates,[12] but then candidate numbers dropped precipitously in many districts. As revealed in Table 7.4, which shows the number of candidates and participation rates in the New York Bank from 1915 to 1927, the participation rate rose from around 37% in 1917 to around 70–90% after 1918, but the number of candidates decreased after 1919 and elections were uncontested except in 1920 and 1926. Although elections for director of the New York Bank maintained high voting rates, uncontested elections led to indifference. Although the New York Bank was not unique, most elections for the Reserve Bank directors, except in Chicago, Dallas, and San Francisco, were uncontested from 1926 to 1934 (Bopp 1935, p. 34, Table II).

Since elections were largely uncontested, the nomination process was crucial. Lawrence E. Clark describes the 1914 election for the New York Bank's directors. "The series of bankers' caucuses initiated by the New York Clearing House banks resulted in the unofficial nomination for Class A directors of candidates all of whom were connected with Group 1, the largest banks."[13] On October 20, 1922, the Committee on Nominations for Directors of the New York Bank, which was appointed by the Bankers' Associations of New York, New Jersey, and Connecticut, recommended Gates W. McGarrah, chair of Mechanics and Metals National Bank of New York, as a candidate for Class A director and Owen D. Young, chair of General Electric Co., as a candidate for Class B director to Group 1

[10]According to James (1938, p. 874), nomination of James B. Forgan as a Class A director for Group 2 was subject to the condition that "the third Class A director [who was appointed by the group 3] and all the Class B directors should come from parts of the district outside Chicago.".

[11]*Federal Reserve Bulletin*, October 1918, pp. 947–948.

[12]In the list of National City Bank of New York (1914, p. 8), James B. Forgan was listed in every category, Groups 1 to 3 for Class A and Class B, in the Chicago Bank.

[13]Of the six directors elected by bankers, four were those recommended by the committee of clearing house, while two Class B directors were the "insurgents" group. Clark (1935, pp. 69–71).

Table 7.4 Elections for Class A and Class B Directors of the New York Bank by Voting Group

Year	Class	Voting Group	Candidates	Votes	Eligible Banks	Participation Rate (%)
1915	B	3	2	122	205	59.5
1916	A	1	2	123	209	58.9
1916	B	1	4	123	209	58.9
1917	A	2	4	83	222	37.4
1917	B	2	2	84	222	37.8
1918	A	3	3	327	479	68.3
1918	B	3	3	331	479	69.1
1919	A	1	1	59	63	93.7
1919	B	1	1	59	63	93.7
1920	A	2	2	141	203	69.5
1920	B*	2	1	110	188	58.5
1921	A	3	1	327	520	62.9
1921	B	3	1	327	520	62.9
1922	A	1	1	63	66	95.5
1922	B	1	1	63	66	95.5
1923	A	2	1	202	256	78.9
1923	B	2	1	202	256	78.9
1924	B	3	1	349	519	67.2
1924	A	3	1	349	519	67.2
1925	A	1	1	60	67	89.6
1925	B	1	1	60	67	89.6
1926	A	2	2	236	316	74.7
1926	B	2	2	236	316	74.7
1927	B**	1	1	59	71	83.1
1927	A	3	1	***n. a.	518	–
1927	B	3	1	***n. a.	518	–

Federal Reserve Bank of New York, *Circular*, 1915–1927, various numbers

Notes *Special election because of the resignation of William Boyce Thompson. **Special election because Owen D. Young switched to Class C director. ***Since 1927 the number of votes has not been disclosed "because the voting was by secret ballot."

member banks.[14] Each election had only one candidate. Even in the early 1930s, Clark reported, "this committee canvasses the situation and recommends someone to the member banks for the nomination."[15]

In some Reserve Banks, member banks had an unofficial "stockholders' meeting." The Boston Bank district held such meetings after 1921, the Richmond Bank district held them from 1925 to 1932, and the Dallas Bank district held them from 1927 to 1931. At these meetings in the Boston and Richmond districts, a committee recommended "one or more name, for the Director to be elected." However, at the fourth meeting in 1930, the Dallas Bank district resolved that there would be "no pledge or promises of votes in favor of any candidate for a directorship" (Bopp 1937, pp. 527–528).[16] Strong bankers, like George M. Reynolds, who served as Class A director of the Chicago Bank for almost 20 years from 1914 to 1933, had a major influence, according to Bopp, even though the governor of the Reserve Bank had some power on the nomination and election of directors through influence or suggestion (Bopp 1935, pp. 33–34).[17]

The FRB in Washington appointed Class C directors, but we have not been able to find an official document describing this process. The FRB, Bopp reports, appointed "strong men" as Class C directors "with hope that they would extend Board control" (Bopp 1935, pp. 38–39).[18] Owen D. Young was an outstanding example when he switched from Class B to Class C for the New York Bank in 1927. He also served as the chair of the board of directors of the New York Bank from 1938 to 1940.

However, in some cases, the story was far more complicated. The search for a successor to the first chair of the New York Bank—Pierre Jay, who served from 1914 to December 4, 1927—proved to be contentious.[19] In the face of Governor

[14]Committee on Nominations for Directors of the Federal Reserve Bank of New York to Young, October 20, 1922, O.D. Young Papers, Box 262, 463B. When O.D. Young switched from Class B director to Class C, George L. Harrison, Deputy Governor, recommended for Young to write each of the presidents of the Bankers Associations of New York, New Jersey and Connecticut. See Harrison to Young, January 8 and 11, 1927, O.D. Young Papers, Box 263, 463D.

[15]Clark (1935, p. 85) insists that "real power in determining who shall sit on the board as Class A and B directors of the Reserve Bank resides in this committee of the bankers' associations of the states in the district.".

[16]We confirmed that there are copies of proceedings of stockholder meetings of the Boston Bank during 1929–1930. At these meetings, governors of the Boston Bank, William P.G. Harding and Roy A. Young, "as is the custom," reported reviews of the operation of the Boston Bank. According to the meeting in 1929, "The Federal Reserve Bank of Boston inaugurated stock-holders' meetings in 1923." The Boston Bank paid "the expenses of one representative from each member bank in the District to the stock-holders meetings," and "attendance at the meeting has been consistently large, averaging over 85% of all members annually." Federal Reserve Bank of Boston (1931, pp. 9, 99–100).

[17]A letter that appeared on the front page of the *Chicago Daily Tribune* (January 4, 1915) alleged that "the reserve bank has been 'stuffed' with Reynolds-Forgan appointees.".

[18]Also see testimony of Governor Miller at U. S. Senate, Committee on Banking and Currency (1935, pp. 766–768).

[19]Pierre Jay served as vice president of [Bank of] Manhattan Company until 1914.

Strong suffering a serious illness, "the senior directors in the Bank felt the need of more strength in the top officer class." The FRB suggested to Owen Young that he switch from Class B to Class C so that he could become deputy chair and eventually chair. But Gates W. McGarrah, who was chair of Chase National Bank and a Class A director during 1923–1925 (he later served as president of the Bank for International Settlements in 1930–1933), was the FRB's choice, supported particularly by Governor Daniel R. Crissinger. The New York Bank's directors recommended Warren Randolph Burgess, who was the 38-year-old Assistant Federal Reserve agent of the New York Bank, for chair.[20] The FRB, however, felt "that it is more desirable at this time to take a man of high position from the banking world for that office than it is to promote a man less well known from the organization itself," and appointed McGarrah as chair and Young as deputy chair.[21]

Although the Federal Reserve Act intended for the FRB to have considerable influence over the Reserve Banks' boards of directors, there are some statements in the literature that raise questions about the FRB's power. Morgenstern (1930, p. 4) says the FRB's influence deteriorated because most Class C directors "began gradually to veer about and no longer to regard themselves as delegates of the central board at Washington."[22] Owen D. Young voiced this concern shortly after switching to become a Class C director:

> I think that the influence of the Federal Reserve Board in our affairs will be less with Gates McGarrah as chairman than it would be with Dr. Burgess as chairman; not that Burgess is not as strong as McGarrah, but he is less well known, and therefore his resistance would be less effective….If equally strong men can be put into the other Reserve Banks in place of the men already there, I feel that we will have insured the System against the very centralization which you fear and against which for so many years you have given such effective resistance.[23]

In a letter to Henry B. Steagall, moreover, Edmond Platt, who was Vice Governor of the FRB from 1920 to 1930, insisted the FRB had in fact seldom appointed Class C directors. "Nearly all the appointments of Class 'C' directors and Federal Reserve agents have been made by the Board on recommendation from the directors of the Reserve Banks themselves."[24]

Consolidation of power was achieved by the Banking Bill of 1935, which combined the post of Reserve Bank chair with the governor, who was to be appointed by the FRB from the Class C directors. Indeed, in a letter to Carter Glass dated October 30, 1935, Charles S. Hamlin, member of the FRB, described the

---

[20]After serving as a deputy governor until 1938, Burgess moved to the National City Bank, where he was executive chair from 1948.

[21]Young to Strong, January 8, 1927, O.D. Young Papers, Box 263, 463D.

[22]A 1975 study on the directors concluded "the so-called public directors appointed by the Board hold views similar to those of directors elected exclusively by bankers." See Harrison (1977, p. 55).

[23]Young to Strong, March 31, 1927, O.D. Young Papers, Box 263, 463H.

[24]*Congressional Record*, May 1, (1935, Vol. 79, Part 6, 74 Cong., 1st Sess., p. 7617); Bopp (1937, p. 530).

process to fill the vacancy stemming from following the death of Alba B. Johnson, a Class C director of the Philadelphia Bank, as follows:

> Governor Norris first submitted a list of 24 names of men whom he thought would be fitted for this position. Fourteen were at once eliminated because of the fact that they are now holding offices as directors of banks, and he was sure they would not be willing to resign. (…) I then went over the remaining 10 names carefully with the assistance of our Division of Examinations. I finally fixed upon one name as probably best qualified for this position.[25]

7.3 Dual Leadership: Reserve Bank Governance Before the Great Depression

As the organization of the board of directors indicates, governance of the Reserve Banks required three kinds of stakeholders to be represented: member banks, industrial customers, and the general public. These stakeholders in turn influenced Reserve Bank governance by choosing both the chair of the board of directors and the governor. The Federal Reserve Act provided that the Federal Reserve agent, who was appointed by the FRB, serve as chair of the board of directors. However, the Reserve Bank Organization Committee (RBOC) recommended that each Reserve Bank "should have a distinct executive head not identical with the Federal reserve agent."[26] Because there was no provision for the head or the governor in the original Act, the RBOC created a dual executive in Reserve Banks comprising the chair and governor.[27]

The board of directors was the highest decision-making body in the Reserve Banks. They had the power to prescribe by-laws, appoint executive officers and employees, fix their compensation, and exercise all power to carry on the business of the banking industry.[28] In general, it could be said that they supervised and controlled the management of the Reserve Banks. They also appointed a member to the Federal Advisory Council, which consisted of each Reserve Bank's representatives from the banking industry and which conferred with and made recommendations to the FRB.[29] The Council was recompense for the lack of direct banker representation on the FRB (Lindley 1985, p. 6).

Controversy surrounded the Council's influence over monetary policy. In 1931, when then-Governor of the New York Bank, George L. Harrison, was fighting for

---

[25]Hamlin to Glass, October 30, 1935, p. 1, C. Glass Papers, Box 64.

[26]U.S. Reserve Bank Organization Committee (1914, p. 21).

[27]One well-known case was that Governor Harrison of the New York Bank suggested continuing open-market purchases of about $25 million a week during the Depression, but the executive committee rejected his "recommendation by a vote of 4 to 1." Friedman and Schwartz (1963, p. 369).

[28]See Federal Reserve Act, Sect. 4; Federal Reserve Bank of New York, Bylaws, Article I, in Federal Reserve Board, *Annual Report*, 1916, pp. 201–202.

[29]Federal Reserve Act, Sect. 12. The Council was a compromise for no direct banker's representation on the Board. Lindley (1985, p. 6).

Table 7.5 Meetings of the Reserve Banks' Board of Directors

Reserve Bank	Frequency of Regular Meeting	Quorum	Powers
Boston	1/week	Majority	• Supervision & control of the Bank • Appoint the officers (governor, deputy governor, secretary, cashier, and legal counsel), and fix their compensation • Appoint special committees • Appoint a member of the Federal Advisory Council • Make regulations
New York	1/week		
Philadelphia	2/month		
Cleveland	1/month		
Richmond	1/week		
Atlanta	1/month		
Chicago	1/month		
St. Louis	2/month		
Minneapolis	1/month		
Kansas City	2/month		
Dallas	1/month		
San Francisco	2/month		

Source Federal Reserve Board, *Annual Report for 1916–1919*, passim

open-market purchases, the Federal Advisory Council expressed the same point of view as the conservative Reserve Bank executives, who insisted on the "danger of stimulating financing" (Friedman and Schwartz 1963, pp. 371–373). Although each Reserve Bank used a common form of bylaws prepared by the RBOR,[30] they provided different meeting schedules. As Table 7.5 shows, the directors of the Boston and the New York Reserve Banks held weekly meetings, while the other Reserve Banks held meetings only once or twice a month.

The directors, except those of the San Francisco Bank,[31] delegated day-to-day management to an executive committee.[32] The schedule of meetings and powers the directors are listed in Table 7.5.

[30]U.S. Reserve Bank Organization Committee (1914, pp. 22–26).

[31]The San Francisco Bank did not call upon the executive committee in practice, even though they set up the committee. "With the exception of Mr. Alden Anderson, Class A director, who lives in Sacramento, three hours distant, all directors live in San Francisco, and their great regularity of attendance at meetings, hold on the first and third Tuesdays of each month, assures invariably larger meetings than a mere quorum of five. Matters both of general policy and to a considerable extent of detail are considered by the entire board. The members of the executive committee of five individually investigate and sign the executive committee report of investments submitted at each directors' meeting, but because of the close touch of the whole board of directors with the bank's affairs formal meetings of the executive committee are rarely called." Federal Reserve Board, *Annual Report for 1916*, pp. 455–456.

[32]In general, power of the executive committee was as follows: (1) pass upon all commercial paper submitted for discount, (2) initiate and conduct open-market transactions, (3) recommend to the board of directors changes in the discount rates, (4) buy and sell securities, (5) apply for and provide for the security to be pledged against the issuing of Federal Reserve notes, (6) employ or delegate to officers and fix their compensation, (7) approve bonds furnished by the officers, and (8) conduct the business of the bank.

Table 7.6 Structure of Reserve Banks' Executive Committee

Reserve Bank	Member					Quorum	Regular Meeting
	Governor	Chair	Class A	Class B	Class C		
Boston	1 (Chair)	1	2	1		3	1/week
New York			4 (in turn)				Every business day
Philadelphia			1 or more				n/a
Cleveland			3 (rotation)				1/week
Richmond*			1				Every business day
Atlanta*			1 (monthly rotation)				Every business day
Chicago			2		1		2/week
St. Louis			2	1			Every business day
Minneapolis			1				Every business day
Kansas City			1				Every business day
Dallas*			3				2/month
San Francisco			3				2/month**

Federal Reserve Board, Annual Report for 1915–1919, passim; Coit (1941, pp. 42–43); Willis (1937, p. 120)

Notes: *Richmond was for 1915; Atlanta & Dallas was for 1919. **The executive committee was called at the same time as the board of directors meeting

The executive committee consisted of the chair, the governor, who presided over the committee, and one or more directors. As Table 7.6 shows, however, the way in which members served in these positions varied. Five Reserve Banks excluded Class C directors other than the chair from the committee while in the Chicago Bank, it consisted of two Class A directors and one Class C director, but Class B was excluded.[33] In three Reserve Banks, the directors served on the committee in rotation.

Executive committee meetings were held every business day in six Reserve Banks, once or twice a week in three districts, and twice a month in two districts. In

[33] Class A directors were Reynolds and Forgan, and Class C director was James Simpson, vice president of Marshall Field & Co. An article in the *Chicago Daily Tribune*, January 4, 1915, p. 2, reported that Class B directors "have taken little interest in the conduct of the institution."

Table 7.7 Board of Directors of the New York Bank in 1936

Regular meeting agendas	Meet every Thursday afternoon
	(1) Minutes of Previous Meetings: Approved
	(2) Advances and Rediscounts: Considering and approved
	(3) Open Market Operations: Informed and approved
	(4) Discount Rates: Informed and approved by vote
	(5) Business and Credit Conditions: Informed
Standing committees	(a) Executive Committee*[5]
	(b) Special Committee on Industrial Loans [5]
	(c) Auditing Committee [3]
	(d) Committee of Directors on the Welfare of the Staff [3]
	(e) Building Committee [4]
	(f) Committee on Foreign Relations [3]
	(g) Committee on Supervision of Member Banks [4]
	(h) Committee on Relations between Reserve Bank and its Directors and between Reserve Bank and FRB [5]

Young to William F. Ploch, December 16, 1936, O.D. Young Papers, Box 268, 463GG
Notes: [ ] Number of the committee members. *This committee does not meet regularly at the present time

the New York Bank, the committee increased its meetings drastically after 1918, which reflected the importance of the committee to financing World War I.[34] Table 7.7 shows the frequency of meetings in New York in 1936.

However, in the San Francisco and Dallas Banks, where meetings were held at longer intervals, most of the executive committee's work was turned over to the governor (Clark 1935, p. 91). The San Francisco Bank reported in 1917 that "the executive committee is rarely convened. Rediscounts and loans are first authorized over the signatures of the governor or deputy governor and the chairman, the other members of the executive committee signing at their convenience and after such investigation as each desires."[35]

Perhaps the most important role of the executive committees and boards of directors in the early days were to take part in Federal Reserve policy formation. Until the Great Depression, most Reserve Banks still considered the discount window for member banks as their most important policy tool. With the executive

[34]There were 53 board of directors meetings and 246 executive committee meetings in 1918. Federal Reserve Board, *Annual Report*, 1916–1918. Despite the Federal Reserve Act permitted [Sect. 15], the Secretary of Treasury designated as fiscal agent of the United States on June 1, 1916, and the sub-treasury, which held a large portion of government deposits until 1920. After the United States entered the Great War, the Reserve Banks started fully the fiscal agency functions and sold huge amounts of the Liberty Bonds and Treasury Certificates, short-term obligations of the government. Taggart (1938, pp. 86–90). In the Chicago Fed, "An Executive Committee was organized with the Governor and Federal Reserve Agent as Chairman and Vice-Chairman". Griswold (1936, pp. 72–74).

[35]Federal Reserve Board, *Annual Report for 1917*, p. 594. See also Willis (1937, p. 120).

committee's increasing importance, the governor, who presided at the meeting of the executive committee, increased his/her influence relative to the chair of the board of directors. The chair of the board of directors also served as the "Federal Reserve Agent." As the "official representative" of the FRB, the Federal Reserve Agent held responsibility for reporting to the FRB [Sect. 4], supervising and regulating Federal reserve notes [Sect. 10-(d), Sect. 16], and investigating collateral securities for notes [Sect. 10-(i)]. The Agent had separate departments for these responsibilities in the Reserve Banks.

Despite the fact that the original Federal Reserve Act did not provide for the position of governor in the Reserve Bank, RBOC viewed the governor as an "executive head." In addition, the FRB positioned this officer as an executive officer and gave him "the title of governor in order to differentiate his functions from those of the president of a member bank."[36] The bylaws of each Reserve Bank gave the governor power to "transfer securities or other property of the bank," which were authorized by the executive committee or board, and to "prescribe the duties of all subordinate officers and agents of the bank." The governor also became chair of the executive committee.

Possible confusion arising from dual leaderships of the chair and governor was avoided or managed in several ways. First, at the initial meeting of the Richmond Bank, the board of directors elected George J. Seay as the Bank's first governor. Seay, a member of Richmond-based banking and stockbroking firm Scott & Stringfellow, was first elected as a Class B director. In addition to governor and Class B director, he was elected a member of the Federal Advisory Council until 1915.[37] As discussed later, most early-period governors came from commercial and investment banks.

Second, in both Atlanta and Kansas City Banks, the chief executive positions were switched. Disagreement between Chair Maximilian B. Wellborn and Governor Joseph A. McCord in the Atlanta Fed surfaced in 1918, when the FRB's chief examiner criticized the Bank's credit department.[38] For a long time "Wellborn was unhappy with the leadership of McCord and with the limited authority of his own position" (Gamble 1989, pp. 26–27).[39] In November 1917, Wellborn described problems of internal organization to W.P.G. Harding, Governor (now Chair) of

[36]Federal Reserve Board, *Annual Report for* (1914, p. 8). In the original Act, the name of governor was given to a member of the Federal Reserve Board as "the active executive officer" [Sect. 10].

[37]Parthemos (1990, p. 8). See also Committee on the History of the Federal Reserve System, Persons and Federal Reserve Banks files, Federal Reserve Bank of St. Louis, FRASER website.

[38]By Sect. 21 of Federal Reserve Act, the Comptroller of the Currency "shall appoint examiners who shall examine every member bank." However, "every Federal Reserve Bank may, with the approval of Federal Reserve agent or the Federal Reserve Board, provide for special examination for member banks within its district." Furthermore, the FRB "shall at least once each year, order an examination of each Federal Reserve Bank," and order "special examination" of the Reserve Bank "upon joint application of ten member banks." Even though the Reserve Banks organized their own examination department in 1917, they had only 18 examiners in that year while the Office of Comptroller of the Currency had 204 examiners. For more details, see White (2013, pp. 31–33).

[39]Also see Temporary Internal Memorandum, Atlanta Bank Visit—February 1955, Comments of Mr. Levis Clark, Vice President of Atlanta Bank, Committee on the History of the Federal Reserve System file on the FRASER website.

the FRB, who had recruited him from his post as president of the First National Bank of Birmingham. As a result, the board of directors met in February 1918, with Harding present. The board went into "executive session," forcing McCord to leave the meeting, and resolved to compel McCord to resign and appoint Wellborn as the governor. At the same meeting, the board appointed McCord as its chair.[40] In the Reserve Bank of Kansas City, Jo Z. Miller, Jr. was appointed first chair and Charles M. Sawyer was selected as first governor. Miller expected to run the Kansas City Bank from the position of chair, but found this impossible. Then, in January 1916, when it "was found that it was the governor who was to run the bank, he arranged so that the two men should switch jobs."[41]

Third, another factor served to further confuse the management of Reserve Banks. Conflict between the two executives could be reduced by equalizing their salaries. The chair was only a director who received "an annual compensation to be fixed by the Federal Reserve Board and paid monthly by the Federal Reserve Bank to which he is designated."[42] Fixing the compensation of every senior officer in the Reserve Banks required approval from the FRB,[43] because Sect. 7 of the Act provided that "after all necessary expenses of a Federal Reserve Bank have been paid" and the stockholders received "an annual dividend of six per centum on the paid-in capital stock,… all the net earnings shall be paid to the United States as a franchise tax."[44] Therefore, it is reasonable to assume that the FRB restrained the pay increase for Reserve Bank officers. In fact, the FRB often vetoed increases to officers' compensation. In 1915, for instance, directors of the Richmond Bank set the governor's salary at $15,000, but the FRB reduced it to $10,000. As a result "a sharp dispute with the Reserve Board erupted" (Parthemos 1990, p. 9). Nevertheless, the governor's salary was influenced by those of commercial bank top executives, while the salary of the chair, who represented public interest and was appointed by the FRB, "was obliged to bear a reasonable relation to the salaries

---

[40]Federal Reserve Board, *Minutes of the Meeting*, Nov. 9, 1917, pp. 616–617; Gamble (1989, p. 27).

[41]"Interview with Mr. John P. Phillips Jr., recently retired as vice president of the Kansas City Bank," June 13, 1955, p. 5, in Committee on the History of the Federal Reserve System file.

[42]Other directors received "in addition to any compensation otherwise provided, a reasonable allowance for necessary expenses in attending meetings of their respective boards." Federal Reserve Act, Sect. 4.

[43]Federal Reserve Act provided in Sect. 4 as follows: "Any compensation that may be provided by boards of directors of Federal Reserve banks for directors, officers, or employees shall be subject to the approval of the Federal Reserve Board." However, most salaries were decided by informal discussions at Board meetings.

[44]All expenses and salaries of the FRB are also levied upon the Reserve Banks [Sect. 3 and 4].

paid such officials in Washington" (Clark 1935, p. 98).[45] Equal salaries were useful for sharing responsibility and efficient operation of the Chicago Bank.[46]

Reducing the salary gap between the two executives was apparently realized when a relatively strong person served as chair. In the New York Bank, equal salaries were accomplished in 1928. As previously noted for the New York Bank, while Governor Strong was ill, Gates W. McGarrah was inaugurated as chair of the board of directors and Owen D. Young switched from a Class B to Class C director. Immediately after Strong's death, McGarrah became acting governor of the New York Bank between October 16 and November 28, 1928. Since McGarrah continued as chair, he executed both jobs so that the bylaws had to be changed. According to Leslie Rounds, who was the controller of account at the Bank at that time and became a vice governor in 1928, the change occurred because "the directors have always felt that the post of governor or president, as it is now, should not be vacant for even one day." Although "it was a foregone conclusion from the very beginning that [George L.] Harrison would be elected" as governor, why did McGarrah become acting governor by changing the bylaws? Rounds suggested that, "Mr. McGarrah apparently felt the position of chairman should not be subordinated to the governorship."[47]

Nonetheless, power of the Reserve Banks' management moved steadily from the chair to the governor. As pointed out above, this partly reflected the fact that the governor was a de facto executive officer of the Reserve Bank, but also because the authority of the chair's position was limited. These limits emerged in the early years because the fact that the Class A (banker) directors "elected the governors made it possible for the governor to assume the leadership rather than the chairman who was an appointee of the Federal Reserve Board" (Clark 1935, p. 97).

[45]Maximilian B. Wellborn, whose salary was $18,000 as president of the First National Bank of Birmingham, accepted a position of chair of the Atlanta Bank in 1914. Gamble (1989, p. 15).

[46]Griswold (1936), pp. 53–54. Both chair and president received equal salaries in 1916 in the Atlanta Bank, in 1920–1924 in the Dallas Bank, in 1919 in the Minneapolis Bank, in 1920–1921 in the San Francisco Bank, in 1927–1935 in the New York Bank, and in 1931–1935 in the Chicago Bank.

[47]By the amendment of the Reserve Bank bylaws, the chair of the board of directors became chair of the executive committee. See J.H. Philbin to Young, February 4, 1927, O.D. Young Papers, Box 263, 463I. Leslie Rounds also held that "the position of the chairman is somewhat ambiguous," and "the reason for that change in the by-laws was simply that McGarrah foresaw the possible occasions when that might be a necessary power to have." Brookings Institution, "Confidential Interview with Leslie Rounds," May 2, 1955.

7.4 Removing Old-Line Bankers: Restructuring Federal Reserve Governance

The Great Contraction spurred a drastic change in governance of the Federal Reserve System. For this purpose, the Banking Act of 1935 formally designated the president, formerly governor, as the sole chief executive of the Reserve Bank, while the Board of Governors of the Federal Reserve System (FRB), which was the new name of the Federal Reserve Board, was deprived of the most important power inherent in the chair of the board of directors, with little or no amendment of the original Act. The 1935 Act provided that "the president shall be the chief executive officer of the bank and shall be appointed by the board of directors, with the approval of the FRB, for a term of five years." Furthermore, "the first vice president of the bank shall be appointed in the same manner and for the same term as the president" [Title II, Sect. 201].

Even though Marriner S. Eccles, FRB, "proposed to combine the offices of the chairman of the board of directors and the governor of the Federal Reserve banks,"[48] the Act did not change the position of the chair of the board of directors. Strong objection from Senator Carter Glass defeated Eccles' plan. Nevertheless, Eccles achieved the result he desired because "the Board of Governors still retained the power to appoint the chairman, who was also Federal Reserve Agent" (Eccles 1951, p. 224). By exercising this power, the FRB "made the chairmanship a purely honorary post which carries no salary"[49] from 1936, despite the fact that the Federal Reserve Act provided that the chair receives an annual salary. The FRB explained this change was due to the fact that "various nonstatutory duties now performed in the office of the chairman and Federal Reserve agent would be placed under the president of the bank." To "obtain the services of men who are not only well qualified, but public spirited to serve as chairmen," the FRB ended the term of the chair of six Reserve Banks (Boston, New York, Philadelphia, Chicago, St. Louis, and Dallas) in April 30, 1936, the terms of four Reserve Banks (Cleveland, Atlanta, Minneapolis, and Kansas City) at the end of 1936, and kept two vacancies (Richmond and San Francisco).[50] These six chairs who resigned in April, did not accept an "honorary basis" position or "a part-time one, without salary."[51] In addition, by prearrangement with Owen D. Young of the New York Bank, James

---

[48]"Comparison of Governor Eccles' Recommendations with Title II as Reported to the Senate," July 3, 1935, p. 3, Box 13, Marriner S. Eccles Papers, University of Utah. In March 1933, O.D. Young, Deputy Chair of the New York Bank received $20 dollars for attendance of each meeting. Receipt issued by Allan Sproul, March 31, 1933, O.D. Young Papers, Box 266, 463V.

[49]Brookings Institution, "Confidential Interview with Leslie Rounds," January 29, 1954.

[50]*Federal Reserve Bulletin*, March 1936, p. 145.

[51]*Commercial and Financial Chronicle*, March 7, 1936, Vol. 142, Pt. 1, p. 1558. The FRB also introduced a new rule for the Reserve Bank chair, who must be younger than 65 when entering office. "This controversial move brought the immediate resignations of six of the Reserve Bank chairmen." Board of Governors to Young, December 4, 1935, O.D. Young Papers, Box 268, 463EE, Box 267, 463AA; Gamble (1989, p. 73).

Simpson, deputy chair of the Chicago Bank, tendered a letter of resignation to Governor Eccles in January 28, 1935.[52] According to his letter, the "Federal Reserve Board has adopted a policy that six years of service represents the maximum period of time during which a [Class C except Chair] director should remain continuously in office."

As a consequence, the standing and spending of the chair and the Federal Reserve Agent in the Reserve Banks changed after 1936. In the Boston Bank, an office was maintained for the Federal Reserve Agent and its function remained legally the same as provided in the original Act, but "actually there is no Federal Reserve Agent" (Taggart 1938, p. 65). Frank H. Neely, who served as a Class C director in 1937 and as a chair of the Atlanta Bank for 16 years from 1938 to 1953, when he was between the ages of 54 and 69, "spent considerable time in his chairman's office at the Bank, where he frequently held long and sometimes animated meetings." He first worked for the Westinghouse Electric & Manufacturing Co. as a Scientific Management specialist, then for the Fulton Bag and Cotton Mills as an executive officer, and then for Rich's Inc., a department store, as president then chair. It "suited him to be a volunteer chairman instead of a professional staff member, and his own agenda for shaking up the Atlanta Bank dovetailed reasonably well with Eccles's agenda for the System" (Gamble 1989, p. 76).

At the same time, the FRB introduced guidelines for the position of Reserve Bank president, who must be younger than 65 when taking office. As a result, the FRB did not reappoint three governors (Philadelphia, Richmond, and San Francisco) and two deputy governors (Philadelphia and Minneapolis).[53] An article in *The Time* reported that the FRB had succeeded in a "wholesale house-cleaning" of old-line bankers who did not support the leadership of Marriner S. Eccles.[54]

The power of the board of directors did not change according to the new bylaws, but the number of meetings decreased, for instance, from weekly to twice a month in the New York Bank.[55] Moreover, because the chair or the Federal Reserve Agent was exempted from executive management, the executive committee's character changed greatly. The president, who had formerly presided over the committee, was excluded and replaced by the chair of the board of directors, which now consisted of only the chair and other directors. Although the executive committee of the New York Bank still had "power to direct the business of the Bank" as seen in Table 7.7

[52]Simpson to Young, January 28, 1935; Simpson to Eccles, January 28, 1935, O.D. Young Papers, Box 267, 463AA.

[53]*Federal Reserve Bulletin*, 1936, March, p. 145; Gamble (1989, p. 73). "The Board agree not to approve for the five year term beginning March 1, 1936, the appointment of any one as President or First Vice President of a Federal reserve bank who is seventy years or more of age or who, before the end of the five years, will have reached that age." Federal Reserve Board, *Minutes of the Board of Governors of the Federal Reserve System*, February 29, 1936, p. 8.

[54]"Business: Reservists Out," *The Time* (1936, March 16).

[55]At the end of May 1935, the board of directors of the New York Bank decided that "the regular meetings of the executive committee during the months of June, July, and August, 1935, be omitted." Allan Sproul to Young, May 31, 1935, O.D., O.D. Young Papers, Box 267, 463AA.

the amendment of the bylaws in March 1, 1936, changed the membership and constitution of a quorum as follows: "All other directors are invited to attend the meetings of the committee, and while so attending shall also be members of the committee for all purposes, including the constitution of a quorum," which was not less than three committee members. Furthermore, the executive committee of the New York Bank did not meet regularly after the governance reforms.[56]

7.5 Economic and Social Backgrounds of the Federal Reserve's Top Executives

Sometimes, the determinants of individual preferences regarding policies do not coincide with those assumed rationally by economists, an outcome that reflects the fact that individuals' behavior is affected not just by their economic interest but by their cultural and social backgrounds as well. Although a few studies have focused on the influence of social backgrounds, such as religious beliefs (Barro and McCleary 2003; Ruhr and Daniels 2003), little research has been conducted on the impact of the social backgrounds of the Federal Reserve's top executives, with the exception of monographs on the FRB Chair like Marriner Eccles, who was a Mormon.

Not until 1954 did the *Committee on the History of the Federal Reserve System* provide "Profiles [of the] Federal Reserve System Top Command" including the board of directors and the presidents of the Reserve Banks, as well as FRB members. The committee surveyed birthplace, education level, business experience, age, and length of service for the top executives of 36 FRB members, 60 presidents, and 590 directors in the Reserve Banks including 79 chairs the Reserve Bank's board of directors for the 1914–1954 period. The committee compiled a composite image of the top executive groups as follows: "Born largely in the Middle West, most of them with at least a high school education and almost half of them college graduate, between fifty and sixty years of age on appointment, with a wide range of business experience behind them, this is the composite picture of decision-makers in the Federal Reserve System. Once they get in, (…) a surprising number went on to serve 11 to 20 years."[57]

However, this snapshot by the *Committee on the History* of the top executives' social backgrounds was quite approximate. It drew the top executives' profile from the simple average of biographical data contained in personal card files for 1914–

---

[56]"Proposed Amendment to By-laws of Federal Reserve Bank of New York, Effective March 1, 1936, To Be Presented to Board of Directors for Action at Meeting of Board on January 2, 1936," December 27, 1935, O.D. Young Papers, Box 268, 463CC. See also Bylaws of Federal Reserve Bank of New York website.

[57]Committee on the History, "Profile of Federal Reserve System Top Command," Entry 164, Box 11, Folder 11, Committee on the History of the Federal Reserve System, Brookings Institution, p. 2.

1955. Few works provide the backgrounds of top Federal Reserve executives, and those that did focused mostly on the post-1950s timeframe and/or offered fragmented background studies that focused on a few elements.[58] To fill this gap in the literature, we use the personal card files from the *Committee on the History* and correct their omissions and errors. We have personal data on 209 Class A directors, 186 Class B directors, 218 Class C directors, 84 chairs, 62 presidents, and 51 FRB members. Data from these personal cards are transformed into annual data from 1915 to 1955 so that we can show chronological changes in their backgrounds before and after the mid-1930s governance reforms.

We select average age, average length of service, industrial origin, highest education, and political and religious affiliations as background traits of the Federal Reserve System's top executive group. In addition, we carefully handle political and religious backgrounds because many executives did not disclose their affiliations in the biographical cards. As we see later, 80.7% of the Reserve Bank directors in 1954 never unveiled their political affiliations, and in 1946, 70.6% withheld their religious affiliation. Nevertheless, it is worthy to compare the revealed affiliations between executive groups on an annual basis so that we can confirm the diverse effects of the mid-1930s governance reforms upon their backgrounds and financial networks.

(1) **Age and Length of Service**

On the one hand, the new FRB carried out a wholesale house-cleaning in the Reserve Banks as well as in the FRB in Washington to purge old-guard cronies from central banking. On the other hand, beginning with appointments made in 1935, the FRB adapted a new guideline for an age limit of 65 when coming into the Reserve Bank office as either chair or president, and a length-of-service limit of two or more consecutive terms of three years each for Class C directors except chairs.[59] The FRB explained that it adapted these rules to the Reserve Banks "against criticism based either upon the fact or the possibility of crystallization of control of their managements by particular individuals or groups through long continuance in power."[60] What effect did the new rules regarding age and terms of the top executives in the Reserve Bank have?

As seen in Figs. 7.1 and 7.2, effects soon emerged. The average age of Class C directors dropped drastically from 63.5 in 1936 to 60.0 in 1938, and the average

---

[58]Andrew F. Brimmer, a member of the FRB in 1966–1974, surveyed age, tenure, industry origins, and educations of the board of directors, including the branch offices in 1957, 1967, and 1972. He pointed out that the "composite director in 1972 is younger than his predecessors, has served less time on his board, is more diverse in his occupant pursuits, and has more formal education than the typical directors of 15 years ago." Furthermore, he insisted there were few directors of minority groups and women then (Brimmer 1972). Miller (1961) and Havrilesky et al. (1973) also noticed a lack of diversity in the boards of directors, especially Class C directors.

[59]FRB, *Minutes of the Board of Governor of the Federal Reserve System*, December 28, 1934, p. 1.

[60]See Note 53.

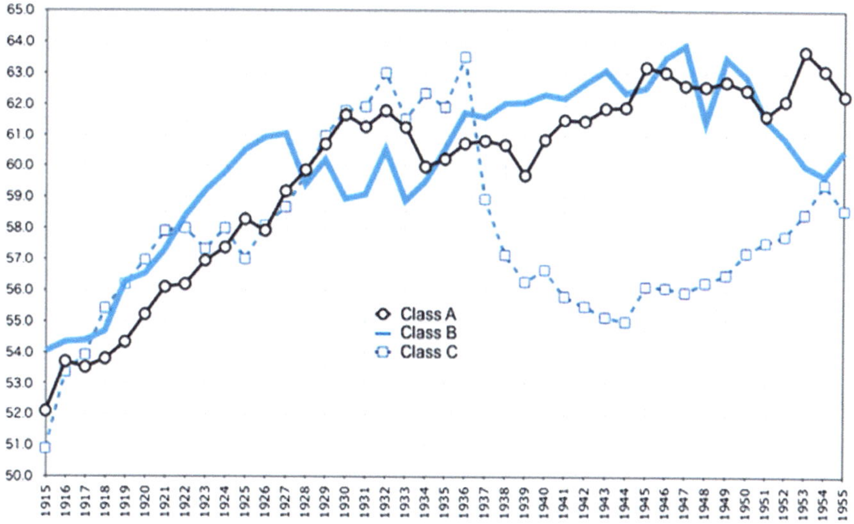

Fig. 7.1 Average age of Reserve Bank Directors by Class

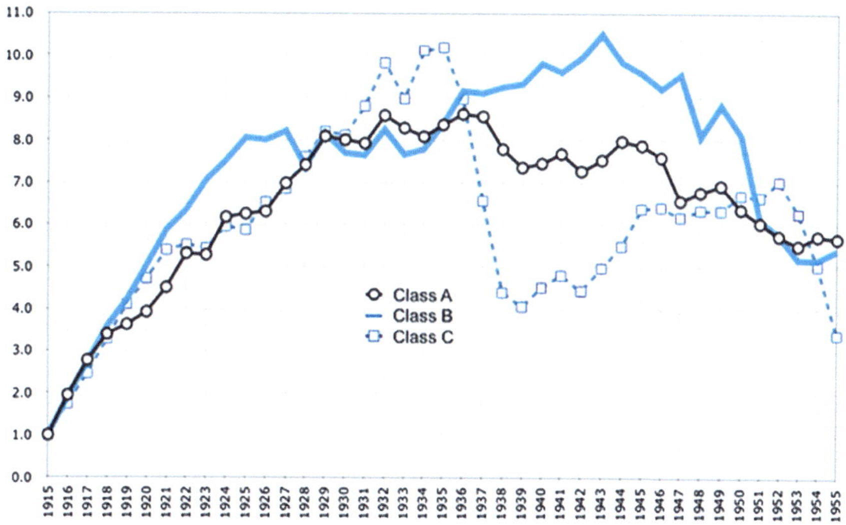

Fig. 7.2 Average years of service of Reserve Bank Directors by Class

years in office of Class C directors dropped from 10.2 in 1935 to 4.1 in 1939. With regards to directors elected by member banks, the average age of Class A directors rose steadily to 63.0 in 1946, and for Class B directors to 63.9 in 1947. The average years in office of Class A directors, however, went up slightly until World War II

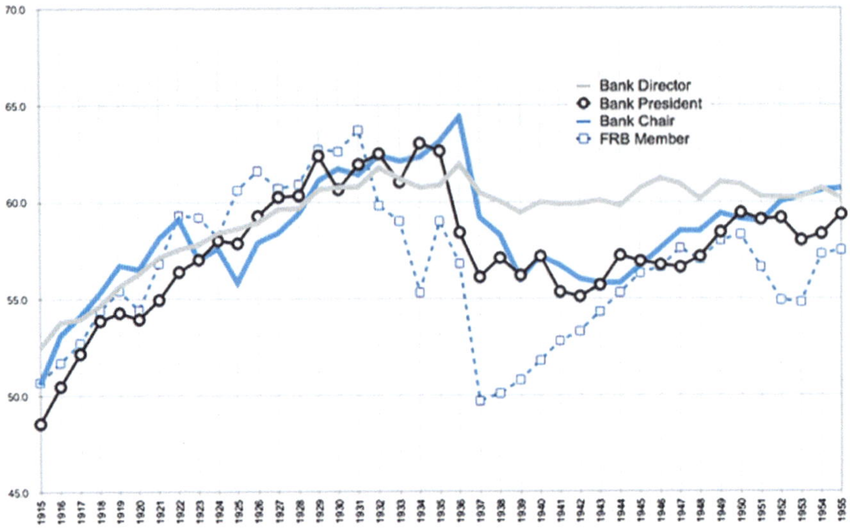

Fig. 7.3 Average age of top executive groups

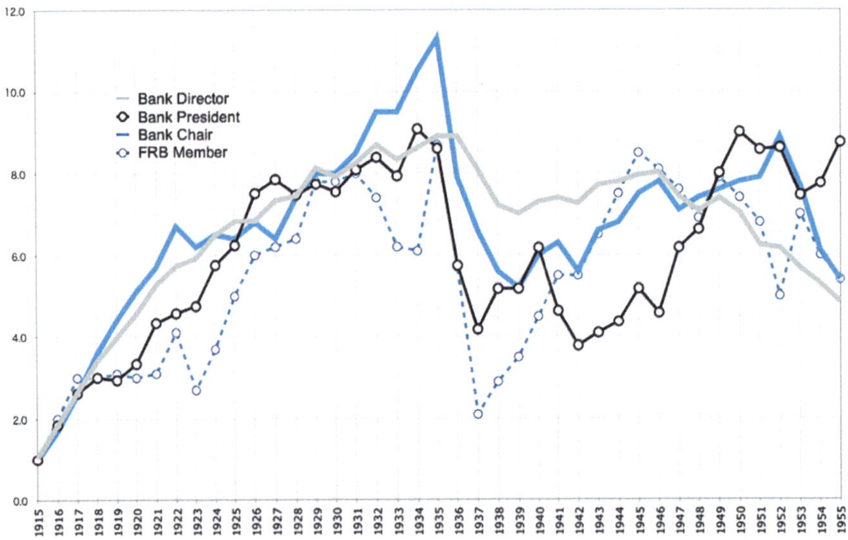

Fig. 7.4 Average length of service of top executive groups

then fell to below 6 years in the early 1950s, while for Class B directors, it rose to 10.5 in 1943 before dropping to a similar level in the 1950s.

Mariner Eccles, Chair of the FRB, targeted exclusions of old-guard cronies from the positions of presidents and chairs in the Reserve Bank as well as in the FRB. For this reason, we compare average age and term between top executive groups in

Figs. 7.3 and 7.4. The average age of the Reserve Bank presidents and chairs initially fell after 1936, but then rose steadily to below 60 in the early 1950s. For the FRB members, it had dropped since the early 1930s, and then more rapidly in 1937 (Fig. 7.3). The average number of service years for presidents, chairs, and FRB members fell more drastically than for the directors, but rebounded quickly during the 1940s (Fig. 7.4). Therefore, the governance reform had a stronger influence on the Reserve Bank presidents and FRB members than Reserve Bank directors. In fact, Eccles shuffled three older members from the FRB. Charles Hamlin, who was 75 years old, had served since 1914, and was a friend of President Roosevelt, was made Special Counsel to the FRB. Seventy-year-old Adolph C. Miller, who had served since 1914, became chair of the FRB's Building Committee. Finally, 66-year-old John J. Thomas, who had served since 1933, became chair of the Kansas City Bank, an appointment converted to an honorarium basis on January 01, 1937.

(2) **Industrial Origins or Experience in the Federal Reserve**

According to the Federal Reserve Act, Class A directors were elected from three groups of member banks, and member banks elected Class B directors who were "actively engaged in their district in commerce, agriculture, or some other industrial pursuit" (Sect. 4). As seen in Fig. 7.5, Class B directors were not selected equally from commerce, agriculture, and industry sectors. Until the mid-1920s, the financial industry contributed more than 10.5% of all Class B directors, while the manufacturing industry contributed 27.8% of Class B directors in 1915, rising to 67.6% in 1947, and maintaining more than 50% even in the 1950s. Agriculture accounted for 20% of Class B members in the early 1930s, dropping to 10% in the 1940s.

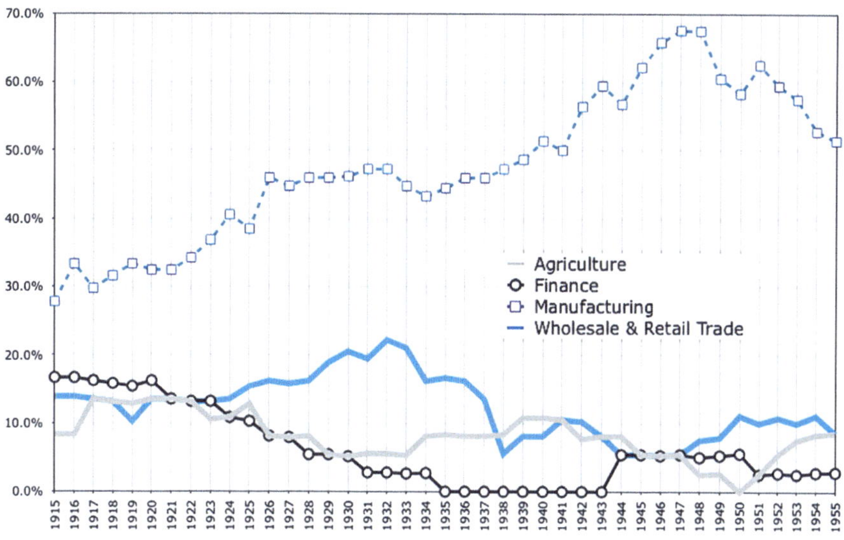

Fig. 7.5 Industry origins of Reserve Bank Class B Directors

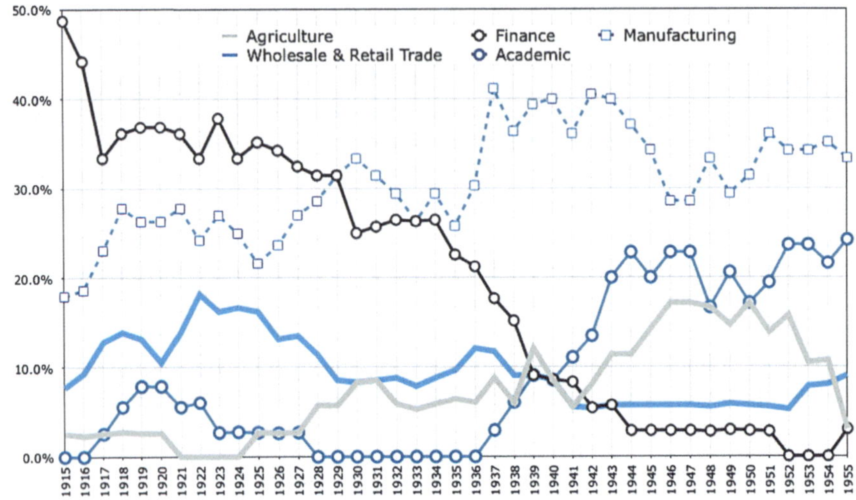

Fig. 7.6 Industry origins of Reserve Bank Class C Directors

The FRB also appointed Class C directors, including a chair and deputy chair, who were required to have "tested banking experience." Therefore, as seen in Fig. 7.6, almost 50% of Class C directors had financial industry backgrounds in 1915, but the share of such directors with finance backgrounds declined rapidly in the late 1930s and finally disappeared in the 1950s. Commerce backgrounds also dropped from 18.2% in 1922 to below 6% in the 1940s. The manufacturing industry, however, has accounted for the greatest proportion of Class C directors since the late 1930s. Instead, of commerce and finance, the percentages of academics and farmers rose sharply, accounting for around 23 and 17%, respectively, by the early 1950s.

Now we will compare the industrial backgrounds of Class B and Class C directors with other top executive groups. Figure 7.7 shows the executive groups originating from banking businesses, and Fig. 7.8 shows the groups with origins in commerce and manufacturing. In 1925, 75% of board of directors' chairs had banking origins. This percentage shrank rapidly in the 1930s before finally disappearing in 1942. Reserve Bank presidents from banking businesses remained around 70–80% of the total until 1936, and then decreased to around 45% in the 1940s. The FRB appointed Reserve Bank chairs from commerce and manufacturing industries after the governance reforms. As seen in Fig. 7.8, chairs from these industries accounted for 70% in 1937, and 91.7% in 1955. While FRB members in Washington who came from banking decreased until 1934, they increased in the 1940s before dropping to 12.5% in the 1950s. In place of candidates from banking, commerce, and manufacturing industries, many government officers were appointed as FRB members; they accounted for 25.0% in 1935, 66.7% in 1939, and 83.3% in

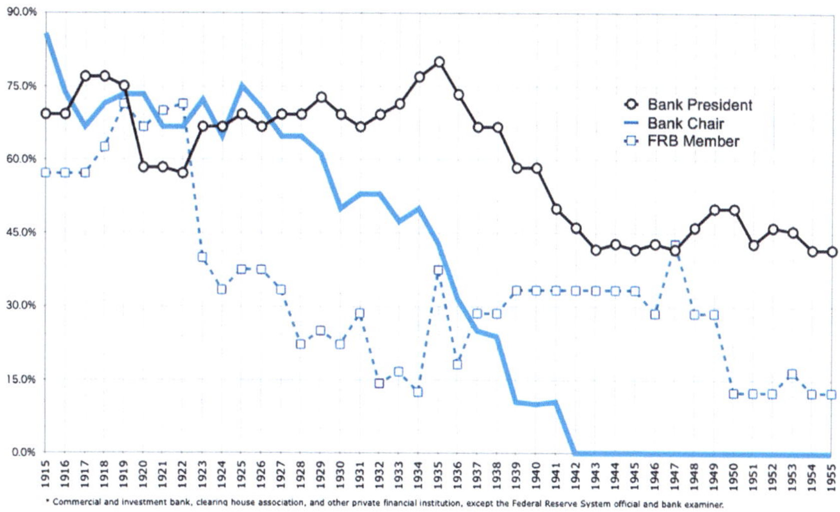

Fig. 7.7 Banking origins of top executive groups. Banking indicates commercial and investment bank, clearing house association, and other private financial institution, except the Federal Reserve official and bank examiner

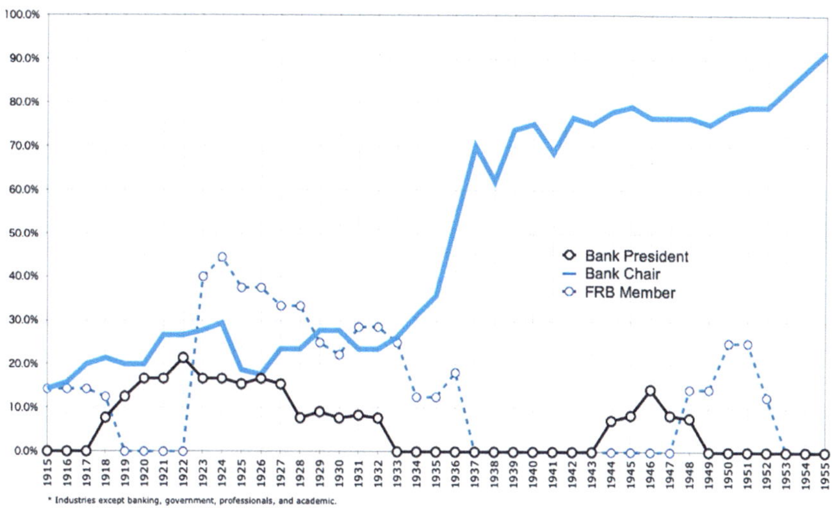

Fig. 7.8 Commerce and manufacture origins of top executive groups. Commerce and manufacture indicate industries except banking, government, professionals, and academia

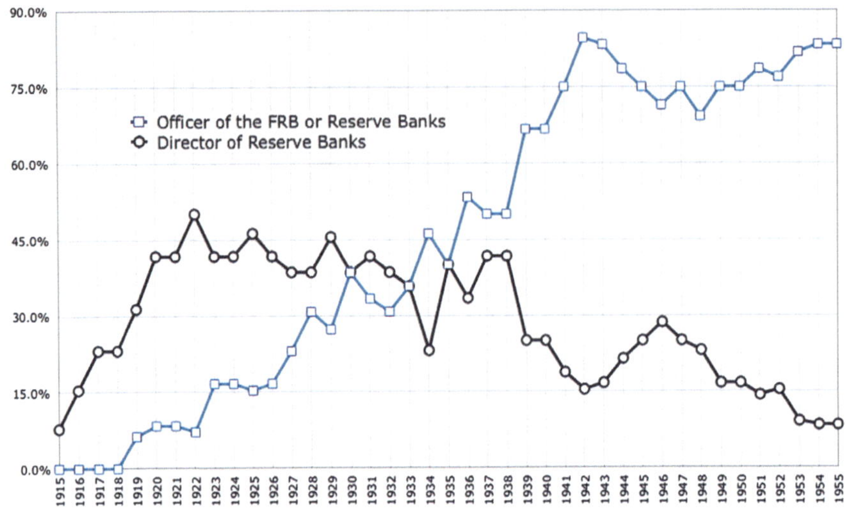

Fig. 7.9 Stepping stone for the Reserve Bank President. Many Reserve Bank presidents had a position in the Federal Reserve prior to taking office as a Federal Reserve Bank president

1953.[61] This change partly reflected the Banking Act of 1935's removal of the sentence of "at least two [of five except ex officio members] shall be persons experienced in banking or finance" from the original Act. However, the Banking Act of 1935 provided that "the President shall have due regard to a fair representation of the financial, agricultural, industrial, and commercial interest, and geographical divisions of the country."[62] As the result of the amendment, some of the FRB members had formerly served as government officials, for instance, Administrator of Agricultural Adjustment Administration (Rudolph M. Evans, 1940–1954), Assistant Secretary of Commerce (Ernest G. Draper, 1938–1950), and Assistant Secretary of Treasury (William M. Martin Jr., 1951–1970).

Brimmer (1972, p. 551) insisted that occasionally, "service as a director is a stepping stone for appointment to a full-time policy position with the Federal Reserve." This pipeline is confirmed in Fig. 7.9, which reveals which Reserve Bank presidents had relationships with Federal Reserve positions before assuming their position of president. While around 40% of presidents had experienced, in fact, being a member of the Reserve Bank board of directors before 1938, officers of the FRB or Reserve Banks held the position of president more than directors of the

[61]For example, Rudolph M. Evans (1940–1954) was formerly an Administrator of Agricultural Adjustment Administration, Ernest G. Draper (1938–1950) was formerly an Assistant Secretary of Commerce, and William M. Martin Jr. (1951–1970) was formerly an Assistant Secretary of the Treasury.

[62]Section 10 of the original Act provided that "the President shall have due regard to a fair representation of the different commercial, industrial, and geographical divisions of the country."

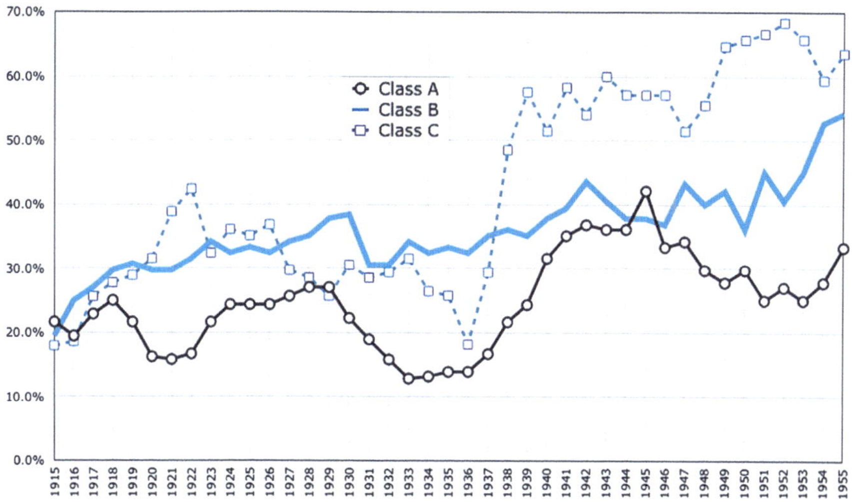

Fig. 7.10 Educational background of Reserve Bank Directors: Upper Bachelor's Degree

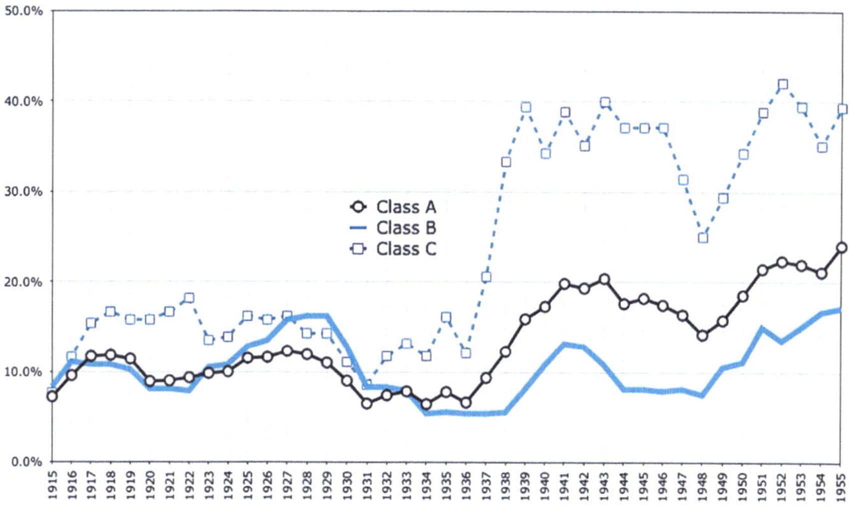

Fig. 7.11 Educational background of Reserve Bank Directors: Advanced Degree (LL.B., Master's, and Doctorate Degree)

Reserve Banks held the position. These officers accounted for 70–80% in the 1940s and 1950s.

(3) **Education**

As shown in Sect. 7.2, the FRB endeavored to appoint "strong men" as Class C directors in order to extend central control over Reserve Banks. In 1927, the FRB appointed Gates W. McGarrah, chair of the Chase National bank and an ex-Class A director of the Reserve Bank, as successor to New York Bank Chair Pierre Jay, while the board of directors intended to appoint Warren R. Burgess, Ph.D. from Columbia University as assistant Federal Reserve agent. How did educational background influence the selection of top executives?

As seen in Fig. 7.10, which shows the percentage of Reserve Bank directors who had bachelor's degrees, Class B and C directors had higher educational attainment than Class A directors until the 1930s.

Class A directors, however, had more advanced degrees than Class B directors from the late 1930s (Fig. 7.11). Interestingly, Class C directors had the highest educational attainment levels out of the three classes from the late 1930s onwards. In the 1940s, almost 40% of Class C directors had LL.B., Master's, or Doctoral degrees. This supports Brimmer's 1972 statement that "educational attainment is higher among directors appointed by the Board of Governors than among Bank-selected directors" (Brimmer 1972, p. 557). However, this was also true from the late 1930s. However, partners of investment banker had more university graduates than the Reserve Bank directors.

Table 7.8 shows directors' highest education by Reserve Bank over the entire period. In the Philadelphia and Kansas City Reserve Banks. Primary or secondary education was the most common, accounting for 40.3 and 36.6% of total director numbers. In the St. Louis Bank, 41.0% of directors had enrolled colleges but not graduated from them. In the Boston, New York, and Richmond Banks, bachelor's degrees were most common, accounting for 36.0, 31.9, and 32.2%, respectively. In the Philadelphia Bank, 10.6% of the directors had a Master's degree and 10.0% of New York Bank directors had a Doctorate. Directors in financial-center districts had higher educational backgrounds than directors in the rural districts.

Did Class C directors' higher level of educational attainment influence other top executive groups? As shown in Fig. 7.12, presidents had the lowest education level until 1927, after which their education level rose steadily, while Reserve Bank directors ranked last from 1928.

Figure 7.13 shows advanced degree holders among the executive groups. FRB members had the highest education amongst the four groups throughout the period. FRB members having advanced degrees, however, dropped from 75.0% in 1936 to 33.3% in 1939, while the education levels of Reserve Bank presidents became similar to those of FRB members by the 1950s.

According to Pak (2013, pp. 140–141, Table 11), between 1920 and 1940, out of 19 partners of the House of Morgan's American branches, J. P. Morgan & Co. and Drexel & Co., 14 (73.7%) had received a BA or higher degree.[63] During the same period, only

[63]Pak (2013, p. 139) suggests, "a university education from an elite university became an informal requirement" for new partners who were not born of high social status.

Table 7.8 Educational backgrounds of Reserve Bank Directors, 1915–1955 (%)

Reserve Bank	Primary/Secondary School	Technical School	College-Not Comp.	Bachelor's degree	LL. B.	Master's degree	Doctoral degree	Unknown	Total
Boston	22.8	1.0	22.0	36.0	0.3	6.6	3.4	7.9	100.0%
New York	13.4	3.7	14.9	31.9	14.7	1.8	10.2	9.4	100.0%
Philadelphia	40.3	1.6	14.9	22.3	1.1	10.6	4.8	4.5	100.0%
Cleveland	21.4	5.3	33.4	32.4	0	2.4	0.3	4.8	100.0%
Richmond	29.2	5.7	31.6	32.2	0	0.8	0.3	0.3	100.0%
Atlanta	27.2	4.9	33.2	3.5	6.7	5.7	7.8	11.1	100.0%
Chicago	27.6	5.1	23.6	23.1	10.5	1.1	1.9	7.2	100.0%
St. Louis	20.4	1.1	41.0	9.9	17.4	2.7	0.3	7.2	100.0%
Minneapolis	29.4	6.4	13.9	24.3	8.6	2.7	1.1	13.6	100.0%
Kansas City	36.6	0	29.2	7.4	10.0	0	0.8	16.1	100.0%
Dallas	24.0	8.1	30.0	11.0	9.4	0.3	0.3	17.0	100.0%
San Francisco	23.4	0	25.3	15.8	7.9	0.8	8.4	18.5	100.0%
Total	26.3	3.6	26.1	20.8	7.2	3.0	3.3	9.8	100.0%

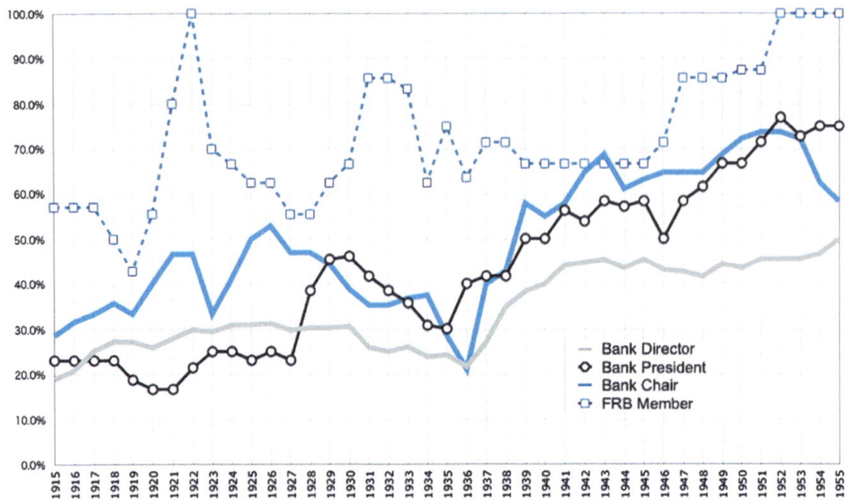

Fig. 7.12 Educational background of top executive groups: Bachelor's Degree

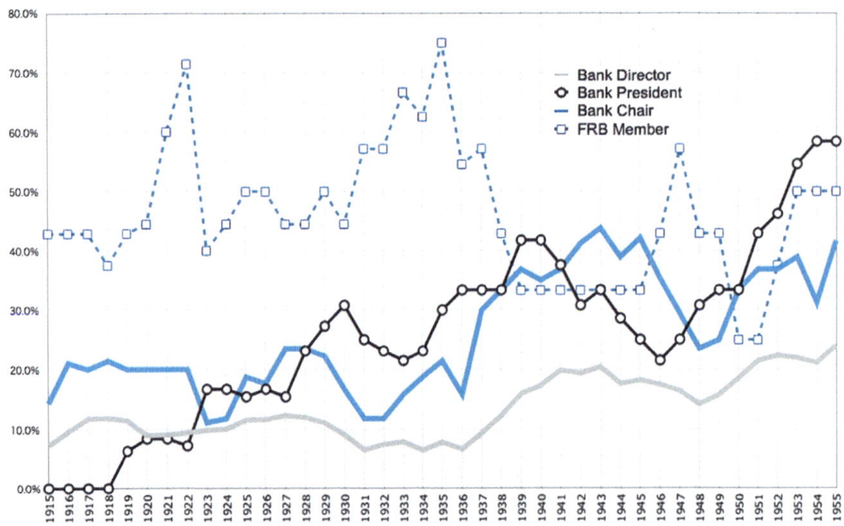

Fig. 7.13 Educational background of top executive groups: Advanced Degree (LL.B., Master's and Doctoral Degree)

20.4% of Class A directors of the Reserve Bank held a BA degree, compared to 33.7% of Class B directors and 34.0% of Class C directors. Even among Reserve Bank presidents, 33.6% received a BA degree. However, the FRB members received approximately same education level (70.0%) as the House of Morgan American branches.

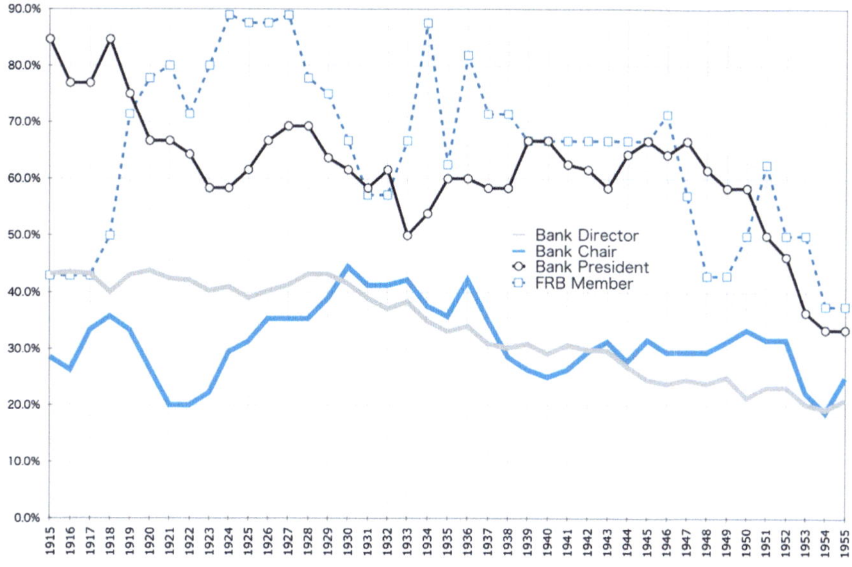

Fig. 7.14 Top executive groups who disclosed their political background

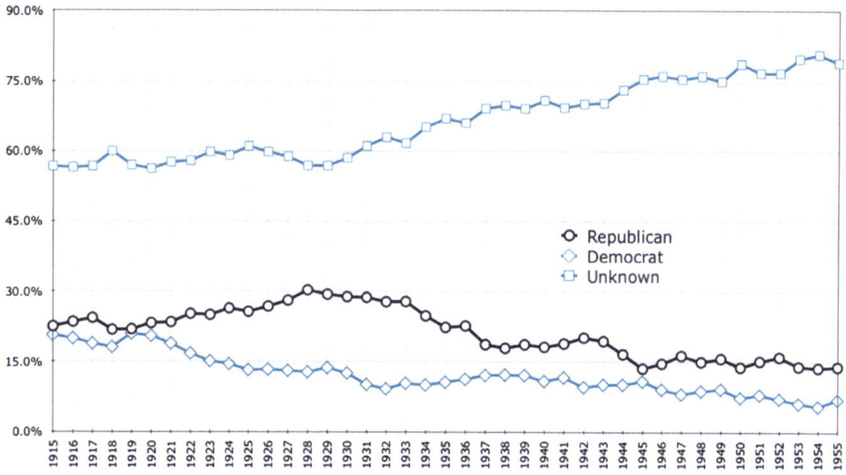

Fig. 7.15 Political affiliations of Reserve Bank Directors

(4) **Political Affiliation**

Senator Glass, father of the Federal Reserve System, highly prioritized having a balance between political parties in the FRB over other factors. However, many top

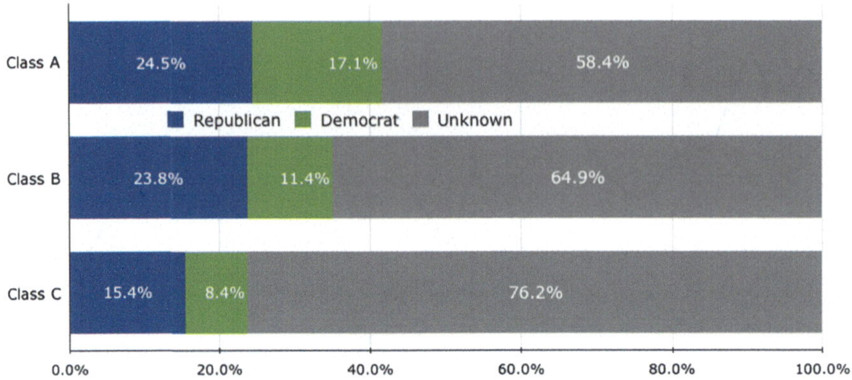

Fig. 7.16 Political affiliation of Reserve Bank Directors by Class, 1915–1955

executive groups revealed less about their political affiliation than other social backgrounds. Figure 7.14 indicates the percentage of top executive groups who revealed their political background, which exhibits a declining trend for all groups. The groups of the FRB members and the Reserve Bank presidents show higher percentages than the Reserve Bank directors. More than 80% of FRB members revealed their political affiliation from 1923 to 1927, and more than 50% of them revealed it until 1953 except in 1948–1949. Also more than 60% of the Reserve Bank presidents revealed their political affiliation from 1935 to 1948 except 1937–1938 and 1943. These data imply that the FRB members and the Reserve Bank

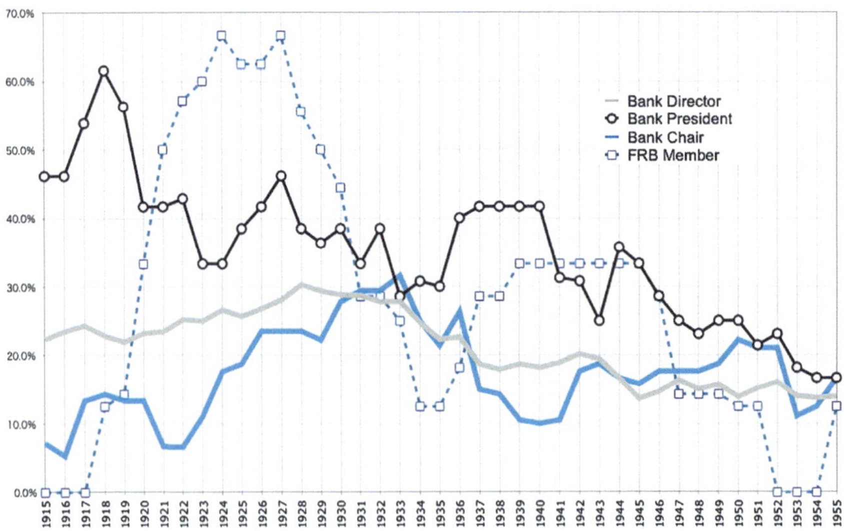

Fig. 7.17 Republicans in the top executive groups

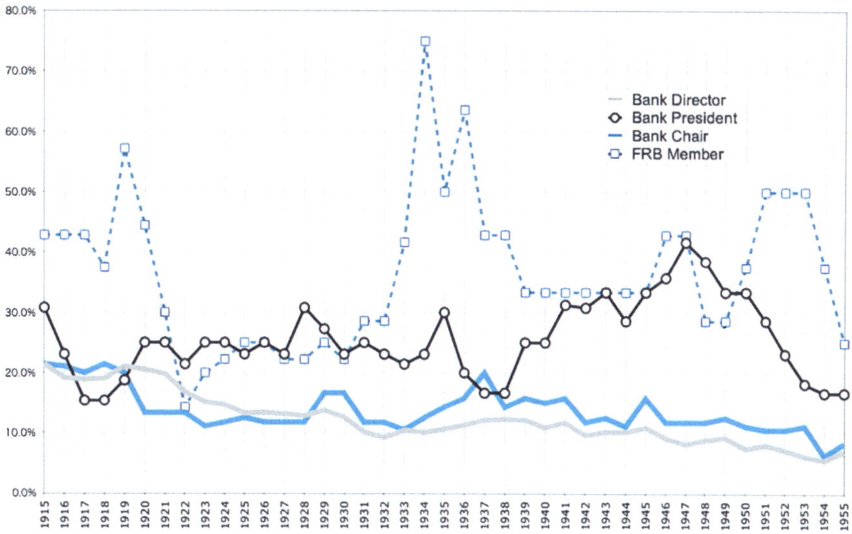

Fig. 7.18 Democrats in the top executive groups

presidents open about their political affiliation were at ease taking a position at the Federal Reserve, or they needed to disclose it in some cases. However, many Reserve Bank directors were unable to be open about their political affiliation given considerations for customer relations.

As seen in Fig. 7.15, Reserve Bank directors who withheld their political affiliation increased gradually since the Great Depression. From the point of view of political balance, parity between Republicans and Democrats initially existed. However, the number of Republicans increased by about 5% during the 1920s. Democrats decreased 11.4% from 1915 to 1932; they increased slightly in the late 1930s, but dropped back to 7% in 1955. Republicans also decreased from 27.8% in 1933 to 14% in 1955.

Figure 7.16 shows the political affiliations of all directors by class from 1915 to 1955. Republicans exceeded Democrats in all three classes, accounting for 24.5% of Class A and 23.8% of Class B, but only 15.4% of Class C directors. Democrats also accounted for 8.4% of Class C directors. This may explain why the FRB shunned the political friction that would arise from appointing Class C directors.

By virtue of Senator Glass's concern about political balance, the proportion of political party affiliates among FRB members swung widely. As seen in Fig. 7.17, Republicans accounted for 66.7% in 1927, but only 12.5% in 1934, and 0% in 1952. Democrats accounted for only 22.2% in 1927, rising to 75.0% in 1934, but 50% in 1952 (Fig. 7.18). Regarding Reserve Bank presidents, Republicans outnumbered Democrats until 1934, but Republicans and Democrats each accounted for 30.0% in 1935. However, Republicans outnumbered Democrats from 1936 to 1940, after which the numbers of Democrats exceeded those of Republicans from 1945 to 1951. The number of Republican Reserve Bank chairs was double that of

Table 7.9 Political backgrounds of the Reserve Bank Directors, 1915–1955

Reserve Bank	Republican (a)		Democrat (b)		Sub-total (c)	Unknown (d)		Total (e)
	Directors	(a)/(c) %	Directors	(b)/(c) %		Directors	(d)/(e) %	
Boston	85	96.6	3	3.4	88	293	76.9	381
New York	123	82.6	26	17.4	149	233	61.0	382
Philadelphia	100	97.1	3	2.9	103	274	72.7	377
Cleveland	109	92.4	9	7.6	118	256	68.4	374
Richmond	3	5.2	55	94.8	58	312	84.3	370
Atlanta	0	0	159	100.0	159	212	57.1	371
Chicago	170	85.4	29	14.6	199	174	46.6	373
St. Louis	23	16.0	121	84.0	144	229	61.4	373
Minneapolis	115	79.9	29	20.1	144	230	61.5	374
Kansas City	97	76.4	30	23.6	127	253	66.6	380
Dallas	7	9.1	70	90.9	77	306	79.9	383
San Francisco	127	85.8	21	14.2	148	220	59.8	368
Total	959	63.3%	555	36.7%	1514	2992	66.4%	4506

Democrats in the same time period, and after 1950. This can partly be explained by the fact that the chair was an executive officer with the president until 1935.

Some contrasts of political affiliation can be observed between Reserve Bank directors. Table 7.9 shows the share of Reserve Bank directors who declared a political affiliation from 1915 to 1955. Republicans outnumbered Democrats in many Reserve Banks; for example, Republicans accounted for around 76.4 to 97.1% in the Boston, New York, Cleveland, Chicago, Minneapolis, Kansas City, and San Francisco Reserve Banks. However, Democrat directors accounted for 100% in the Atlanta Bank, 90.9% in the Dallas Bank, and 84.0% in the St. Louis Bank. This could reflect these being part of the "southern democrat" stronghold. Data from political backgrounds suggest political power shifts and political divisions had no small effect on the governance structure of the Federal Reserve.

(5) **Religious Affiliation**

Top executive groups were more candid about religious affiliation than political leanings. Figure 7.19 indicates the percentage of top executive groups who disclosed their religious background. It exhibits a declining trend for the Reserve Bank director group since the early 1920s with the exception of the chair of the board of directors. Again, customer relations issues could have hindered Bank directors from being open about their religious affiliation, as seen above in terms of political affiliation disclosure. In contrast, the percentage of Reserve Bank chairs open about their religious affiliation increased from 47.1% in 1924 to 66.7% in 1930, and decreased sharply from 62.5% in 1934 to 25.0% in 1940. However, the percentage of the Reserve Bank presidents disclosing a religion increased from 38.5% in 1934 to 60.0% in 1936, and then decreased sharply from 50.0% in 1947 to 33.3% in

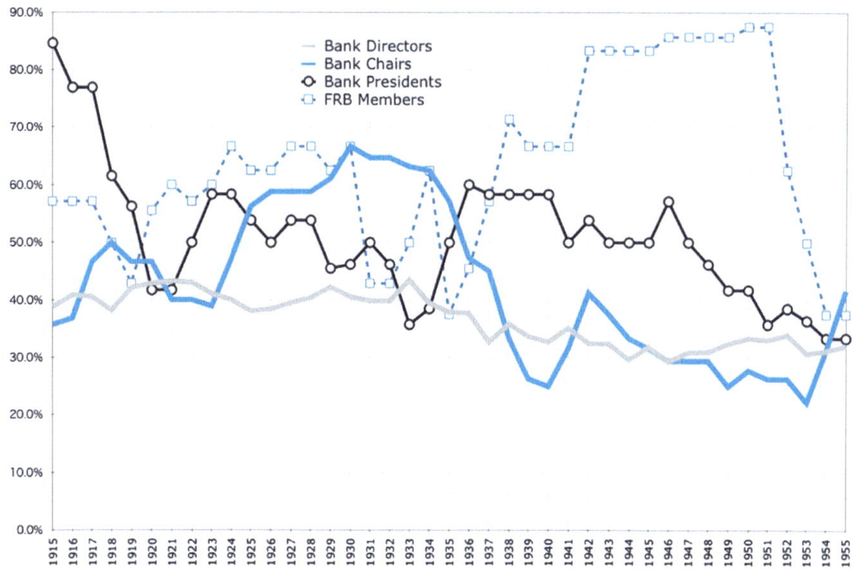

Fig. 7.19 Top executive groups who disclosed their religious background

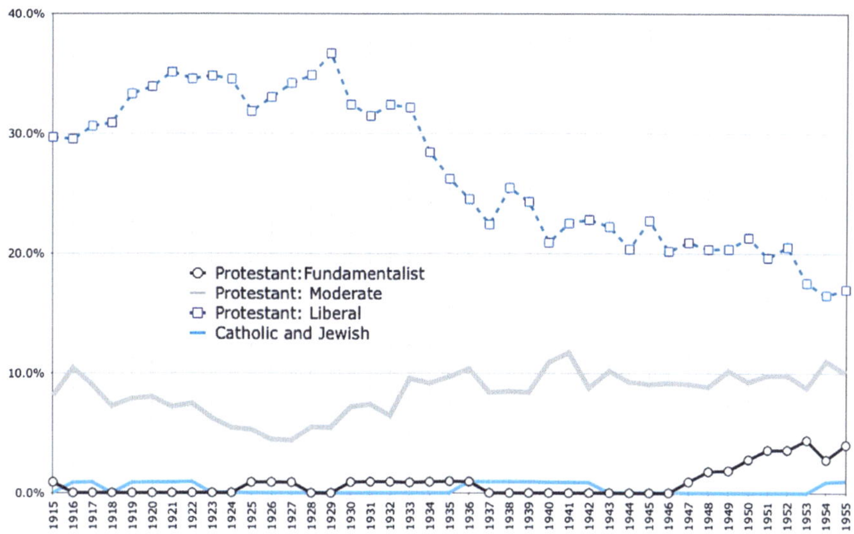

Fig. 7.20 Religious background of Reserve Bank Directors

1955. FRB members show quite a different line, in that more than 80% revealed their religious affiliation, going from 37.5% in 1935 to 87.5% in 1951.

What kind of religions or denominations did top executive groups of the Federal Reserve believe? First, we will examine the religious affiliations for the Reserve

Table 7.10 Religious backgrounds of District Bank Directors by Class, 1915–1955

Classifying*			Class A		Class B		Class C		Total	
			Directors	%	Directors	%	Directors	%	Directors	%
Protestant	Fundamentalist	Baptist	10	1.9	8	1.5%	15	2.6%	33	2.0%
		Evangelical	0	0	6	1.1	0	0	6	0.4
	Moderate	Lutheran	0	0	3	0.5	6	1.0	9	0.5
		Methodist	121	23.0	147	26.8	92	15.9	360	21.8
		Reformed Church	3	0.6	5	0.9	0	0	8	0.5
	Liberal	Disciples of Christ	9	1.7	4	0.7	10	1.7	23	1.4
		Congregationalist	68	12.9	15	2.7	70	12.1	153	9.3
		Episcopalian	78	14.8	149	27.2	111	19.2	338	20.5
		Presbyterian	221	41.9	193	35.2	231	40.0	645	39.0
		Unitarian	17	3.2	16	2.9	23	4.0	56	3.4
	Unknown		0	0	0	0	6	1.0	6	0.4
Catholic			0	0	2	0.4	9	1.6	11	0.7
Jewish			0	0	0	0	4	0.7	4	0.2
Subtotal			527	100%	548	100%	577	100%	1652	100%
Unknown			980	65.0	984	64.2	890	60.7	2854	63.3
Total			1507	100%	1532	100%	1467	100%	4506	100%

* Classified by Smith (1990)

Table 7.11 Religious backgrounds of reserve bank directors, 1915–1955 (%)

Classifying*			Boston	New York	Philadelphia	Cleveland	Richmond	Atlanta	Chicago	St. Louis	Minneapolis	Kansas City	Dallas	San Francisco	Total
Protestant	Fundamentalist	Baptist	6.7	4.6	0	1.7	1.9	5.6	0	0	0	0	0	0	2.0
		Evangelical	0	0	0	3.3	0	0	0	0	0	0	0	0	0.4
	Moderate	Lutheran	0	0	0	1.7	0.0	2.4	0	0	0	0	0	0	0.5
		Methodist	0	3.3	5.1	17.1	12.4	45.8	26.8	39.1	0.7	0	61.8	3.8	21.8
		Reformed Church	0	5.3	0	0	0	0	0	0	0	0	0	0	0.5
	Liberal	Disciples of Christ	0	0	0	0	0	1.6	0.0	13.0	0	13.7	0	0	1.4
		Congregationalist	53.3	6.0	0	8.8	0	0	7.6	0	22.9	0	0	48.1	9.3
		Episcopalian	18.1	31.1	18.5	24.3	14.3	7.6	19.7	29.0	37.1	12.3	15.3	36.5	20.5
		Presbyterian	3.8	47.0	75.2	39.8	71.4	36.7	41.4	18.8	15.0	74.0	22.9	7.7	39.0
		Unitarian	18.1	2.6	0	0	0	0.4	0	0	21.4	0	0	3.8	3.4
	Unknown		0	0	0	3.3	0	0	0	0	0	0	0	0	0.4
Catholic			0	0	1.3	0	0	0	4.5	0	0	0	0	0	0.7
Jewish			0	0	0	0	0	0	0	0	2.9	0	0	0	0.2
Sub-total			100%	100%	100%	100%	100%	100%	100%	100%	100%	100%	100%	100%	100%
Unknown			72.4%	60.5%	58.4%	51.6%	71.6%	32.3%	46.9%	81.5%	62.6%	80.8%	55.6%	85.9%	63.3%
Total			100%	100%	100%	100%	100%	100%	100%	100%	100%	100%	100%	100%	100%

* Classified by Smith (1990)

Table 7.12 Religious background of top executive groups (%)

Classifying*			District Bank			Board member
			Director	President	Chair	
Protestant	Fundamentalist	Baptist	2.0%	15.0%	5.1%	1.0%
		Evangelical	0.4	0	0	0
	Moderate	Lutheran	0.5	0	0	0
		Methodist	21.8	12.7	14.9	8.6
		Mormons	0	0	0	10.7
		Reformed Church	0.5	0	0	0
	Liberal	Disciples of Christ	1.4	7.5	0	0.5
		Dutch Reformed Church	0	0	0	5.6
		Congregationalist	9.3	9.7	4.1	5.6
		Episcopalian	20.5	27.0	21.7	36.5
		Presbyterian	39.0	25.5	49.8	21.8
		Quaker	0	1.5	0	0
		Unitarian	3.4	1.1	0	2.0
	Unknown		0.4	0	2.0	0
Catholic			0.7	0	2.4	3.0
Jewish			0.2	0	0	4.6
Sub-total			1652 (100%)	267 (100%)	295 (100%)	197 (100%)
Unknown			2854 (63.3%)	255 (48.9%)	405 (57.9%)	118 (37.5%)
Total			4506 (100%)	522 (100%)	700 (100%)	315 (100%)

* Classifying by Smith (1990)

Bank directors. As seen in Fig. 7.20, Catholicism and Judaism comprised at most 1.0% in 1955, while the other 99% of directors were Protestant throughout that same period. Following Smith (1990), we further classified Protestants into three denominations (for details see Table 7.10). As seen in Fig. 7.18, the Liberal denominations had the largest share over the entire period, accounting for 36.7% of Protestants in 1929, dropping to 22.4% in 1937, and 16.5% in 1954. The Moderate denomination was the second-largest group, accounting for 4.4% in 1927, rising to 11.7% in 1941. The Fundamentalist group was the smallest, rising from 0.9% in 1947 to 4.0% in 1955.

Table 7.10 shows religious affiliations of the Reserve Bank directors by Class in the 1915–1955 period. Of those who disclosed a religious affiliation, Class A directors were 41.9% Presbyterian, 23.0% Methodist, and 14.8% Episcopalian; similarly, Class B directors were 36.2% Presbyterian, 27.2% Episcopalian, and 26.8% Methodist; Class C directors were 40.0% Presbyterian, 19.2% Episcopalian, and 15.9% Methodist.

Table 7.11 shows the religious affiliations of all Reserve Bank directors in the 1915–1955 period. Presbyterian was the largest denomination in New York (47.0%), Philadelphia (75.2%), Cleveland (39.8%), Richmond (71.4%), Chicago (41.4%), and Kansas City (74.0%); Congregationalist was the largest denomination in Boston (53.3%) and San Francisco (48.1); Methodist was the largest denomination in Atlanta (45.8%), St. Louis (39.1), and Dallas (61.8%); and Episcopalian was the largest in Minneapolis (37.1%). Catholicism accounted for 4.5% in Chicago and 1.3% in Philadelphia, and Judaism accounted for 2.9% in Minneapolis.[64]

Lastly, we consider the top executive groups of the Federal Reserve System across the entire study period. As seen in Table 7.12, Presbyterians comprised the largest denomination among directors (39.0%) and chairs (49.8%) of Reserve Banks, and Episcopalians were the largest affiliation among Reserve Bank presidents (27.0%) and FRB members (36.5%). Catholics accounted for 3.0% of FRB members, 2.4% of Reserve Bank chairs, and 0.7% of Reserve Bank directors; Jews accounted for 4.6% of FRB members and 0.2% of Reserve Bank directors.[65] Moreover, of the executives who did not disclose their religious affiliations, 63.3% were directors, 57.9% were chairs, 48.9% were presidents in the Reserve Banks, and 37.5% were FRB members.

While FRB members disclosed their religious affiliation more than other group affiliations, they also faced higher publicity and visibility than other executives. Smith (1990) classified Mormons as Fundamentalist. Eccles, a well-known Mormon, who was a "pragmatic, conservative liberal" (Back 1976, p. xii), induced Lawrence Clayton, who was a vice president of Eccles' own First National Bank of Ogden and also a Mormon, to serve as a FRB member in 1947. This highlights the significance of religious background and financial networks of Federal Reserve System executives.

Partners of investment banks had maintained close religious networks as well as kinship ones. However, Kuhn, Loeb & Co., the leading German-American Jewish bank, moved forward with Americanization around the First World War so that new partners came from different religions (Carosso 1976). Although J.P. Morgan & Co. maintained "anti-Semitism" until 1930s, some partners had different denominations. According to Pak (2013), between 1920 and 1940, of the 19 House of Morgan American partners 15 (78.9%) were Episcopalian, one each was Methodist and Presbyterian, and two were unknown (pp. 140–141, Table 11). Top executives of the Federal Reserve had a weaker religious network than investment bank partners. Most of them were Protestant, and belonged to networks encompassing

[64]Class C director (1916–1917) at the Philadelphia Bank and Class C director (1936–1942) at the Chicago Reserve Bank were Catholic, and Class C director (1919–1922) at the Minneapolis Reserve Bank was Jewish.

[65]With regard to the FRB members, Jews Paul M. Warburg served 1914–1918, Eugene Meyer served 1930–1933, and Henry Morgenthau, Jr. served 1934–1936, and Catholic James F.T. O'Connor served 1933–1936.

different denominations by executive groups and Federal Reserve districts in case of the board of directors.

7.6 Conclusions

During the Great Depression, monetary policy was ineffective. One source of this problem was policy conflicts among top executives in the Federal Reserve System, particularly at some of the Reserve Banks. First, we traced the evolution of governance and membership of the directors and governors/presidents of the Reserve Banks. When the Federal Reserve Act was enacted in 1913, the design of the Reserve Banks was only generally outlined, with many details about the management structure left to the Reserve Banks themselves. Consequently, the character of these institutions developed a surprising degree of heterogeneity, which may have contributed to their different policy positions in the late 1920s and early 1930s. When confronted by the financial crisis, Congress restructured the Reserve Banks by imposing greater uniformity in structure and control by the FRB, and Chairman Eccles accomplished a partial purge of the Federal Reserve's governance without revision of the Federal Reserve Act. As the result of this reform, old-line bankers were removed from the Reserve Banks as well as well from as the FRB, and the executive committee of the board of directors also lost responsibility for managing the Reserve Bank.

Second, we examined how governance reforms after the Great Depression influenced the economic and social backgrounds of the top executive groups in the Federal Reserve, especially Reserve Bank directors and presidents. Most elements we surveyed were influenced by the governance reforms following the Banking Act of 1935, especially the expulsion of old-line executives and the conversion of the chairmanship of the Reserve Bank's board of directors into "a purely honorary post." Average age and length of service of Reserve Bank chairs and FRB members decreased dramatically after 1936, but returned to their previous levels by the end of the 1940s. Even though "the dead hand" revived somewhat, bankers never took the chair's position, while many manufacturers served as chairs as an honorary post. Reserve Bank directors had higher education levels following the governance reforms, partly because the FRB appointed academic experts as Class C directors of Reserve Banks. To the extent that executives revealed their political or religious affiliations, all executive groups were Republican except the FRB members in the New Deal period, and all executive groups were of liberal Protestant denominations. Although we found no clear influence from the governance reform on trends in executives' religious backgrounds, some economic and social networks, including political and religious affiliations, were identified in the Federal Reserve's top executive groups.

Despite the drastic reforms to the Federal Reserve's governance in the mid-1930s, the Federal Reserve System has preserved the structure of independent regional central banks. Reserve Bank directors have influenced monetary policy by setting their District's discount rate and by appointing the Bank's president, who sits on the FOMC, and approving the Bank's budget, overseeing its operations, and appointing the Bank's officers, especially the president. Because of these powers of the directors, Class C directors have been required to be in the public interest since the 1960s, and Class A directors lost their voting power for Reserve Bank presidents in the Dodd-Frank Wall Street Reform Act of 2010.

References

Back, G.L. 1976. Foreword. In *Marriner S. Eccles: Private Entrepreneur and Public Servant*, ed. S. Hyman. Stanford: Stanford University Graduate School of Business.

Barro, R.J., and R.M. McCleary. 2006. Religion and Political Economy in an International Panel. *Journal for the Scientific Study of Religion* 45 (2): 149–175.

Barro, R.J., and R.M. McCleary. 2003. Religion and Economic Growth Across Countries. *American Sociological Review* 68 (5): 760–781.

Bopp, K.R. 1937. Reserve Bank Directors. *Journal of Political Economy* 45 (4): 517–531.

Bopp, K.R. 1935. *The Agencies of Federal Reserve Policy*. Columbia: University of Missouri.

Brimmer, A.F. 1972. Characteristics of Federal Reserve Bank directors. *Federal Reserve Bulletin*. 550–559.

Carosso, V.P. 1976. A Financial Elite: New York's German-Jewish Investment Bankers. *American Jewish Historical Quarterly*. 66 (1): 67–88.

Clark, L.E. 1935. *Central Banking Under the Federal Reserve System*. New York: The Macmillan Company.

Coit, C.G. 1941. *The Federal Reserve Bank of Richmond*. New York: Columbia University Press.

Eccles, M.S. 1951. *Beckoning Frontiers: Public and Personal Recollections. S*, Hyman ed. New York: Alfred A. Knopf.

Federal Reserve Bank of Boston. 1929–1931. *Stockholders of the Federal Reserve Bank of Boston*. Retrieve from FRASER website of the Federal Reserve Bank of St. Louis.

Federal Reserve Bank of New York. 1914–1941. *Circular*. New York: Federal Reserve Bank of New York. Retrieve from FRASER website of the Federal Reserve Bank of St. Louis.

Federal Reserve Bank of New York. 1919–1935. *Annual report*. Washington: GPO.

Federal Reserve Bank of New York. n.d. Bylaws. Retrieve from the Federal Reserve Bank of New York website.

Federal Reserve Board. 1915–1936. *Annual report*. Washington: GPO.

Federal Reserve Board. 1915–1936. *Minutes of meeting*. Retrieve from FRASER website of the Federal Reserve Bank of St. Louis.

Friedman, M., and A.J. Schwartz. 1963. *A Monetary History of the United States, 1867–1960*. Princeton: Princeton University Press.

Gamble, R.H. 1989. *A History of the Federal Reserve Bank of Atlanta, 1914–1989*. Atlanta: Federal Reserve Bank Atlanta.

Griswold, J.A. 1936. *A history of the Federal Reserve Bank of Chicago*. St. Louis: J. Mulligan Print. & Pub. Co.

Harrison, W.B. 1977. Regionalism: A Sample of Views Held by Federal Reserve District Directors. *Journal of Economics and Business* 30: 46–56.

Havrilesky, T., et al. 1973. The economic affiliations of directors of Federal Reserve district bank. *Social Science Quarterly* 54 (3): 608–622.

Havrilesky, T. 1986. The effect of the Federal Reserve Reform Act on the Economic Affiliations of Directors of Federal Reserve banks. *Social Science Quarterly* 67 (2): 393–401.

Irwin, N. and D. Cho. 2010. Financial reform would shift Fed's authority away from regional banks. *Washington Post*. March 17.

James, F.C. 1938. *The Growth of Chicago Banks*. New York and London: Harper & Brothers, Vol. II.

Lindley, J.T. 1985. *An analysis of the Federal Advisory Council of the Federal Reserve System, 1914–1938*. New York: Garland.

Miller, E. 1961. Public Interest Representation on Federal Reserve Bank Directorates. *Review of Economics and Statistics* 43 (4): 380–384.

Morgenstern, O. 1930. Developments in the Federal Reserve System. *Harvard Business Review* 9 (1): 1–7.

National City Bank of New York. 1914. *United States Securities, Government Finance, and Federal Reserve Organization*. National Archives, Record of the Reserve Bank Organization Committee.

Pak, S.J. 2013. *Gentlemen Bankers: The World of J.P. Morgan*. Cambridge, Mass and London: Harvard University Press.

Parthemos, J. 1990. The Federal Reserve Bank of Richmond: Governor Seay and the Issue of Early Years. *Economic Review* (Federal Reserve Bank of Richmond) Jan./Feb., 7–17.

Ruhr, M., and J.P. Daniels. 2003. The Relationship between Religious Affiliation, Region, Race, and Attitudes. *Faith & Economics* 42: 26–39.

Smith, T.W. 1990. Classifying Protestant Denominations. *Review of Religious Research* 31 (3): 225–245.

Taggart, J.H. 1938. *The Federal Reserve Bank of Boston*. Boston and New York: Bankers Publishing Co.

U.S. Reserve Bank Organization Committee, Preliminary Committee on Organization. 1914. *Report to the Reserve Bank organization Committee*. Retrieve from FRASER website of the Federal Reserve Bank of St. Louis.

U.S. Senate, Committee on Banking and Currency. 1935. *Banking act of 1935, Hearings on S. 1715 and H. R. 7617*. 74th Congress, 1st Session, Washington DC.

White, E. 2013. To Establish a More Effective Supervision of Banking: How the Birth of the Fed Altered bank Supervision. In *The Origins, History and Future of the Federal Reserve: A Return to Jekyll Island*, ed. M.D. Bordo and W. Robards. Cambridge: Cambridge University Press.

Willis, P.B. 1937. *The Federal Reserve Bank of San Francisco: A study in American central banking*. New York: Columbia University Press.

Author Biography

Isao Suto is a professor of economic history at Meiji University, Tokyo. He gained his Ph.D. in economics from Nagoya University. He recently coedited *American economic history, 1929–2008: the emergence of a troubled superpower*, with Akitake Taniguchi. His books include *Shaping of the post-war Federal Reserve policy: from New Deal to "the Accord"* (2008) and *American big business and banking: the formation and reorganization of the Federal Reserve system, 1863–1935* (1997). Among his many articles are "U.S. international monetary policy for the IMF," and "Early twenty-century Japanese worker saving: precautionary behaviour before a social safety net" and "Savings and early economic growth in the United States and Japan" written with John A. James.

The manufacturer's authorised representative in the EU is Springer Nature Customer Service Centre GmbH, Europaplatz 3, 69115 Heidelberg, Germany. If you have any concerns regarding our products, please contact ProductSafety@springernature.com

Printed and bound by CPI Group (UK) Ltd, Croydon, CR0 4YY
25/09/2026
02222892-0001